② Jane Weltch ^Knots daughter of John Weltch
when Catholics took over contro[l]
of the country, began to persecute
Protestants - non-Catholics + her Hus[band]
John Welch preatching "the Faith" w[as]
arrested + imprisoned, long time lat[er]
the Catholics come
her + in does days
the Rome controlled
the world
they controlled
both the church and
politics + told her
"he will realesed"
husband from prison
of the man she loved
if she con get him
to renounce this
protestant | Faith
she gathered up her
apron + said,
the brother catch his
head in this, + held her
apron up high.

9 Sige of Philip

... ell

"Get ①
Iven
Aven Spencer's Biography
written after he died =
Founder of Lon Bible Intitution
As a Student preatched in
Divine Healing

Ez 13:10, 15-16
micah 3:5, 8
Ez 12:15-16 Jer 24:1-10 1:10
6

138 - 139

③ Jesse Penn Lewis
what the Lord showed ^her

God Only requires
total Faith and total
Holyness in total
Discipleship

48 *
Book

In time of trail = Faith
In time of Temptation = Faithfulness

Biographies by Mary Drewery

WINDOW ON MY HEART

RICHARD WURMBRAND

BADEN POWELL: THE MAN WHO LIVED TWICE

WILLIAM CAREY

A Biography

Mary Drewery

OF THE ZONDERVAN CORPORATION
GRAND RAPIDS, MICHIGAN 49506

Zondervan Publishing House, 1415 Lake Drive, S.E., Grand Rapids, Michigan 49506

Zondervan edition 1979

Published by special arrangement with Hodder and Stoughton Limited, Mill Road, Dunton Green, Seven Oaks, Kent, England.

Library of Congress Cataloging in Publication Data

Drewery, Mary, 1918-
William Carey : a biography.

Includes bibliographical references and index.
1. Carey, William, 1761-1834. 2. Missionaries—India—Biography. 3. Missionaries—England—Biography.
BV3269.C3D7 1979 266'.6'10924 [B] 79-14886
ISBN 0-310-38851-1

Printed in the United States of America

83 84 85 86 87 88 — 10 9 8 7 6 5 4

Contents

Foreword

MANY, many books have been written about William Carey during the past hundred and forty years. My thanks go to all those scholars who have mined so thoroughly the material about him that has survived. Of particular help was Dr. E. Daniel Potts' carefully researched book: *Baptist Missionaries in India, 1793–1837* .

Detailed though all these previous works are, however, I yet found myself wishing for more information about the personal life of this extraordinary man and the effect on it of the momentous times through which he lived. This gap I have attempted to fill – less than adequately, I fear, as there is so little material extant. I trust that, in so doing, I have been able to add some warmth and colour to Carey's portrait.

My thanks are also due to the Librarian of the Baptist Missionary Society and to the Principal of Regent's Park College, Oxford for their assistance – and to my family for their encouragement.

MARY DREWERY
Pulborough, West Sussex.
1978.

1

Schoolboy and Shoemaker

1761–1784

IT HAS BEEN written of William Carey that he came from an 'obscure village in the dullest period of the dullest of all centuries'.[1] Although the age that saw the stirrings of modern Parliamentary democracy in England, the War of Independence in America and the turmoil of the Revolution in France can hardly be described as 'dull', the classification of Paulerspury as an 'obscure village' holds true, even today.

It lies some ten miles south of Northampton and straggles over about a mile of quiet countryside that can have changed scarcely at all since the third quarter of the eighteenth century when William Carey was born. Not that this helps any biographer in his endeavours to recreate Carey's childhood. Had he been born a nobleman's son, there would no doubt have been portraits extant of the child at varying stages of his development; there would have been a great house to visit; furnishings to admire; toys; a cradle, perhaps – intimate possessions as carefully cherished as his memory.

Carey, however, was only a weaver's son and there is little in the 'Carey country' either to honour or to recall the great Christian who spent his first thirty-two years exploring its woods, tramping its roads, cobbling and teaching and preaching in its villages. Of the grey stone cottage at Pury End, Paulerspury, where he was born, nothing remains but a small cairn with a memorial plaque giving the wrong month of his death. The history of the parish church of St. James the Great, where he worshipped as a boy, ante-dates his birth by ten years. In Hackleton and Piddington, the poor cottages and shoe-maker's shops where he scraped a living during the seventeen-eighties have been cleared to make way for neat new housing estates. Only at Moulton has Carey's cottage been preserved and a few meagre records gathered together to assist the student of his career.

Fortunately, Carey himself wrote a brief memoir of his early years and his sister, Mary, recorded her recollections. These two documents, together with some brief comments by the few people who could be traced after his death who had known him before he left England, provide enough information to sketch in an outline of his formative years.

William Carey was born on 17th August, 1761, one year after King George III ascended to the throne and (appropriately, in view of Carey's later career) in the year when the surrender by the French of Pondicherry left England virtually free from competition in India. It was the year in which Gainsborough held his first exhibition of paintings in London. Hogarth's career was almost at an end. Dr. Johnson's monumental *Dictionary of the English Language* had been in circulation for five years. It was the time of Gray's *Odes*, of Sterne's *Tristram Shandy*, of Rousseau's *Social Contract.* It was the heyday of 'Capability' Brown who landscaped the gardens of some of the great houses built with the profits of the slave trade. However, these great names and events would have had little impact on the quiet village where William's father, Edmund Carey, worked as a journeyman weaver. The term describes a man who received his raw materials from a 'manufacturer', worked on them on a loom in his own cottage, then returned the finished product to the manufacturer for distribution. Factories or workshops in the modern sense, where a number of employees worked for a fixed weekly wage in one large building, were at that time rare in England. Indeed, they did not really come into common use until about 1785 when the steam engine was introduced into factories. During the seventeen-sixties, home industry was the usual practice. Edmund Carey produced the type of woollen cloth known locally as 'tammy', a fine worsted of good quality, often with a glazed finish. He would probably have earned ten shillings a week.*

With a loom occupying a large part of the living-room, the mean cottage must have been very crowded, particularly as William, Ann, Mary, Thomas and Elizabeth were born into

* 50p in today's money though, of course, the modern equivalent would be much more.

the family. The household was completed by William's widowed grandmother, Ann Carey – 'a woman of remarkable tenderness' and of a 'calm and even disposition'[2] – who helped to care for the children. Their father was a man of 'the strictest habits of integrity and uprightness'[3] but somewhat stern. 'He was a man that never discovered any partiality for the abilities of his children, but . . . tended a little to discourage them.'[4]

Paulerspury was divided then, as now, into two 'Ends' separated by a small stream. 'Pury End', where William was born, was on rising ground at the west end of the village. When he was six years old, the family moved to 'Church End', the larger and more prosperous eastern part of the village. The reason for this improvement in status was that Edmund Carey had been nominated to the position of Parish Clerk. With this position went the appointment as schoolmaster at the village free school which had been endowed by two local landowners. Except for the well-to-do who sent their sons to public schools, there was no education obtainable at this time except in the charity schools (and these were not universally distributed throughout the country) where the children of the poor, between the ages of seven and twelve, were taught reading, writing, arithmetic and the catechism. Edmund Carey's father before him had been Parish Clerk and schoolmaster, and he himself occupied the position from 1767 to 1816. A free house went with the post of schoolmaster – a much larger house than the Pury End cottage – so that William was early able to enjoy a bedroom to himself. This was a rare privilege in a family of their station. Even so, life for the Careys was hard. 'My parents were poor,' William wrote some years later, 'and unable to do much for me.'[5]

From his earliest years, the boy displayed a passionate interest in his surroundings, particularly in plants and animals. If he had set his heart on obtaining any particular flower or insect for his collection, he was heedless of dirt or discomfort in the pursuit of it. His bedroom was filled with specimens, with birds and insects both alive and dead, which would indicate that his mother must have shown commendable tolerance of her son's enthusiasms.

Whittlebury Forest, covering hundreds of acres, still stands today within walking distance of Paulerspury. Hawthorns foaming with blossom and thickets of hazel still screen the dark mysteries of oak woods within, as they would have done in Carey's day when the forest extended almost to the edge of the village. The boy spent happy hours exploring the woodland glades, returning home with his pockets bulging with treasures to add to the collection in his room.

William's uncle, Peter Carey, also lived in Paulerspury. He had served as a soldier in the wars against the French in Canada until hostilities ended with the capture of Quebec by General Wolfe two years before William was born. After that, Peter Carey returned to England and settled down in his home village where he worked as a gardener. His tales of far-off countries must have made exciting listening and have opened up new horizons for young William. 'He often had his nephew with him, not having any child of his own,'[6] writes William's sister Mary and she describes how the uncle cherished in William such a love of gardens that 'while brother continued at home he seldom left any part of his father's garden uncultivated, he was so fond of flowers.'[7]

As Parish Clerk, William's father had an important part to play in church and village affairs. The poet, William Cowper, describes some of the clerk's duties: 'Not only must the clerk pronounce the *Amen* to prayers and announce the sermon. He must also be universal father to those he guides to the altar and he is god-father to every new-born babe.' In fact, the clerk's duties were even more numerous. He led the chants and gave the responses during services; he kept the church accounts, registered baptisms, marriages and burials; he saw that the surplices were laundered and the church cleaned; he 'chased dogs out of church and forced unwilling youngsters in.'[8] In return for all these duties, the clerk received £2 a year, plus the fees for marriages and funerals.

On Sundays, in order to be able to carry out his part in the service, William's father sat at a table beneath the pulpit in the parish church. His family occupied a small gallery rising up behind the pulpit. William described his early church-going in the following terms:

> I have no doubt but the constant reading of the Psalms, Lessons, &c., in the parish church, which I was obliged to attend regularly, tended to furnish my mind with a general

> scriptural knowledge. Of real experimental religion I scarcely heard anything till I was fourteen years of age; nor was the formal attendance upon outward ceremonies, to which I was compelled, the matter of my choice.[9]

The studied neutrality of this statement suggests a young boy's boredom with an Established Church which in his day was largely sunk in worldliness and lethargy.

From a visit to the Gothic church in Paulerspury, it is easy to imagine young William's attention wandering during Rev. Nicholas Jones's sermons. Sitting high in the gallery, he could see over the heads of the congregation and perhaps catch the eye of his friends among the bell-ringers under the tower. Did he ever peer over his shoulder, fascinated by the life-sized effigies on the tombs in the North Chapel: Sir Laurence Paveli and his wife, the fourteenth century Lord of the Manor who gave the village its name; Sir Arthur Throckmorton, brother-in-law of Sir Walter Raleigh, reclining forever in alabaster effigy with his wife Anne, each smiling blandly at the other? Did he ever struggle with his self-taught Latin to interpret the inscriptions on the memorial slabs in the chancel floor, diapered in blue and crimson where the Sunday morning sun slanted through the stained glass windows: *Hic jacet corpus Svzanne Carter, uxoris Henri Carter* who died on 20th July, 1685? It is on record that at the age of twelve Carey mastered the short grammar in Dyche's *Latine Vocabulary* and learned practically the whole of the vocabulary by heart.

If compulsory regular church attendance was the penalty for being the son of the parish clerk, this was more than compensated for by being the son of the schoolmaster because this would enable William to have access to at least some books. His sister records that their father was 'a great reader'.[10] 'I chose to read books of science, history, voyages, &c., more than any others,' William wrote of his boyhood.[11]

Carey does not specify in what branch of science his interest lay but it was an age in which great advances in knowledge were being made in all fields, wnether it was Edmund Halley studying the action of the trade winds, variations of the compass and the behaviour of what is now known as 'Halley's Comet', or Joseph Priestley discovering oxygen and investigating the nature of electrical discharges; whether it was

Richard Arkwright's 'water frame' and James Hargreaves' 'spinning-jenny' revolutionising the cotton industry, or James Watt turning Newcomen's early steam engine into a working proposition. The newspapers of the day (and there were many provincial newspapers by the time Carey was born) must have given extensive coverage to such developments. There was much to stimulate a boy such as William who had a quick mind and a natural love of learning.

There is no record, either, of the titles of the books he read on 'history, voyages, &c.'. An account of Captain Cook's first voyage (1768–1771), during which he charted the east coasts of New Zealand and Australia, was published in 1773 when William was twelve years of age but it is unlikely that anyone in his social position would have access to a copy immediately on its publication. Moreover, accounts indicate that he did not see the records of Cook's voyages until he was twenty-two. He is more likely as a boy to have read Hakluyt's *Principall Navigations, Voiages, Traffiques and Discoveries of the English Nation* which had already become a classic by the mid-eighteenth century. It described the voyages of John and Sebastian Cabot to Newfoundland and America; Drake's circumnavigation of the globe; Martin Frobisher's search for the North-West Passage and many other expeditions of courage and enterprise such as would fire the enthusiasm of an imaginative boy.

As England's commercial interests spread wider throughout the known world, so the demand for travel literature increased and, during the first half of the eighteenth century, the output of books of travel, whether real or imagined, was second only to books of theology. Daniel Defoe's *Robinson Crusoe* (1719) and Jonathan Swift's *Gulliver's Travels* (1726) are two that have survived.

There is a tradition that William Carey used to be nicknamed 'Columbus' by the village boys. Perhaps, if the tradition is true, it was because of his passionate interest in voyages of exploration. There is another – less likely – tradition that the village boys would taunt William: 'Well, if you won't play, preach us a sermon.' It is said that William would mount the stump of an old wych elm and hold forth. This possibly wishful picture of a budding missionary hardly squares with Carey's own account:

> My companions were at this time such as could only serve to debase the mind, and lead me into the depths of that gross conduct which prevails among the lower classes in the most neglected villages . . . I was addicted to swearing, lying and unchaste conversation; which was heightened by the company of ringers, psalm-singers, foot-ball players, the society of a blacksmith's shop, etc., &c.: and though my father laid the strictest injunctions on me to avoid such company, I always found some way to elude his care.[12]

Even allowing for the exaggeration of a man now dedicated to missionary work looking back on his early years, it would appear that William Carey was a very natural, boisterous, lively village lad, if above average in intelligence. And such he might have remained, doomed to a future as an agricultural labourer at five shillings a week, had he not suffered from a skin disease that made it painful for him to go out in full sun. There does not seem to have been any visible rash but if his face and hands were exposed to the sun for any lengthy period, he would suffer distressing agony throughout the night. Thus, after an unsuccessful attempt on leaving school to cope with work in the fields, it became necessary for the boy to find an indoor trade.

Northampton and its surrounding district was then, as it is today, important as a centre for shoemaking. Some time during the seventeen-seventies (Carey says at 'about fourteen'[13]; his sister Mary says 'in his sixteenth year'[14]) he was bound as an apprentice to a cordwainer in Piddington, a village about seven miles away from his home. A cordwainer was more skilled than a mere shoemaker. He did not just effect repairs but was a craftsman who made up an entire shoe – sole, vamp and uppers. The Piddington cordwainer was one Clarke Nichols, a strict churchman and a very moral man, though not above requiring his apprentice to deliver goods on the Lord's Day. Carey tells us that 'he sometimes drank rather too freely'[15] and 'was an inveterate enemy to lying, a vice to which I was awfully addicted'.[16] Apprenticeship to this man was to have important consequences for William.

Up to his mid-teens, the boy had probably never questioned the faith in which he had been reared. If his attention had wandered during the services he attended, he had, nonetheless, absorbed, through sheer repetition, a good deal of liturgical and scriptural knowledge. He says he 'avoided books of religion'[17] but he had read Bunyan's *Pilgrim's Progress* 'with eagerness', even though 'to no purpose'.[18] He had also read Jeremy Taylor's *Sermons*, Spinker's *Sick Man Visited* and other similar improving works. If asked to state his convictions, he would have said he was an Anglican and that he held Dissenters* 'in contempt'.[19]

The Anglican or 'Established' Church at this time could best be described as being 'latitudinarian' or broadly tolerant in its outlook. 'The Church of England', said an eighteenth century bishop, 'is a happy mean between the meretricious gaudiness of the Church of Rome and the squalid sluttery of fanatic conventicles.'[20] The eighteenth century was 'the Age of Reason'. Enthusiasm in any extreme form, whether in literature or religion, was anathema to the well-bred man of the period. Thus the clergy of the Established Church were more often witnesses to the reasonableness of Christian doctrines (particularly with new scientific thought in mind) than chastisers of sin. The Church preached morality rather than salvation.

In contrast, the Evangelical Movement, spearheaded by John and Charles Wesley and George Whitfield, had rediscovered Luther's great doctrine of Justification by Faith: that salvation is achieved, not by a man's own works or merit, but by his faith in the redeeming power of Jesus Christ. These men were at the peak of their influence during Carey's formative years. Whitfield died when Carey was nine; Charles Wesley when he was twenty-seven; John Wesley in Carey's thirtieth year. In addition, the Quaker and Baptist denominations had increased in strength owing to the greater official religious tolerance of the age. The Test and Corporation Acts which barred Dissenters from paid offices of state, from holding commissions in the Army and Navy, and so on, were not at this time always strictly enforced. They were the legacy of the bitter religious struggles of the later Stuart reigns. Although

* A Dissenter was a person who was not 'in communion' with the Established Church of England; that is, who refused to accept its doctrines and practice. The term, although it could include Roman Catholics, was more often applied to protestants such as Baptists, Congregationalists, Presbyterians and Quakers.

there was still prejudice – at times, bitter – against Dissenters and although they were excluded as a class from higher education and civil rights, there was no longer persecution. That would no doubt have been too 'extreme' for the Age of Reason, too 'enthusiastic'. It was left to the Dissenting Churches to stress the self-discipline and active zeal which were missing from the Established Church of the period.

In Piddington, Carey found himself working alongside a senior apprentice named John Warr who was some three years older than himself. Warr was a Dissenter and did not hesitate to seek to convert the new employee to his views. Both William and his sister speak of the influence of this young man and the passionate arguments over religion in which their employer, Mr. Nichols, also joined. Carey, with the stubborn arrogance of youth, could not bear to be bested in argument. He confesses how he would bolster up the weakness of his case by an assumed confidence of manner, stifling within himself the growing conviction that the reasoned beliefs of the Dissenters were preferable to the dogma of the Anglican Church.

At this time, also, his general conduct was causing his master some concern. 'He had before been rather inclined to be gay, which gave his parents, as well as his master, some little uneasiness,'[21] writes his sister of this period. This sounds very much like the typical teenage syndrome of bouts of rebellion alternating with agonising crises of conscience, the search for an identity which is part of the process of growing up. 'I wanted something,' Carey wrote, 'but had no idea that nothing but an entire change of heart could do me good.'[22]

It is impossible to know whether argument and discussion alone would have brought about in Carey the conversion which was to have so profound an effect on his future career. It is certain, however, that his outlook was changed by an incident to which he confesses in the letter to Andrew Fuller from which most of the few facts known about his youth are drawn. It was an incident which he must have kept secret from his family for his sister writes of his conversion merely: '. . . the conduct, together with the powerful arguments, of his young friend, *connected with some other trifling circumstances*, (Author's italics) made an impression on his mind. . . .'[23]

Carey tells us that it was a custom at Christmas time that apprentices should be allowed to collect Christmas-boxes from tradespeople with whom their master had dealings. He was given permission to collect such small sums as he journeyed round the district making deliveries for Mr. Nichols. No doubt he looked forward to having a few pence for himself. When William called on one particular ironmonger, imagine his surprise when the tradesman asked him if he would prefer to have a sixpence or a shilling. A shilling! A whole silver shilling! Probably equivalent in value to a pound or more by today's values. Naturally, he chose the shilling and gleefully put it in his pocket. After several more calls from which he gathered together a few more pence for himself, he decided to buy some articles on which he had set his heart. To his dismay, when he counted out his money to pay for them, he discovered that the ironmonger's shilling was a counterfeit. William wanted his purchases very badly so, stifling his conscience, he made up the sum with a shilling out of the money he had collected on his master's behalf. However, that left him with the problem of how to account to his master for the missing shilling. Mr. Nichols was a stern man and William was afraid of him. Let Carey continue the story in his own words:

> I . . . therefore came to the resolution to declare strenuously that the bad money was his. I well remember the struggles of mind which I had on this occasion, and that I made this deliberate sin a matter of prayer to God as I passed over the fields home. I there promised, that if God would but get me clearly over this, or, in other words, help me through with the theft, I would certainly for the future leave off all evil practices; but this theft and consequent lying appeared to me so necessary, that they could not be dispensed with. A gracious God did *not* get me safe through. . . .[24]

This was the 'trifling circumstance' of Mary Carey's letter!

On hearing William's account of the transaction, Mr. Nichols sent his other apprentice back to the ironmonger with a request that he be reimbursed for the bad shilling. The tradesman replied that he had paid his account with good coin but that he had played a joke on young Carey over his Christmas-box money. Thus the boy's conduct became known to the ironmonger, to Mr. Nichols and to Carey's fellow-apprentice. Carey's shame and remorse were acute and for a long time he dare not go out in public or attend any place of worship, so convinced was he that everyone would know of his crime and point an accusing finger.

In order to understand Carey's anguish, it must be appreciated that theft (or larceny) was a grave crime, visited with dire penalties, in the seventeen-seventies. It is easy from the distance of the twentieth century to regard the incident lightly; a shilling seems such a small sum, even allowing for depreciation. Indeed, the changing standard of values of today's society regards cruelty as more blameworthy than dishonesty. In contrast, eighteenth-century England (and not least, in the law) was extremely crude and its punishments barbaric. There were two hundred crimes against property that carried the death penalty at this time, whereas crimes against the person (other than murder, mayhem and rape) were relatively lightly punished. Property was held in greater respect than human life. It is little wonder that the slave trade was considered acceptable commercial practice.

In Carey's time, the theft of more than a shilling in money or 'money's worth' was 'grand larceny' which was a capital offence. The corpse of the criminal was sometimes hung in chains in public and left to rot as a warning to others. This was known as 'gibbeting' and there was an instance of it at Leicester as late as 1832. The theft of a shilling or less was 'petty (*petit*, or small) larceny' which, apart from imprisonment, carried the penalty of forfeiture of goods and chattels, whipping or transportation for seven years to the plantations of the West Indies or America. Thus, as late as 1806, a woman was transported for seven years for 'the theft of a felt hat, value 6d.'[25] Young Carey must have been aware that grave penalties of a greater or lesser degree awaited a convicted thief. Roadside gibbets were a common sight in his day and he regularly tramped the main roads from Bedford to Kettering and Northampton. Moreover, the newspapers reported the gruesome sentences pronounced at each Assize.

It is ironic, in view of the importance that has attached over the years to 'Carey's shilling' that, as the law stood in the year 1777, no felony had in fact been committed. Failing any other evidence than his own account, Carey was not guilty of theft, even though he dishonestly appropriated to himself a shilling of his master's. By today's law, his dishonest intention 'permanently to deprive' his master of the shilling would indeed constitute theft. However, as the law stood in Carey's time, larceny was an offence whereby an item was taken without consent from another's *possession*. Because Carey had not yet handed over the money either actually or constructively to his employer, it had not yet become his employer's money. He therefore could not steal something which was not yet in another's possession. It was to remedy this anomaly in the law that Parliament created the crime of 'embezzlement' in 1799.[26]

The offence which Cary had in fact committed was to 'utter' (that is, knowingly pass as genuine) a counterfeit coin. So much counterfeit money was in circulation in the early eighteenth century that the *Counterfeiting of Coins Act* was passed in 1742. Among the various penalties provided under the Act, imprisonment was laid down as the appropriate sentence for a first offence of 'uttering'.

However, the niceties of legal argument would be beyond the appreciation of a sixteen-year-old. Carey had had a strict moral upbringing. In his own eyes and (he was sure) in the eyes of God, he was a thief and a sinner. He was deeply ashamed. In the long term, the incident had a profound effect on the future pattern of his life; in the short term, he attended prayer meetings much more regularly.

He was still nominally a member of the Anglican Church but on 10th February, 1779 – a date clearly imprinted on his memory – he made the decision to cease attending 'a lifeless, carnal ministry'[27] in preference for one 'more evangelical'.[28]

Thaι particular Sunday had been declared by King George III a day of national fasting and prayer, for the war with the rebellious American colonies was going badly.

Trouble with the colonies had been simmering for the past two decades. That same conquest of Canada in which Peter Carey had played his small part in the seventeen-fifties had removed one of the reasons that had kept the American colonists loyal to the home country. The defeat of France meant that her threat to the expansion west of the colonies had been removed. There was no longer so great a need to rely on the presence of British troops in America for security. Without the need for troops, there was less justification for the taxes to which the colonists were subjected – taxes which were imposed without any representation of the colonies in the London Parliament. Moreover, the colonies smarted under restrictive Trade Laws which limited their markets, and under bureaucratic control which they felt infringed their liberties – particularly the 'writs of assistance' which allowed British Customs officers to search private houses.

Open hostilities with the mother country broke out in 1775 with the Battle of Lexington. At first the colonists fared badly but the Declaration of Independence in 1776 stiffened their resolve and when first France and then Spain allied themselves with America, Britain found herself harassed on several fronts at once. By the national day of prayer in February 1779, Gibraltar was blockaded, Britain had lost command of the sea and, in addition to losing ground in America, her garrisons in the West Indies were bottled up by the French. The outlook for Britain was grave.

Carey went with John Warr to the service of intercession at the Meeting House at Hackleton. There, the preacher, Thomas Chater, made a powerful appeal in his sermon for complete commitment to Christ. He quoted Hebrews 13:13, 'Let us therefore go out unto him without the camp, bearing his reproach'. This somewhat obscure verse seemed on this occasion to speak directly to Carey. Its meaning took on clarity and personal significance. In the closed community of a small English village, those who were Dissenters were despised, were outcasts. Surely God was telling him to leave the Church of England ('the camp') and to join the Dissenters ('without the camp'). Only there would he find guidance along the way of the cross which he could not find in the Established Church.

Thus did young Carey join with his fellow-apprentice, John Warr, and a few older Christians in forming a 'congregational' church in Hackleton.

This village was really another part of Piddington, just as Church End and Pury End made up the village of Paulerspury. Even had Carey not become a Dissenter, he could not have worshipped in the Established Church for there was no satisfactory Anglican church in Hackleton. The squire had long appropriated to himself the living of that village (worth

£300 a year) along with its tithes and glebe, merely sending his private chaplain 'at times'[29] to take services.

Another far-reaching consequence of Carey's apprenticeship with Mr. Nichols was that his master allowed him access to his books among which was a New Testament commentary containing a number of passages in Greek. Mr. Nichols did not understand the language but this did not deter Carey from satisfying his curiosity about these strange characters. There was at that time working in Paulerspury as a weaver a young man, Tom Jones, who had 'dropped out' from University. On his periodic visits home, Carey would carefully copy out passages in Greek and would ask the former undergraduate to interpret them for him. This the weaver did, explaining the terminations of the words and the grammar. Carey's natural gift for languages must have been quite exceptional for, with only this small assistance, added to his own powers of perseverance, he soon mastered the Greek language.

In September 1779, Clarke Nichols died and Carey's apprenticeship was transferred to a relative of his former master, a Mr. Thomas Old of Hackleton. William was by now eighteen years of age, small in stature and slight of build. Rev. Thomas Scott, vicar of Olney, has set on record how he used to visit Mr. Old two or three times a year and was greatly impressed by the young apprentice and by the sensible questions he asked. 'I from the first thought young Carey an extraordinary person.'[30]

This man, Thomas Scott, had succeeded Rev. John Newton at Olney. John Newton became an outstanding figure in the anti-slavery campaign in England. Before taking Holy Orders, he had himself been a ship's master engaged in the slave trade. Indeed, he composed the hymn 'How sweet the name of Jesus sounds' during the course of a voyage with a cargo of slaves! He referred to himself as 'the old African blasphemer'. It is possible – indeed, probable – that Carey heard him preach during his ministry in Olney. Carey tells us that he attended many different churches in the district, seeking guidance and inspiration from the various preachers. Olney was only six miles from Piddington/Hackleton – no distance at all for a youth who tramped many miles further than that in a day delivering his master's goods. Slavery was certainly a burden on Carey's heart. 'He (William) was always, from his first being thoughtful, remarkably impressed about heathen lands, and the slave-trade. I never remember his engaging in prayer, in his family, or in public, without praying for those poor creatures.'[31]

Before William reached the age of twenty, he took on the responsibility of a wife, marrying his master's sister-in-law, Dorothy (Dolly) Plackett, on 10th June, 1781. She was nearly six years older than William, her christening being recorded as taking place on 25th January, 1756. She was a girl from a Puritan background and her father was the leader of the Hackleton Meeting. There is no evidence as to whether the marriage was a love-match. Carey always speaks of his wife with respect and a certain tenderness but their relationship must have had limitations. Dorothy was unable at that time to write. The entry of their marriage in the Piddington Parish Register, a copy of which can be seen in the Carey Museum at Moulton, is signed by her with a cross. Presumably, therefore, she would be unable to read either which, for a man already as studious as the young Carey, must have placed bounds to the scope of their conversation. In fairness to Dorothy, only a privileged few girls of her status in that period received anything in the way of education. Perhaps if she had been able to set down her own views on paper, she might have suffered less at the hands of Carey's biographers. 'Never had minister, missionary or scholar a less sympathetic mate, due largely to . . . latent mental disease' writes Dr. George Smith; and again, in the same book, 'Not only did she remain to the last a peasant woman, with a reproachful tongue . . .'[32] 'The marriage did not prove suitable,' writes John Brown Myers.[33]

However, they were happy in their first home in Hackleton, even though they were extremely poor. Carey planted and tended the first of the many gardens he was to create throughout his life; and within a year their marriage was blessed by the addition of a daughter who was named Ann after William's grandmother.

Already Carey was beginning to develop the talents which would eventually lead him into the mission field. Ever since his apprenticeship with Clarke Nichols, he had discussed and read and argued about Christian principles. Within a year of his marriage he was preaching regularly at Earls Barton – eight miles' walk each way – though the church there was so small that 'he did not receive from the poor folks enough to pay for the clothes he wore out in their service.'[34] Many of the tiny Nonconformist churches at this time could not afford a paid minister but had to rely on visiting lay preachers such as Carey. He also preached once a month in his home village of Paulerspury and it must have been a source of great gratification, if some bewilderment, to his mother to be told by a neighbour that her dissenting son would one day be a great preacher. Of course, William's views must have caused a certain embarrassment to his father, being the Parish Clerk. Mary Carey writes: 'Our parents were always friendly to religion; yet, on some accounts, we should rather have wished him to go from home, than come home to preach.'[35] However, Mr. Carey Senior did slip into the assembly on one occasion, unseen by his son, and 'was highly gratified'[36] by what he heard.

In prayer with his family at home on these occasions, William gave less satisfaction. His sister describes her resentment at his over-zealousness. 'Like Gideon, he seemed for throwing down all the altars of Baal in one night.'[37] She says how self-righteous he was in his Dissenting beliefs and how antipathetic to the Anglican church. 'Often have I felt my pride rise while he was engaged in prayer, at the mention of those words in Isaiah, "that all our righteousness was like filthy rags." I did not think he thought *his* so, but looked on me and the family as filthy, not himself and his party. Oh, what pride is in the human heart! Nothing but my love for my brother would have kept me from showing my resentment.'[38]

If Carey did indeed have any pride in himself – and he frequently castigates himself for such a sin – his faith was shortly to be put to a severe test. Some time towards the end of 1782 or early in 1783, his baby daughter Ann was carried off by a fever. William himself was also smitten by the same disease and all but died. His mother came over to Hackleton to help nurse him and was appalled at the impoverished circumstances in which the little family lived but which they had sought to keep a secret. It says much for the loving and united family feeling that William's young brother Thomas, still only in his 'teens, saved what he could from his own small earnings and gave it to William and his wife. A collection was raised also in his home village which enabled Carey and his wife to buy a small cottage at Piddington.

William recovered from the fever but was left with a cough and an ague which troubled him constantly as long as he lived in that low-lying district which was marshy and often fog-bound. A further consequence of the disease was that it left the young man quite bald and he was obliged to wear a wig to hide this disfiguring condition.

It was probably some time during June, 1782 that Carey first heard Rev. Andrew Fuller preach – though he could not at the time know how closely their lives would be intertwined in the future. In a subsequent letter to Fuller, Carey describes the occasion as follows, illustrating at once his zeal and his abject poverty:

> . . . I cannot say in what year it was, but you will recollect. At the Association at Olney, when Mr. Guy preached from "Grow in grace", &c., and you, from "Be not children in understanding"; I, not possessed of a penny, that I recollect, went to Olney. I fasted all day because I could not purchase a dinner; but towards evening, Mr. Chater, in company with some friends from Earl's Barton saw me, and asked me to go with them, where I remember I got a glass of wine . . .[39]

Still, however, the young man was undecided in his views on religion, apart from abandoning the formalities of the Anglican Church. He was struggling to crystallise his beliefs, to establish foundations on which to build his faith. 'Having so slight an acquaintance with ministers,' he was to write in later years, 'I was obliged to draw all from the Bible alone'.[40] However, one day he was loaned a recently published book by Robert Hall entitled *Help to Zion's Travellers.*[41] This book had a profound effect on his mind for in it he 'found all that arranged and illustrated which I had been so long picking up by scraps. I do not remember ever to have read any book with such raptures as I did that . . . and I rejoice to say, that those doctrines are the choice of my heart to this day'.[42]

This book, together with a sermon he heard preached at an infant baptism, turned his thoughts and discussion to the question of believer's baptism. His deliberations confirmed the opinions he had formed from constant study of the New Testament. The case for believer's baptism seemed to him unanswerable; he could find no scriptural authority for what he termed '*rhantism*' or 'infant sprinkling'.[43]

> The eunuch said, See, here is water; what doth hinder me to be baptized?
> And Philip said, *If thou believest with all thine heart*, thou mayest.[44]

On 5th October, 1783 Carey was baptised in the waters of the River Nene at Northampton by Rev. John Ryland – an event which Ryland recorded in his journal: 'This day baptised a poor journeyman shoemaker.'

Carey needed all the grace that his baptism bestowed on him to help him cope with the problems of the next few months.

On 31st December 1783, Thomas Old died and was buried in the churchyard at Piddington three days later. William took over the business (and also the responsibility of caring for his master's widow and four children). It was not a good time to be in business without the backing of capital. Trade was bad following Britain's humiliating defeat in America. One customer, taking advantage of Thomas Old's death, countermanded a large order, leaving the goods on Carey's hands and no return for all his hard work. If he had been more experienced, he might have successfully demanded payment for he had fulfilled his part of the contract, but he was only a diffident twenty-two year old, wholly inexperienced in the running of a business. The winter of 1783/1784 was one of the coldest on record, with nine weeks of continuous frost. Carey tramped the icy roads from village to village, trying to sell the surplus goods.

Yet there were compensations. It was about this time that he was able to borrow the volumes of *Captain Cook's Voyages*, the news of which journeys had so many years before captured his imagination. 'Reading Cook's voyages was the first thing that engaged my mind to think of missions,' Carey said many years later.[45] Would it be too fanciful to imagine Carey's lonely winter journeys shortened by eager thoughts of the great field that awaited a harvester on the other side of the world?

2

Young Radical
1785–1792

Everyone who ever worked alongside William Carey pays tribute to his dogged persistence.

His sister writes of him: 'Whatever he began he finished: difficulties never seemed to discourage his mind'.[1]

His brother Thomas says: 'I . . . recollect that he was, from a boy . . . always resolutely determined never to give up any point or particle of any thing on which his mind was set, till he had arrived at a clear knowledge and sense of his subject. He was neither diverted from his object by allurements, nor driven from the search of it by threats or ridicule . . .'.[2]

Carey himself said to his nephew: 'Eustace, if after my removal any one should think it worth his while to write my Life, I will give you a criterion by which you may judge of its correctness. If he give me credit for being a plodder, he will describe me justly. I can plod. I can persevere in any definite pursuit. To this I owe everything.'[3]

Certainly the young shoemaker must have required all the doggedness of which his character was capable during the years he spent in Piddington. He admitted that though he could cope with shoe-making, he was not successful at running a business. Under-nourished and constantly struggling against the persistent cough and fever that plagued him, Carey endeavoured not only to scrape a living for seven people, but also to preach and study.

It must have brought him a dizzying sense of relief when, early in 1785, an opportunity arose to move to Moulton as preacher to the small Baptist community there.* The church

* It must be understood that there can be no straight comparison between an Anglican and a Baptist church. Quite apart from hierarchical differences, the Anglican church tends (though not exclusively) to draw its members from a parish, a geographical area. A Baptist church is a

at Moulton had been without a minister for ten years. Services had become infrequent and the actual church building had fallen into disrepair. According to an account written at the time, the congregation ran 'the risque of being buried'. The stipend was only £10 a year, supplemented by £5 from a fund in London, so that Carey was no better off financially than at Piddington. However, the local schoolmaster had recently left the village and Carey was able to supplement his meagre salary by teaching.

He moved to Moulton on Lady Day, 25th March, 1785.

The village lies about five miles out of Northampton on the road to Kettering, on slightly higher ground than Piddington and consequently better for Carey's health. He had a cottage with a small garden close by the Baptist church.

It was a pleasure to be free of the burden of shoe-making and Carey threw himself with enthusiasm into the task of rallying the congregation. His ministry – albeit still probationary – must have been reasonably effective for the Church Minute Book speaks of him with affection as 'Our Beloved Pastor'. He raised sufficient funds locally to have the church building repaired and slightly enlarged. The school, it would appear, was less successful.

> There might be another reason why his school succeeded so ill (his sister writes). He probably had much less faculty for teaching than for acquiring. And then he could never assume the carriage, nor utter the tones, nor wield the sceptre of the schoolmaster. He would frequently smile at his incompetency in these respects.[4]

Carey himself was obviously a natural scholar. It is on record that in a matter of weeks he taught himself sufficient French and Dutch to be able to read books in those languages. Yet it is not uncommon for a teacher to be too intelligent for his pupils, unable to understand their lack of comprehension of what seems so easy to him; impatient at their lack of interest in what is to him of such burning concern. It can well be imagined that the twenty-four year old Carey would feel

---

'gathered' church; that is, a coming together or voluntary association of men and women who feel they have experienced saving grace and who are fully conscious of a commitment individually made before God. They give witness of their faith in the sacrament of 'believer's baptism'.

similarly frustrated before a class of children from largely unlettered homes. Yet he must have tried. As evidence of this, there is in the small Carey Museum at Moulton a reconstruction of Carey's world map made by Dr. Selwood in collaboration with Carey's great-grandson and biographer, S. Pearce Carey. Carey's friend, Andrew Fuller, describes the original map as follows:

> I remember on going into the room where he employed himself at his business, I saw hanging up against the wall a very large map, consisting of several sheets of paper pasted together by himself, on which he had drawn, with a pen, a place for every nation in the known world, and entered into it whatever he met with in reading, relative to its population, religion, etc . . .[5]

If Carey had had more money, no doubt he would have had a globe on which to locate the places he found described in books or to trace the latest discoveries of Captain Cook who had made two more great voyages of discovery in 1772 and 1776. Terrestrial globes had been used for navigation since the fifteenth century, but by the late eighteenth century they had become a required piece of equipment in every well-appointed home. They were often of very beautiful workmanship such as the two at Parham Park, West Sussex, that belonged to Sir Joseph Banks, Bart. (later to become President of the Royal Society). He had been botanist on Cook's first voyage in the *Endeavour*. But Carey had no money. Instead, he had to make do with a sheet map of the world and (it is said – though it has not been possible to find confirmation of this) a home-made globe fashioned out of pieces of leather (which, no doubt, his pupils would rather have kicked around the village green). In the reproduction sheet map there is confirmation that Carey had by the time he was in Moulton read the published accounts of Cook's voyages. In the bottom right hand corner of the map, roughly where Australia would be on a Mercator projection, is the entry:

> Australia = New Holland
> 12,000,000 Pagans
> 1 or 2 ministers here

It would be interesting to know how the estimate of population was arrived at.

The entry for Easter Island reads:

> People thieves. Large statues.
> No wood. Plantains. Yams.
> Potatoes. Sugar Cane.

He goes into greater detail for China:

> The Chinese are middle-sized, broad faces.
> Their eyes are black & small, noses blunt,
>   high cheekbones, large lips.
> Emperors and princes wear yellow.
> Some mandarins wear black, some red.
> Common people wear blue.
> White is for mourning.

In view of Carey's later great work in the mission field, it is interesting to note what little he knew at this time of the Indian sub-continent:

> Indoostan.
> 110,000,000
> Mahometans and Pagans.
> Brahmins, Sitris, Beise and Sudders.
> Rice, Pomegranates, Oranges,
>   etc. banyan roots.
>   yams, radishes.
> 8,000,000 Indians are
> Pagans, vigilant, cruel, warlike.

There is a sweeping simplicity about the entry, reminiscent of Hendrik van Loon's later and very effective description in *The Home of Mankind*: 'India is very full of people.'

S. Pearce Carey writes in his *William Carey D.D., Fellow of the Linnaean Society*: 'His pupils saw sometimes a strange sight, their master moved to tears over a geography lesson as, pointing to continents, islands and peoples, he would cry, "And these are pagans, pagans!"'[6] That biography, though undoubtedly a work of love, tends throughout to be somewhat emotional in tone and, as the author rarely quotes the authority for his statements, it is possible that this story – like the one of the boy Carey preaching from the stump of the wych-elm – is apocryphal. Certainly there is nothing in the records to suggest that the intelligent, enquiring lively village lad with his quietly dogged and dutiful pursuit of his trade would be likely within two or three years to become so emotional. Nor do any of the records of Carey's public utterances on the need for foreign missions show an emotional approach. Passionate enthusiasm, yes, but always backed by reason and facts.

The school in Moulton did not last long for the former schoolmaster, William Chown, returned to the village and opened a rival establishment. He had always enjoyed a high reputation as a teacher and, as there were not enough children in the village to warrant two schools, Carey's pupils deserted him. Once again he had to return to shoe-making to supplement his stipend. This time he did not attempt to be his own master – his experiences in Hackleton and Piddington had shown him only too clearly the disadvantages – but became a journeyman shoemaker, as his father had been a journeyman weaver. He worked for a Government contractor in Northampton, a Mr. Thomas Gotch, who supplied the Army and Navy with footwear. Once a fortnight, William made the ten or eleven mile round trip into Kettering on foot, taking in a batch of completed boots and shoes and returning with a fresh supply of leather. For each fortnight's work he received nine or ten shillings. Little wonder that Andrew Fuller was to write later: 'I have been assured that he and his family have lived for a great while together without tasting animal food, and with but a scanty pittance of other provision.'[7]

To say that Carey was preaching at Moulton Baptist Church and was receiving a stipend would imply that he was already an ordained minister, but this was not the case. Indeed, he was not even yet in membership with a Baptist Church although he had undergone the sacrament of believer's baptism. Even today, it is quite common for a man with sufficient gift to be invited to preach regularly in a Baptist Church without being 'set apart' for the ministry. Moreover, no minister is directed to a church; he is invited or 'called' to be pastor by the members of a church after they have heard him preach, have interviewed him and have decided that he is God's choice for them. In Carey's case, he applied for membership to the Baptist Church at Olney where he was received into fellowship on 14th July, 1785. This church, whose pastor was John Sutcliff, had a large membership; the premises could accommodate a congregation of seven hundred. Carey intimated to the church that he wished to enter the ministry but, after hearing him preach, the members at Olney decided that he needed a period of probation before ordination. A Mr. Hall of Arnsby, when criticising one of Carey's pulpit exercises, said 'Brother Carey, you have no *likes* in your sermons. Christ taught that the Kingdom of Heaven was *like* to leaven hid in meal, *like* to a grain of mustard, &c. You tell us what things are; but never, what they are like.'[8] Not until April, 1787 was he considered satisfactory. The Minute Book of the Church at Moulton records:

> *1787. May 3.* At our Church meeting our Brother Wm. Carey was received by a letter of Dismission (i.e. transfer) from the Baptist Church at Olney in the Double Character of a Member and Minister and his Ordination was settled or appointed to be on Wednesday, Aug. 1st.

Three ministers – John Sutcliff of Olney, John Ryland of Northampton and Andrew Fuller of Kettering – officiated at the service of ordination. In this way, the four cornerstones of the Baptist Missionary Society came together.

Even before his ordination, Carey's thought had been turning to the need for missionary effort. After the move to Moulton, he had the opportunity of meeting other ministers of the Baptist denomination at their periodic meetings, the Ministers' Fraternals of the Northampton Association. Baptist Churches were then, as now, grouped together in about ten regional Associations, somewhat in the manner of Methodist circuits. Although these Associations had no authority over member churches, they afforded a forum for the exchange of ideas; a meeting together for fellowship; a means of obtaining recognition for the denomination and an opportunity to present a united front and a united voice for the Baptist Church. The Northampton Association in Carey's day stretched from St. Albans to Lincoln.

There was an occasion during 1786 (recorded by Mr. Morris, minister of Clipstone) when the ministers gathered together for their Fraternal in Northampton under the chairmanship of Mr. Ryland, Senior (father of the John Ryland who baptised and was present at the ordination of William Carey). He invited the younger members of the company to

suggest a subject for discussion. Carey could not keep back the question that had begun to possess his thought. 'Was not the command given to the Apostles, to teach all nations,' he asked, 'obligatory on all succeeding ministers to the end of the world, seeing that the accompanying promise was of equal extent?'

This was in complete contradiction to the interpretation of the Gospels generally held at that time. The comfortable doctrine of the eighteenth century moderates was that the evangelisation of the heathen was the personal privilege of the Apostles; that the work had been fulfilled in previous ages; that the heathen world could therefore be assumed to have rejected the Gospel and now had to await its fate on Judgment Day. The 'Particular' Baptists, of whom Mr. Ryland, Senior, was one, maintained that God would enlighten the heathen in His own way without human aid. Either way, there was an adequate argument for doing nothing about missions. This was expressed forcibly by the aged Chairman at the Northampton meeting, who reproved Carey with the words: 'You are a miserable enthusiast for asking such a question. Nothing can be done before another Pentecost.'

Mortified by the censure he had brought down upon himself, Carey fell silent – but he did not change his views. It is difficult to appreciate today the hyper-Calvinistic view of Mr. Ryland, Senior that demanded no responsibility for personal evangelism. Perhaps a clue to his reasoning lies in the two words 'miserable *enthusiast*'. For Carey, the obligation lay on *all* Christians.

'Obligation' was indeed the main burden of his argument. After his public rebuke in Northampton, he set down on paper a detailed analysis of the state of the world as he saw it, the need for missionary enterprise and the methods by which it should be carried out. In addition, he took in turn each of the arguments advanced against missionary endeavour and proceeded to demolish it. The study was logical, lucid and persuasive. A friend offered him money to have it published but he did not take up the offer at that time – a decision which, with the benefit of hindsight, proved to be a wise one, for William himself needed to mature before he could hope to win over men of influence to his views.

There was work to be done in Moulton to build up the

church. There was a growing family to provide for – three sons born in quick succession: Felix, William and Peter. And at the beginning of October, 1787, only two months after he was ordained, William had what for him must have been the inestimable joy and privilege of baptising his wife, Dorothy. There was more time for study, too, thanks to Mr. Gotch, Carey's 'Manufacturer'. Gotch was a deacon at Andrew Fuller's church in Kettering. Perhaps Fuller discussed with him the talented young man at Moulton and how hard he worked at the study of languages. Whether or not that was the reason, Mr. Gotch, hiding his generosity under grudging words, told Carey: 'I do not intend you should spoil any more of my leather, but you may proceed as fast as you can with your Latin, Greek, and Hebrew, and I will allow you from my own private purse 10s. a week.'[9]

This sum, with the five shillings a week stipend from the church, was all that Carey had to sustain himself and his family during the four years he spent in Moulton. That the church recognised his poverty is apparent from a Church Minute for 2nd April, 1789 that reads 'Our Beloved Pastor *who had been in considerable straits for want of Maintenance* informed us that the Church at Leicester had given him an invitation to make trial with them . . .' On May 7th, Carey told his Moulton congregation that he had accepted a call to Leicester.

The Harvey Lane Church, Leicester, in addition to having 'become a scandal'[10] owing to the depravity of its deacons and the ineffectiveness of its pastor, was almost as poor and run down as the one in Moulton so, materially, Carey was only fractionally better off. Indeed, he had once again to take up teaching in order to be able to provide even the basic necessities for his family. However, according to the accounts of visitors to the house, its poverty was brightened by the beautiful flowers Carey kept on the windowsill of his downstairs room. Another child, Lucy, was born in Leicester but, like the Carey's first daughter, died before she was two years old.

Amidst admiration for Carey's dedication to missions and his application to study, thought should be spared for Dorothy Carey who flits through his story like a pale and unhappy shadow. Almost nothing is known about her but it is not unreasonable to imagine that life must have been desperately hard for her, struggling to make ends meet, constantly pregnant yet seeing two of her babies carried off by sickness. Whether, if they had been better nourished, Anne or Lucy might have survived can only be speculation; the rate of infant mortality at that period was high even in better-off homes. But the strain must have been particularly great for Dorothy with her young husband so completely absorbed in his preaching and studying – interests which it would be difficult for an unlettered girl to share. She must have felt at times very much alone. That Carey drove himself relentlessly, disciplined himself and used every minute of every day is apparent from a letter he wrote to his father at this time:

> Leicester, Nov. 12th, 1790
>
> Dear and Honoured Father,
>
> . . . I have no excuse to make for not writing to you before now . . . but when I review my hours, I am sometimes inclined to think that it is out of my power.
>
> Polly's affectionate letter I received with pleasure and shame; pleasure to hear of your welfare, and shame that she has any occasion to complain. I hope to amend for the future; but if I send you an account of the partition of my time, you will see that you must not expect frequent letters.
>
> On Monday I confine myself to the study of the learned languages, and oblige myself to translate something. On Tuesday, to the study of science, history, composition, &c. On Wednesday I preach a lecture, and have been for more than twelve months on the book of Revelation. On Thursday I visit my friends. Friday and Saturday are spent in preparing for the Lord's-day; and the Lord's-day, in preaching the word of God. Once a fortnight I preach three times at home; and once a fortnight I go to a neighbouring village in the evening. Once a month I go to another village on the Tuesday evening. My school begins at nine o'clock in the morning and continues till four o'clock in winter, and five in summer. I have acted for this twelvemonth as secretary to the committee of dissenters; and am now to be regularly appointed to that office, with a salary. Add to this, occasional journeys, ministers' meetings, &c.; and you will rather wonder that I have any time, than that I have so little. . .

S. Pearce Carey describes his distinguished great-grandfather as being an enthusiastic member of the

Philosophical Institute. Perhaps those were the 'friends' he visited on Thursdays. Such Literary & Philosophic Societies were, along with the growth of circulating libraries, an expression of the thirst for knowledge and culture which activated the late eighteenth-century middle-classes every bit as much as the aristocracy. At the Leicester Institute there would foregather reformers like Howard; scientists like Priestley; Carey's friend Gardiner talking on 'gravitation' and 'comets'. There would be ardent discussions on science and philosophy. The founder of Leicester's Institute was Richard Phillips, a Quaker, whose newspaper (Leicester's first) was criticised for its boldness in supporting the great revolutionary struggle that was now raging in France.

The Revolution was at first strongly supported in thinking circles. Thomas Paine (who wrote *The Rights of Man*) was made an honorary citizen by the Republican government. Coleridge wrote a poem to celebrate the Destruction of the Bastille. Wordsworth eagerly embraced the republican ideal of democracy and even, for a time, moved to Paris. The Revolution 'symbolised the destruction of despots in Church and State, and the chance of an era in which human personality, freed from the shackles of the past, could achieve a new fulfilment'.[11] Dissenters in particular, critical of authority derived from tradition, welcomed the way in which the French had thrown off 'the iron yoke of slavery'.[12] Carey saw the French Revolution as 'a movement towards a completer humanity', 'a glorious door opened . . . for the gospel, by the spread of civil and religious liberty, and by the diminution of the papal power'.[13] As Secretary of the Dissenters' Committee, he would no doubt have hoped that the 'religious liberty' he felt confident was coming to France would find equal expression in England. There was already pressure at Westminster for the repeal of the Test and Corporation Acts which placed restrictions on Dissenters. The rejection by Parliament of a motion to this effect in 1790 could only have reinforced Carey's radical opinions.

With all this activity, there could not have been much time left over for family life – although it must be recorded to Carey's credit that, despite the task he felt called by God to carry out, which demanded from him so much in the way of study and preparation, he was yet able to maintain the warm affection of his children and their devoted support for the rest of his life.

There is no doubt that Carey did feel called by God. He continues the letter to his father above-quoted with the words: 'I am not my own, nor would I choose for myself. Let God employ me where he thinks fit, and give me patience and discretion to fill up my station to his honour and glory.'

There is a resolution, a sense of commitment in this letter that over-rides the ties of family affection. 'You will see that you must not expect frequent letters' has about it already the ring of authority of a man who knows his course. It echoes the commitment of his Master, Jesus, as pictured by the gospel-writer Luke: 'He stedfastly set his face to go to Jerusalem.'[14] It had not yet been revealed to Carey where *his* Jerusalem lay although, his imagination fired by the voyages of Captain Cook, he hoped it might be in the South Pacific. However, he was willing to wait patiently upon his Lord for guidance. A letter written to his sister Mary at this time is worth quoting for the illumination it throws on his Christian outlook:

> Leicester, 14th Dec. 1789
>
> . . . Again do you doubt because you have not seen visions, heard voices, or felt impulses. This I know is what many Christians placed dependance upon. But suppose that you have felt nothing of all this, there is no reason for you to despair and if you have been favoured with repeated instances of this nature this is no proof of your Christianity. I apprehend that too many place too much confidence in things of this nature and make a shining light an audible voice, or the sudden application of a passage of Scripture an evidence of their being the children of God. But where is the part of God's Word that informs us of any such evidence of religion as these are . . .
>
> You will observe that conviction flows from illumination to see our sin, and the demands of God's righteous law. . . Real religion consists in all these, conviction, repentance, faith, obedience, submission, zeal and consolation.

On 27th April, 1791 at the Northampton Association Easter Meeting of ministers at Clipstone, two great sermons were preached by John Sutcliff and Andrew Fuller. If emphasis is laid on the impact of sermons on Carey's thoughts and actions, it must be remembered that in Dissenting Churches great emphasis has always been placed on the sermon as a method of teaching. This was even more important with the only partly literate congregations of the eighteenth century than it is today. The two sermons on this occasion seemed to Carey to indicate that the speakers were of a like mind to himself. Both preachers made a call to missionary work; Fuller went further and castigated 'the pernicious influence of delay'. It is on record that Carey was deeply moved and urged his fellow ministers there and then to organise a missionary society on the lines he had set down on paper five years before. Still they hesitated – even Fuller. The scheme was too ambitious; the time was not ripe. At least, however, Carey's enthusiasm did move the meeting to encourage him to publish his paper so that all could read it. Furthermore, he was invited to preach at the next annual Association Meeting which would be held in Nottingham in the following spring.

The pamphlet was published on 12th May, 1792, shortly before that 'next Association Meeting'. The price was one shilling and sixpence, the proceeds to go towards the work of the foreign missions proposed therein. The title, as was usual at that time, was cumbrous: '*An Enquiry into the Obligation of Christians to use means for the Conversion of the Heathens in which the Religious State of the Different Nations of the World, the Success of Former Undertakings, and the Practicability of Further Undertakings, are Considered*.'

Rev. J. B. Middlebrook in his study *William Carey* writes of the *Enquiry*: '. . . even now, over a century and a half later, it is only the statistical pages that are out of date . . . Here for all time, with an absence of rhetoric, is the classical presentation of the argument for the World Mission of the Church.'

The *Enquiry* is too long to quote in full but it is worth while examining how effectively Carey removes the five main excuses he felt would be raised against missionary work: the distance of the 'heathen' lands; their barbarous ways; the physical danger to missionaries; the difficulties of procuring necessary supplies; the barrier to communication of foreign language.

> *FIRST*, As to their distance from us, whatever objections might have been made on that account before the invention of the mariner's compass, nothing can be alleged for it with any colour of plausibility in the present age. Men can now sail with

> as much certainty through the great South Sea as they can through the Mediterranean or any lesser sea . . .

The manner in which he cites the latest technological developments in navigational instruments has a modern ring about it that would appeal to the explorer of outer space. No doubt Carey was aware that Captain Cook on his second voyage in 1772, with the *Resolution* and the *Adventure*, had been testing the reliability of Harrison's Chronometer as a means of ascertaining longitude.

'Commerce shall subserve the spread of the gospel', Carey continues in this section, showing already a practical grasp of the economics of missionary work.

> *SECONDLY*, As to their uncivilised and barbarous way of living, this can be no objection to any, except those whose love of ease renders them unwilling to expose themselves to inconveniences for the good of others. It was no objection to the apostles and their successors, who went among the barbarous Germans and Gauls, and still more barbarous Britons. . . It *is* no objection to commercial men. It only requires that we should have as much love to the souls of our fellow-creatures . . . as they have for the profits arising from a few otter-skins. . .

There is heavy sarcasm here and the scorn of a man who has struggled at starvation level to serve his God for the reluctance of many to abandon their creature comforts.

> *THIRDLY*, In respect to the danger of being killed by them . . . I greatly question whether most of the barbarities practised by the savages upon those who have visited them, have not originated in some real or supposed affront, and were therefore, more properly, acts of self-defence, than proofs of ferocious dispositions. No wonder if the imprudence of sailors should prompt them to offend the simple savage, and the offence be resented. . .

No doubt Carey was again thinking of Captain Cook, killed in a sudden quarrel with the natives of Hawaii in 1779 – a particularly tragic end when one of his outstanding qualities was his ability to make friends with natives of all sorts through treating them with kindness and justice.

> *FOURTHLY*, As to the difficulty of procuring the necessaries of life, this would not be so great as may appear at first sight; for, though we could not procure European food, yet we might

procure such as the natives of those countries which we visit, subsist on themselves. . .

Once again, Carey's poverty was to prove to have been part of his training for missionary work. What hardship would a diet of rice and fish be to one who had 'lived for a great while together without tasting animal food'?[15]

Carey continues with enthusiasm to outline his plans for a small community of men, accompanied by their wives and children, all working together for the common good. Inevitably, the enthusiastic gardener is heard:

> . . . In most countries it would be necessary for them to cultivate a little spot of ground just for their support, which would be a resource to them, whenever their supplies failed. . . So small a number would, upon receiving the first crop, maintain themselves. . .
>
> *FIFTHLY*, As to learning their languages, the same means would be found necessary here as in trade between different nations. In some cases interpreters might be obtained . . . and . . . the missionaries must have patience, and mingle with the people, till they have learned so much of their language as to be able to communicate their ideas to them in it. It is well known to require no very extraordinary talents to learn, in the space of a year, or two at most, the language of any people upon earth. . .

Confident, prophetic words!

Two other brief extracts from the *Enquiry* are of importance. The first shows how realistic and humble was Carey's approach to missionary work:

> They (the missionaries) must be very careful not to resent injuries which may be offered to them, nor to think highly of themselves, so as to despise the poor heathens. . . They must take every opportunity of doing them good . . . they must instruct, exhort, and rebuke . . . and, above all, must be instant in prayer. . .

The second and last extract shows Carey ahead of his times, looking to the modern practice of training up indigenous missionaries to minister to their own people:

> It might likewise be of importance . . . for them to encourage any appearance of gifts amongst the people of their charge; if

> such should be raised up many advantages would be derived from their knowledge of the language and customs of their countrymen; and their change of conduct would give great weight to their ministrations.

On Wednesday, 31st May, 1792 at 10 o'clock in the morning, less than three weeks after the publication of the *Enquiry*, when the breadth of his vision was no doubt still challenging and disturbing his fellow ministers, Carey preached his invitation sermon at the Baptist Association Meeting in Nottingham. He preached from Isaiah 54:2, 3 ('Enlarge the place of thy tent . . .') and with all the passion of which he was capable, implored his hearers to catch wider visions, to dare bolder programmes. He castigated not only the lifeless Anglican church but also his own Baptist denomination for its feebleness, for the time wasted in barren disputations, for its spent enthusiasm, for its lack of vision. 'Expect great things from God; Attempt great things for God' was the call he made which would forever be associated with his name. Have faith. That was the first requirement. With that, the necessary power would flow into man so that he could achieve the seemingly impossible. God's promises were so generous, so unmistakable to Carey, steeped as he was in the Word of God as revealed in the Bible. 'Seek ye first the kingdom of God and his righteousness, *and all these things shall be added unto you*.'

It must be remembered that he was not preaching to a wealthy, influential congregation but to a gathering of fellow Baptists in only one of the various Associations that made up the denomination throughout the country. The ministers there were mostly, like himself, in charge of small, poor village churches where the minister's spiritual horizons could well be clouded by the effort needed merely to subsist. They were ordinary, good but unimaginative men. Carey was an embarrassment to them; he had a 'bee in his bonnet' about missions.

Not surprisingly, there was no reaction from the gathering to Carey's sermon.

The following morning there was a business meeting. Out of the Association's grand annual income of £21, it was decided to make small allocations to two worthy causes; half a guinea was voted towards the travelling expenses of each of the four poorest ministers attending the meetings; and it was agreed to contribute the sum of five guineas towards the fight against the slave trade. Routine decisions on routine matters. Any other business?

It looked as if they would disperse without any reference to Carey's sermon of the previous day. William turned to Andrew Fuller who was sitting next to him. Gripping his arm, he implored him: 'Is nothing *again* going to be done?'

Perhaps the very unexpectedness of this direct appeal jolted the older man into decision. Certainly the conviction was already there, waiting to be catalysed into action. Andrew Fuller was a man of influence in local Baptist circles. When he joined his support to Carey's fervour, things began to happen.

Before the Assembly dispersed at noon on that first day of June, 1792, it had been resolved on a proposition from Andrew Fuller 'that a plan be prepared against the next Ministers' Meeting at Kettering, for forming a Baptist Society for propagating the Gospel among the Heathens.'

The implications of that brief resolution of the Nottingham Assembly were so vast and so much has stemmed from it since that it is a pity it did not achieve notice at the time in the local newspaper. However, the Nottingham weekly *Journal* that appeared on Friday, 2nd June 1792 reported no more than an average week. The latest developments of the Revolution in France were discussed at some length, including a long letter from a Paris correspondent. There had been riots in Birmingham, executions at Newgate. The Tory Party were furious at the latest outburst from Tom Paine. There had been an eloquent Whitsuntide sermon at St. Mary's Church, etc., etc. The proceedings of the Baptist Assembly in Friar Lane Meeting House did not rate even a line.

On 2nd October, the 'next Ministers' Meeting' took place in Kettering. This town was where Andrew Fuller had his church. The twelve ministers who gathered for the meeting were, as at Nottingham, from tiny churches in the district and half of them had been absent from the Nottingham assembly. They would not, therefore, have heard Carey's impassioned address or Fuller's intervention at the business meeting. The ministers of Roade and Thrapstone churches represented congregations of less than twenty-five. What unlikely material they were to prepare 'a plan for forming a Baptist Society for propagating the Gospel among the Heathens'! It could so easily have failed.

In the evening after the day's services were over, the twelve ministers gathered together in the small back parlour of Mrs. Beeby Wallis's house in Kettering. Her husband, who had recently died, had been a deacon at Andrew Fuller's church and the couple were noted for their hospitality to visiting preachers. The purpose of the gathering that evening was to formulate 'the plan'.

It is always assumed that Carey was present on this occasion although there is no positive evidence that he was. His name does not appear among the list of subscribers to the projected Mission. If he was indeed there, no doubt he would have pointed to the successful work of the Moravians in Africa and the West Indies. But did any of those twelve good men that night, save Carey and Fuller, have the vision to see that their decisions would have such far-reaching consequences?

> Humbly desirous of making an effort for the propagation of the Gospel among the Heathen, according to the recommendations of Carey's *Enquiry*, we unanimously resolve to act in Society together for this purpose; and, as in the divided state of Christendom each denomination, by exerting itself separately, seems likeliest to accomplish the great end, we name this the Particular Baptist Society for the Propagation of the Gospel among the Heathen.

Grand words! A noble cause! But what were they to propagate the gospel among the heathen *with*?

Andrew Fuller, newly appointed Secretary of the Mission, had a snuff-box embossed on the lid with a picture of St. Paul's conversion. This became their treasury. Each minister present wrote down what he felt he was able and willing to give.

Reynold Hogg, of Thrapstone, promised two guineas. Edward Sharman (who was shortly to take over the Moulton Church at a stipend of 7s. 6d. per week) promised one guinea. John Ryland promised two guineas – a great sacrifice when it is appreciated that his wife had to keep school to help out his small income. Joshua Burton of Foxton, like Carey, ran a school to supplement his stipend, yet promised half a guinea. 'Anon.' (who was later revealed as a young student by the name of Staughton) promised 10s. 6d.*

In all, the promises that evening totalled £13 2s. 6d. It seemed a tiny sum to use to change the world, yet the men at that meeting had faith that it would be sufficient. They were aware of other miracles.

> There is a lad here, which hath five barley loaves, and two small fishes: but what are they among so many?[16]

* It would be irritating for the reader for each of these figures to be converted individually into decimal currency. For those unfamiliar with the old pounds, shillings and pence, one shilling is equal to 5 new pence, and 6 old pennies have 2½ new pence as their modern equivalent. A guinea was worth £1 1s. 0d. in old currency.

3

'No power on earth can hinder you . . .'

January–May, 1793

It is ironic that, after having been the prime mover of Baptist evangelism among the heathen, Carey should have to take second place in the appointment of missionaries.

The Baptist Missionary Society had come into being but there seemed to be no guidance as to the part or parts of the world to which it should direct its efforts. Then Carey heard of John Thomas, a Baptist and former naval surgeon, who had gone out to Bengal in the service of the East India Company as a ship's doctor aboard the *Oxford*. Thomas had felt a call to missionary work so had stayed on in India ministering to the sick, learning the language, preaching the gospel and endeavouring to translate the scriptures into Bengali, though he had not got beyond the first two Gospels. The closing months of 1792 found him in England trying to establish a fund to support a mission in Bengal.

Andrew Fuller was despatched to London to meet Thomas and was sufficiently impressed to recommend him to his colleagues. A meeting of the Society was called at Kettering for 9th January, 1793. Unfortunately, neither Ryland nor Sutcliff could be present and Thomas himself had injured his foot so seemed unlikely to attend. Even so, on hearing Andrew Fuller's report, the Society decided to invite Mr. Thomas to return to India under their patronage and they promised to find him a companion 'if a suitable one could be obtained'.

Towards the end of the meeting, Thomas arrived, having determined to reach Kettering despite his injured foot. His enthusiasm dispelled any doubts that might have lingered over the rightness of the Society's decision. He spoke elo-quently of the work to be done in India. He described in evocative words the millions awaiting the good news of the gospel. He was confident about the relatively small amount of money that would be required to launch their missionary enterprise in India. He was sanguine in his forecast that missionaries would be able to support themselves in Bengal. To Carey, Thomas's words must have seemed the living embodiment of all that he had set out in his *Enquiry*. Immediately he offered himself as the 'suitable companion' and was accepted. 'It is a great undertaking, yet surely it is right', Fuller wrote to Ryland.

Everything seemed easy in the glow of the meeting but the preparations for the venture soon ran into difficulties.

First of all, Carey's own church at Leicester were dismayed at the prospect of losing their pastor. They had been praying regularly for the spread of Christ's Kingdom among the heathen but did not anticipate that *they* would be the first to be required to make a sacrifice – particularly as under Carey's ministry their church was growing in numbers as well as grace. That opposition gave way before the combined eloquence of Rev. Sutcliff and John Thomas himself who was able, as he had with the Society's Committee, to fire his listeners with enthusiasm for the project. Eventually, the church gave way and agreed to Carey's appointment.

William's family was less tractable. 'Is William mad?' was Edmund Carey's reaction when, a week later, Carey wrote to his father to tell him of his decision. How could he who had never been able to endure even the weak sun of an English summer stand up to the tropical heat of Bengal?

Dorothy Carey's position was pitiable. On the one hand, there was William burning with missionary fervour, confident that he was, to quote his own words, 'devoted to the service of God alone',[1] impatient to be on his way to one of the many countries of which he had thought and prayed over the years. On the other hand, there was Dorothy – unlettered, unimaginative, almost certainly never even having seen the sea, let alone a foreign country. She was to be expected to venture half-way round the world to a country with a strange people, strange language, strange climate and customs, with no settled home to go to. Only three days after Carey's acceptance for missionary service, France had declared war on England so that the long sea voyage would be fraught with danger from enemy attack, over and above the normal hazards of a sea voyage. She had three little boys to care for and, in addition, was five months pregnant with yet another child. If the departure took place as planned on 3rd April, her baby would be born at sea and the only woman in attendance so far as she was aware would be Mrs. Thomas whom she had not even met. Even had Dorothy shared her husband's missionary zeal – and there is no evidence that she did – the prospect would have been daunting. At all events, she was adamant: she would not go to India. Did she hope by her refusal to change her husband's decision? If so, she had under-estimated his determination, dedication and sense of commitment. Though he dearly wished his wife to accompany him, the gospels Carey searched so constantly left no doubt in his mind as to where his duty lay should there be a conflict of loyalty. Perhaps if he went out to India to explore the opportunities, he could send for Dorothy later? Carey determined, if his wife would not accompany him, to journey to India without her, taking eight-year-old Felix for company.

These were the personal problems – but there were others.

Their departure was fixed for 3rd April but passages to India – particularly when the journey lasted five months or more – were costly. Moreover, provision would have to be made for setting up home in India. There were less than three months in which to raise enough money to finance the enterprise.

The Society was young and had as yet only meagre funds. Carey and Thomas went up and down the country preaching and talking about their projected mission. William visited the northern churches and was able to say goodbye to his soldier brother, Tom, who was a corporal with a Yorkshire regiment. Baptist churches in Yorkshire made a generous response. The southern churches, however, were more cautious, even sceptical. The London Association allowed individuals to contribute to the fund but would not commit the Association. Donations came in but only to just a sufficient total to cover the missionaries' passage. Yet, such was the faith of the early leaders of the Baptist Missionary Society that, although they had as yet no certainty of continued financial support, they were confident that, because their cause was 'of God', the means to pursue it would be forthcoming.

So the arrangements went steadily forward. Carey moved his wife and children back to Piddington where they would share a cottage with Dorothy's unmarried sister, Kitty. He took his last regular Sunday service at the Harvey Lane Church.

On 20th March, 1793, Carey and Thomas were 'set apart' for their missionary work like Barnabas and Saul seventeen centuries earlier. All those who had been at Mrs. Beeby Wallis's house six months before were present, and fourteen of Carey's fellow ministers from the Northampton Association. Dr. John Ryland was there from Northampton, Samuel Pearce from Birmingham, John Sutcliff from Olney and Andrew Fuller from Kettering – all to prove loyal friends over the coming years.

It is often represented as a fact that Andrew Fuller exclaimed: 'There is a gold mine in India but it seems almost as deep as the centre of the earth!' to which Carey is reputed to have replied: 'I will venture down but remember that you must hold the ropes.' In fact, as Fuller himself records in a letter to Christopher Anderson (later to be a Secretary of the Society after him) this was the *gist* of what was said. The actual words used are unimportant; what emerged on that momentous occasion in Leicester was a pledge by the home team that they 'should never cease till death'[1] to stand by the missionaries.

After a few days at Piddington, Carey took leave of his wife on Tuesday, 26th March. Dorothy was still adamant that she would not accompany her husband to India so he could only promise to return for her after three years, by which time he would hope to have a settled home prepared for her. As he had written to his father in January, he had 'set his hand to the plough'. If that entailed separation from his wife, so be it. Thus resigned, he set off with Felix to join his colleague in London.

He and Thomas could not be choosing to go out to India at a less propitious time. Quite apart from the new dangers arising from the war which France had declared against England and Holland on 11th February, there was the impossibility of obtaining a permit to go to Bengal as missionaries. Any European wishing to reside in British India needed a licence from the Court of the East India Company, a body which looked with disfavour on anyone likely to disturb the peace of the regions it administered. Missionaries fell into this category. In fairness to the Company (many of whose officers in India were devout Christians) there was a genuine belief that unrest and even insurrection would follow in the wake of missionary teaching. New ideas can be disruptive, particularly if they speak of freedom and equality. Charles Grant, a member of the Court of Directors of the East India Company and a former friend of Thomas in Calcutta, took a different view. As early as 1787, when he was Commercial Resident in Malda, he had written home suggesting that Anglican missionaries be sent to Bengal but there had been no response. Now back in England, he had enlisted the aid of William Wilberforce, Member of Parliament for Yorkshire, in an endeavour to have included in the renewed Charter of the East India Company a clause declaring that Britain's duty to the Indian populace included its 'religious improvement'. Such a clause would make it clear that missionaries and schoolmasters were to be encouraged. This and other proposed innovations were being fought strenuously by the Company. In such a climate, it was obviously futile even for Anglican would-be missionaries to apply for licences, let alone Baptists who, as Dissenters, were accused of bringing about a state of disorder even in England.

Grant's and Wilberforce's campaign was unsuccessful and when, by autumn of 1793, the Act renewing the Company's Charter was passed, the clauses relating to the 'religious improvement' of the natives were deleted. Wilberforce wrote sadly in his diary: 'The East India Directors and Proprietors have triumphed, all my clauses were last night struck out on the third reading of the Bill . . . and twenty millions of people . . . are left . . . to the providential protection of – Brama.'[2]

This was the 'abominable East India monopoly' that Carey refers to in his 1793 *Journal*. William's nephew, Eustace Carey, in his 1836 *Memoir of William Carey*, condemns the Company's policy in even harsher and, to some extent, undeserved terms:

> The conduct of the British authorities in India, upon the subject of religion, was strangely anomalous and absurd; arising partly from ignorance of the true genius of christianity, and the legitimate means of diffusing it; and partly from a profane

> indifference to the spiritual welfare of the millions they governed, and a repugnance and hostility to whatever might seem only to interfere with their own secular ambition and cupidity.

In fact, the British authorities in India were concerned with administering their possessions in an orderly, and preferably profitable, manner. In their view, missionaries constituted a risk to good order and were therefore not acceptable.

Even Charles Grant, when approached by Carey for advice and help, could do no more than warn him of the difficulties. Moreover, although respecting Thomas's undoubted sincerity over missionary work, Grant was unenthusiastic about encouraging his return to Bengal. Thomas had caused embarrassment there during his previous stay owing to his lack of tact in the close English community and even more by the extent of his unpaid debts.

At length, however, Captain White of the *Earl of Oxford*, in whose ship Thomas had formerly been surgeon, agreed to risk taking them without licences. Such deception did not please Andrew Fuller but he reluctantly agreed. Nor was Carey entirely happy about the arrangement. He went to see the ex-slaver, Rev. John Newton, now vicar of St. Mary's Woolnoth, Lombard Street, London. 'What,' asked Carey, 'if the Company should send us home upon our arrival in Bengal?' Newton, paraphrasing the comment of Gamaliel in a similar context, replied 'Then, conclude that your Lord has nothing there for you to accomplish. But, if he have, *no power on earth can hinder you*.'[3]

S. Pearce Carey states that during this same week Carey met young William Ward. Dr. George Smith in his *Life of William Carey – Shoemaker & Missionary* puts the meeting in Hull during William Carey's Yorkshire tour earlier in the year. Both, however, agree on the importance of the meeting. When Carey learned that Ward was a printer, he told him of his hopes to translate the Bible into the language of his new country. 'If the Lord bless us, we shall want a person of your business to enable us to print the scriptures. I hope you will come after us,' he said.

Carey, his son Felix, and Thomas with his wife and daughter boarded the *Oxford* in the Thames on 4th April. If the vessel had been able to proceed direct to India, it could have arrived by the end of August or early in September. However, contrary winds and the very real threat of attack by the French delayed the voyage. They reached the Solent and spent six frustrating weeks waiting for a convoy to assemble. Carey and Thomas would have liked to have lodged in Portsmouth during this period but accommodation was too expensive. They were able to find cheaper lodgings in the village of Ryde in the Isle of Wight.

The horrid truth was being borne in upon Carey that his new colleague was deeply in debt. Thomas's creditors hunted him 'as a partridge'.[4] This was humiliation enough but the bitterest blow came when Carey and Thomas found their luggage summarily put ashore at Portsmouth and themselves denied any further passage. The captain of the *Oxford* had received an anonymous letter warning him that there was a person or persons on board without a licence to reside in India. Whether or not someone in London had 'informed' of the captain's connivance in the missionaries' passage to India or whether (as Thomas suspected) a disgruntled creditor sought to prevent his leaving the country is not known, but the captain dare not risk his command. It may be, also, that Carey himself was a not particularly desirable passenger in the Captain's eyes. He had openly shown his radical sympathies by refusing to join in the Loyal Toast on board ship. Fuller's comment on this incident was: 'Even an imprudent action may overturn all you are doing! It made me and many more tremble for the cause of Christ that was in your hands to hear of Bror. C's refusal to drink a certain health in the "Earl of Oxford". . . . Let nothing but conscience induce such conduct; & beware that conscience itself be not misguided. . .'[5]

The convoy sailed for India on 23rd May carrying with it Mrs. Thomas and her daughter but leaving the two missionaries and little Felix behind.

Carey could well, at this setback, have taken John Newton's words to heart and have concluded that the Lord had 'nothing in India for him to accomplish'. Instead, though distressed at this check to his plans, he was yet able to write in faith to Andrew Fuller: 'All I can say in this affair is, that however mysterious the leadings of Providence are, I have no doubt but they are superintended by an infinitely wise God.'[6] And so it proved to be.

It was an act of faith also to leave their luggage in Portsmouth while they returned to London. Carey was all for making an attempt to procure a licence or, if this was not forthcoming, travelling overland to Bengal. Thomas set his hopes on a foreign ship. Even if it did not go the whole way to India, they might be able to pick up another ship in a foreign port that would take them on to their destination. The season was far advanced and, if they were to reach India before the end of the south-west monsoon period, they could not risk any further delay. Leaving Carey to write to his wife, Thomas went to a coffee-house where he knew he might pick up information regarding any Swedish or Danish ship that might put in to an English port that season on its way to the East Indies. Perhaps the waiter in the coffee-house was used to unlicensed travellers seeking a passage to India by other than East India Company vessels. He did not speak openly to Thomas but slipped into his hand a piece of paper on which was scribbled: 'A Danish East Indiaman – No. 10 Cannon Street.'

If they could but obtain a passage in her, they could sail to India honourably. No licence would be required in a Danish ship so no-one would be able to accuse them of duplicity as might have been the case had they proceeded in the *Oxford*. Moreover, the captain of a foreign ship was not required to supply the authorities with a list of his passengers. Thus the missionary party would be able to arrive unnoticed. What would happen over the question of a work permit when they reached India was another matter; for the moment, their concern was simply to reach that country.

Thomas and Carey hurried to the Cannon Street address. Yes, the information was correct. The Danish ship was expected shortly in the Dover Roads. Yes, she had vacant berths – £100 for each passenger, £50 per child, £25 for an attendant. Their newly-raised hopes seemed dashed again. Carey had only been able to obtain a refund of £150 of the passage money paid over to the *Oxford*. That was not enough even for himself, Thomas and Felix, let alone – as he now faintly hoped – for his wife and the rest of his children. William had heard early in May that Dorothy had given birth to another son whom she had named Jabez.

> 'Received yours,' Carey had written to her from Ryde[7] 'giving me an account of your safe delivery.' (Presumably her sister or a friend had written the letter to Dorothy's dictation or else she had mastered the art of writing during the ten years of her marriage.) 'This is pleasant news indeed to me . . . My stay here was very painful and unpleasant, but now I see the goodness of God in it . . . You wish to know in what state my mind is. I answer, it is much as when I left you. If I had all the world I would freely give it all to have you and my dear children with me; but the sense of duty is so strong as to overpower all other considerations; I could not turn back without guilt on my soul. . . You want to know what Mrs. Thomas thinks, and how she likes the voyage. She would rather stay in England than go to India; but thinks it right to go with her husband. . .'

A stern letter from a husband not yet thirty-two, though possibly Carey dare not give way to sentiment. However, now that the baby was born and he had been so providentially delayed until after the event, he dared to hope that Dorothy would agree to accompany him. Time was of the essence. The ship was due in five days' time and if they missed this one, there might not be another sailing that season.

Once again, the prospective missionaries acted in faith. They had not sufficient money; they had no agreement from Dorothy; but they made a tentative booking for a considerably larger party than originally envisaged to travel to India in the Danish vessel. Then the two men took the overnight coach to Northamptonshire in the hope that they could solve both problems at once.

They breakfasted at Piddington where William was able to have a joyous reunion with his family after two months' separation. But it was no good. Dorothy was still obdurate in her determination: she would not go to India.

She could hardly be blamed. The baby was only three weeks old, yet William was expecting her to pack up her home at a few hours' notice and journey into the unknown with four children under nine years of age. Even so, she must have been a woman of exceptional stubbornness or else Carey must have been more than usually tender and considerate for, at that period, women were completely subject to the dictates of their husbands. They had no rights of property. Even if Dorothy had had any independent means (which she had not) those would have passed to her husband on marriage.

Although the Society had undertaken to support her and the children during Carey's absence in India, nonetheless it must have taken courage, unless it was ignorant obstinacy, for her to refuse his pleadings.

William was terribly cast down. Thomas attempted to reason with Mrs. Carey, but to no avail. The missionaries set out for Northampton to see Mr. Ryland who was acting as the Society's Treasurer. If they could not succeed with Mrs. Carey, at least they might be able to obtain sufficient money for their own passage. As they journeyed, it was obvious to Thomas that his companion was still deeply unhappy at the prospect of leaving his family behind. Thomas proposed that they return to Piddington and try further persuasion but Carey over-ruled him, saying it was of no use. Thomas insisted until Carey gave way, saying 'Well, do as you think proper – but I think we are losing time.' They did return and Thomas, without mincing his words, told Dorothy that her refusal would cause her family to 'be dispersed and divided for ever – she would repent it as long as she lived.'[8] This dire warning had its effect. At last, reluctantly, Dorothy agreed to the Indian journey, provided her unmarried sister, Kitty, could accompany them.

Carey was overjoyed and with quickened steps he and Thomas hurried to Northampton. Yet the solving of one problem created another. The party was now eight and the sum required for fares would be enormous:

		£
Dr. Thomas, William, Dorothy, Kitty	@ £100 each	400
Felix, William, Peter, Baby Jabez	@ £50 each	200
Plus fitting out, say	....	100
	Grand Total	£700

Where was the additional money to come from? Mr. Ryland revealed that, having already paid over £250 for the passages in the *Oxford*, there only remained £9 in the Mission funds. He could add £4 or £5 at the most out of his own pocket. This, with the refund of £150, would make £164 at best. There was no time for an intensive fund-raising campaign for the ship was due in a matter of days.

Could it have been that 'your Father knoweth what things ye have need of, before ye ask him'?[9]

Quite unexpectedly, Andrew Fuller received £200 from a Mr. Fawcett who had heard Carey on his Yorkshire tour. That made the total £364. This sum gave them all hope. Ryland immediately sat down and wrote letters to John Newton and others in London begging for immediate contributions – but would they be received in time? Could the missionary party even be ready in time? While Carey helped his wife and sister-in-law to pack, Thomas hurried back to London to see if he could negotiate a cheaper price for their 'package'. Once again, the hand of God can be seen in the negotiations. The shipping agent said later that what influenced him was that such a large family party were prepared to sail, and at such short notice. Thomas generously offered that only Mr. and Mrs. Carey should go as 'passengers' (i.e. sitting at the captain's table). He and Kitty would be prepared to go as 'attendants' and would eat with any other servants on board. They would be prepared to pack into two cabins only, but all the money he could spare to pay for their passages was 300 guineas (£315). The agent relented and the passages were booked. All that remained now was to get their impedimenta aboard.

Carey took his wife, children and sister-in-law direct to Dover. Thomas hurried to Portsmouth to collect the luggage. He decided that, as it would take several days to take the luggage to Dover by road from Portsmouth, it might be better to take it by sea so that, if the East Indiaman had already sailed, he would be able to intercept it as it hugged the English coast on its way down the channel. Once again, the desperate shortage of money nearly brought the trip to grief. Several boatmen Thomas approached refused to undertake the trip at all. It was too hazardous, they said; the channel was full of French privateers hovering close to the English coast. At last one boatman was found willing to undertake the trip but, with special 'danger money', the passage would cost twenty guineas. Still too much. For two frantic days, Thomas searched the waterfront until at last a fisherman undertook to take him for nine guineas. They sailed only during the night hours. Whether there were indeed any privateers and their little open craft managed to avoid them in the dark is unknown. It was sufficient that Thomas reached Dover just in time to board the *Kron Princessa Maria* before she sailed on 13th June, 1793.

In a euphoric letter scribbled to a friend in London, Thomas must have echoed the feelings that were in Carey's heart also as their vessel slipped anchor and stood out into the Channel:

> The ship is here! the signal made; – the guns are fired; – and we are going with a fair wind. Farewell, my dear brethren and sisters, farewell! May the God of Jacob be ours and yours by sea and land, for time and eternity; most affectionately, adieu![10]

Carey, equally optimistic but ever with an eye to the future extension of the work of the Missionary Society, wrote from the ship:

> . . . Africa is but a little way from England, Madagascar but a little further. South America and all the numerous and large islands in the India and China Seas, I hope, will not be passed over. A large field opens on every side. Oh, that many labourers may be thrust out into the vineyard of our Lord Jesus Christ. . .[11]

4

Passage to India

June–November, 1793

To Dorothy Carey, with a tiny baby to tend and feed, and three other lively boys to watch over, it must have felt as if they were indeed passing over the 'India and China seas'. The journey to Bengal took five months, during which time they did not put in to any port, not even to take on fresh water.

Their course took them through the Bay of Biscay and down the bulging west coast of Africa. Once approaching the tropics, the north-east trade winds would carry them almost to South America. After passing the island of Trinidad off the coast of Brazil, their vessel would pick up the north-westerly winds of the 'Horse Latitudes' which would take them across the South Atlantic, past Tristan da Cunha, into the area of strong westerly winds, the 'Roaring Forties'. These would carry them round the Cape of Good Hope and into the Indian Ocean. Here, they could pick up the south-east trade winds as far as the equator where, if they were not too delayed in their voyage, the end of the south-west monsoon would sweep them into the Bay of Bengal to their destination at Calcutta.

East Indiamen were the largest timber ships in service, often reaching a thousand tons. Copper-bottomed for greater speed and with 'royals' to give an extra spread of canvas on their three masts, they were able (given favourable winds) to make the round trip to India and back in under twelve months. The *Kron Princessa Maria* was slightly smaller than the average British East Indiaman, being of six hundred tons, 130 feet long in the keel.

Accounts of the missionary party's voyage to and safe arrival in India did not reach England for many months. Carey had hoped to send a first packet of letters by the frigate *Triton* which escorted them through the waters in which French privateers were known to be operating. However, when the time came for the ships to part company, the weather conditions were too hazardous for a small boat to take the mail across from the *Kron Princessa Maria* to the *Triton* and the letters had in consequence to wait to be posted until they reached India.

The master of the vessel, Captain Christmas (an Englishman who had taken Danish nationality) proved to be a man of exceptional kindness. Despite that the missionary party were travelling at less than half the price their fellow passengers had paid, he allotted the best and largest cabin to William, Dorothy and the children. He also allotted single cabins to Thomas and Kitty, even though some of the other passengers who had paid full fare were having to share. He was kindness itself when they were seasick crossing the Bay of Biscay, sending soup and wine to tempt the appetites of the sufferers.

'Poor Mrs. Carey,' Thomas wrote back to England from the Bay of Bengal in October, 1793 'has had many fears and troubles; so that she was like Lot's wife, until we passed the Cape; but ever since, it seems so far to look back to Piddington, that she turns her hopes and wishes to our safe arrival in Bengal!'

It is interesting to speculate on the nature of the 'fears and troubles' of the journey. Quite apart from the dangers of a long sea passage (particularly in time of war), the monotonous diet and the restriction of movement, it must also be remembered that Dorothy and her young sister were, as far as it is possible to ascertain, the only women on board, with the exception of a 'black woman'[1] who died off the Cape of Good Hope. Carey writes of the voyage as being among 'carnal men' and, although the word 'carnal' was used at this time to mean 'worldly', it is possible also that the women may well have hade to cope with some unwelcome advances during the voyage, particularly as no calls were made at any port en route for India.

Fortunately, the children kept well and enjoyed the voyage. They 'were complete sailors', Carey was able to tell his sisters.[2] Baby Jabez grew into 'a stout fellow'.

Every morning and evening, the party met for family prayers, and each Sunday they held two services. Unfortunately, these were rarely attended by any of the other four passengers or by the crew, a circumstance which grieved Carey and Thomas greatly. Carey seized opportunities at other times to discuss and argue matters of religion with his fellow travellers. There was, in particular, a Frenchman who was a 'deist'.* With this man Carey seems to have had regular, if frustrating, arguments. He records these in his *Journal* of the voyage – an account that swings from extremes of joy to black depression. He describes his studies of Bengali under Thomas's tutorship. With his knowledge of Hebrew, he was able in return to assist Thomas with the translation into Bengali of the Book of Genesis. He describes the progress of their voyage and scrupulously records the latitude and longitude and the direction of the wind. He comments on the things he sees:

> 1793. June 24.25. Fell in with the tradewind in lat.39° N., and the next day passed the island of Madeira. It was in sight the greatest part of the day. A French privateer hoisted English colours, and pretended to be bound for Sierra Leone. . .

No doubt this was a device of the privateer safely to approach their ship in order to ascertain her nationality but, as Denmark was a neutral country, the *Kron Princessa Maria* was not attacked.

> . . . On the 24th saw a number of flying-fish. Have begun to write Bengali, and read Edward's Sermons, and Cowper's Poems. Mind tranquil and serene. . .
>
> July 1. But little wind. Had a long conversation with the deist today; but never found a man so hardened and determined to turn scripture into ridicule as he. Oh how dreadfully depraved is human nature!

As the vessel moved through the tropics and contrary winds delayed her passage, Carey went down with a bilious complaint. The entries in his *Journal* are despondent:

> . . . (July) 23–Aug. 2. Last night passed the tropic of Capricorn. . . Sometimes I am quite dejected when I see the impenetrability of the heart of those with us. They hear us preach on the Lord's-day, but we are forced to witness their

* A 'deist' was someone who acknowledged the existence of a god but rejected any 'revealed religion'.

> disregard to God all the week. O may God give us greater success among the heathen. I am very desirous that my children may pursue the same work; and now intend to bring up one in the study of Sanscrit, and another of Persian. O may God give them grace to fit them for the work! . . .

All his children were still under nine years of age!

Carey had anticipated that the ship might have called in at the Cape of Good Hope and, once again, had a batch of letters written ready for despatch to his friends in England. In addition, he had hoped to call on some Dutch missionaries in order to question them about their missionary experiences. However, Captain Christmas was anxious to reach Bengal before the end of the monsoon in mid-October, so pressed on, not even stopping to take on fresh water.

The voyage was not all flying-fish and sun-filled days. Cape Agulhas, the southernmost tip of Africa, is one of the worst places in the world for storms. Indeed, when the Cape of Good Hope was first rounded by the Portuguese Bartholemew Diaz, in 1486, he named it the 'Cape of Storms'. Even during the southern summer, there is an average of gale-force winds for twenty per cent of the time. The *Kron Princessa Maria* was negotiating Cape Agulhas during the southern winter. Beyond the Cape, a reef stretches some two hundred miles into the Southern Ocean. The strong currents here have swept many a ship to destruction on the rocks, and prudent sailors put plenty of sea between them and the area of the reef. However, the further south a vessel sails into the 'Roaring Forties', the heavier the seas it encounters for, with virtually no land in these latitudes, the seas can build up and roll onward almost right round the world in front of the prevailing westerly winds. Waves often reach forty, fifty, sixty feet and more in height.

The *Kron Princessa Maria* had taken a southerly course to avoid the reef and at about one o'clock in the morning of 26th August, Carey was wakened by the violent motion of the ship. Stools and tables were rolling about the cabin and presently pots, glasses – in fact, anything not fastened into position – crashed to the floor. Carey scrambled out of his bunk and staggered about the heaving cabin trying to secure their scattered possessions. He made all as safe as he could and was about to retire again when Thomas came to the cabin-door with grim news: the main- and fore-topmasts had been carried away by the storm.

By this time, Dorothy and the children were also awake but Carey urged them to stay in their bunks. They could so easily break a limb on the lurching floor of the cabin. Up on deck the fitful moonlight revealed a shocking scene. Masts, yards, sails and rigging hung over the ship's sides in tangled confusion. The crew scrabbled among the heaving chaos to cut the wreckage loose. Beyond the deck, mountainous seas bore down on the ship seemingly from all directions. Then the vessel rose balanced on a wave-top higher than a house from which she had to plunge almost perpendicularly into the trough beneath. It seemed she could never recover. Carey gasped a prayer and clung to whatever was nearest to him. The downward plunge of the vessel was dreadful, terrifying, and the jib-boom was carried away, but in a moment the ship steadied and rose on yet another sea as mountainous as the first.

With enormous effort, the wreckage was cleared and the vessel rode out the storm safely – and another, of equal violence four days later. It took eleven days to repair the damage to the ship and, only two days after the work was completed, another violent storm carried away the new main-topmast, so the crew had to rig a jury-mast.

The ship was only victualled for a four-month voyage, expecting to take on fresh stores at the Cape, with the result that there was by now a shortage of drinking water. Had the winds been favourable, the captain could have taken the ship into Mauritius for a refit and to take on fresh supplies. However, unexpectedly strong northerly winds drove them back. Providentially, they were blessed with several heavy rain showers from which they were able to replenish their supply of drinking water and, as the state of the ship and the lateness of the season demanded no further delay, the captain decided to head straight for Bengal.[3]

The ship's carpenter caught a chill after his exertions in the storm and this turned to pleurisy. He was already debilitated through scurvy consequent upon the inadequate diet of the voyage and could put up no fight against his illness. His death caused great distress in the ship.

For over two months after the storm, they were not to see

another vessel. At times, Carey must have felt like Noah in his Ark after the rain had stopped – nothing but an expanse of water and no sign of land or life. They entered the Bay of Bengal but the monsoon had ended and they were consequently beaten back for weeks by contrary winds. Many might have given way to despair at having to endure further frustration after so many months at sea. So certain was Carey that he was carrying out God's purpose for him that he could read a lesson even in the delay:

> Nov. 9, 1793. . . For near a month we have been within two hundred miles of Bengal, but the violence of the currents set us back when we have been at the very door. I hope I have learned the necessity of bearing up in the things of God against wind and tide, when there is occasion, as we have done in our voyage. We have had our port in view all along, and there has been every attention paid to ascertain our situation by solar and lunar observations: no opportunity occurred that was neglected. Oh that I was but as attentive to the evidence of my state, as they to their situation! A ship sails within six points of the wind; that is, if the wind blow from the North, a ship will sail E.N.E. upon one tack, and W.N.W. upon the other; if our course is North, we must therefore go E.N.E. for a considerable way, then W.N.W.; and if the wind shifts a point, the advantage is immediately taken. Now, though this is tiresome work, and (especially if a current sets against us) we scarcely make any way; nay, sometimes, in spite of all that we can do, we go backwards instead of forwards; yet it is absolutely necessary to keep working up, if we ever mean to arrive at our port. So in the Christian life, we often have to work against wind and currents; but we must do it if we expect ever to make port.[4]

Here is the enquiring boy grown man, interested in every detail of the new environment in which he finds himself, eager to acquire new knowledge, new skills – and ever determined to achieve the goal he has set himself.

Had they but known it, they were fortunate not to have encountered any other shipping. Earlier in the year, according to the *Memoirs* of William Hickey, Rear-Admiral Cornwallis had returned to England with all his fleet except for the *Minerva*. The French, seeing the shipping lanes across the Indian Ocean unprotected, sent out 'a host of privateers which scoured the ocean in every direction, sadly annoying the British commerce by capturing every vessel that ventured to sea'.[5] Eventually a flotilla of East Indiamen was armed and put under the command of Captain Mitchell of the *William Pitt*, with the purpose of clearing the Bay of Bengal of privateers. Even so, in December 1793 Hickey is still lamenting the 'sad havoc amongst the British merchant vessels'.

However, Carey's ship did make port. A brief notice in the Calcutta *Gazette* of 14th November, 1793 announced the arrival in the River the previous Monday of the *Kron Princessa Maria*. No details were given of her passenger list, so that it was merely as part of a cargo of 'Sundries' that John Thomas, William Carey and six members of his family arrived in India.

5

In the Wilderness

November, 1793–May, 1794

No idea could be more erroneous than to suppose that Britain set out deliberately to conquer India with a view to territorial aggrandisement. The origin of British interest in that continent was much more mundane and much more in line with the French gibe against the British as being 'a nation of shopkeepers'.

The Portuguese were the first to appreciate the trading potential of the Far East when Vasco da Gama in 1498 made his voyage of discovery beyond the Cape of Good Hope and so opened up a sea route to the Indies and beyond. During the sixteenth century the Portuguese had a virtual monopoly of the rich trade with India and the fabled Spice Islands. Inevitably, however, other great maritime nations were eager to profit from the new markets, particularly the Dutch and the English. On 31st December, 1600, Queen Elizabeth I granted a charter to the East India Company, the first organised attempt by private enterprise to establish trade with India; in 1602, the Dutch formed their own United East India Company. Competition was bitter and only after bloodshed did the two companies settle their respective spheres of influence, the Dutch retaining the East Indies, Britain concentrating on India and Persia.

In India, the British came to have trading stations in Surat and Bombay on the west coast. These were good natural harbours but were poor centres of distribution as the Western Ghats, the line of mountains that extend down the western coast of India, made communication with the rest of the country difficult. Another trading station was established at Madras on the east coast of the Deccan but landings here could only be effected in small boats as the shore is a shallow, surf-beaten strand. The natural gateway to the sub-continent from the sea was the vast delta at the head of the Bay of Bengal where two great rivers of India – the Ganges and the Brahmaputra – debouch into the sea. Here in 1690 Job Charnock established on the River Hooghli (one of the streams that make up the delta) a settlement which developed into Calcutta.

During the first half of the eighteenth century, there were probably not more than fifteen hundred English in the whole of India, including wives, children, soldiers of the East India Company and seamen awaiting their ships. Trade, and trade alone, was the reason for the British presence. Sir Thomas Roe, first English Ambassador to the Indian continent, sent by James I in 1615 to the court of the Emperor Jahangir of the Mogul Empire, wrote home: 'Let this be received as a rule that if you will profit, seek it at sea, and in quiet trade; for without controversy, it is an error to affect garrisons and land wars in India.'[1]

The British settlers seem to have made a genuine attempt to work in harmony with the Indians. They adopted Indian habits in food and dress, frequently married Indian women and displayed an intelligent curiosity regarding the customs and culture of the country in which they had made their homes. Trade went two ways: cotton, silk, muslin, embroideries and spice went west in exchange for British woollens, metals, hardware and so forth; opium and grain went to China and Japan in exchange for tea to satisfy the growing demand in Europe and North America.

In some ways, native India at this time resembled Europe in the Middle Ages. Just as, after the death of Charlemagne, the Holy Roman Empire had disintegrated into a collection of feudal states, so in India, after the death of the Emperor Aurungzebe in 1707, the great Mohammedan Mogul Empire which had controlled practically the whole continent, broke up into warring factions. Afghans swarmed through the mountain passes into north-west India; the savage Hindu Mahratta tribes seized control of practically the whole of central India; Hyder Ali became master of Mysore; other Indian princes, such as the Nawabs of Bengal and Oudh, declared themselves independent.

In such a situation, the French (who had established rival ports to Madras and Calcutta) saw the possibility of making vast fortunes and also of attacking the British with whom they were at war almost constantly throughout the eighteenth century. Any native leader who was prepared to attack either the British themselves or any pro-British ruler could be sure of French support with money or arms. In this way, the French hoped to gain a fair measure of control in India and, if possible, drive out the British. The policy was defeated largely by the efforts of Robert Clive, a young 'writer' or clerk with the East India Company. He had escaped from Madras when it was captured by the French in 1746 after which he joined the East India Company's army and rapidly proved himself to be a brilliant officer. Even so, until the complete defeat of France in the Napoleonic Wars, it was necessary for Britain to have an army presence in India to supplement the Company's own troops. Until 1815, there was always the danger that native troops, trained by French officers, would attack any British positions which appeared weak and undefended. As the quotation from Hickey's *Memoirs* has already indicated, there was still a need for vigilance against French attack when Carey arrived in India in 1793.

Over the years, the East India Company acquired a virtual monopoly of trade in India and, in Bengal at least, held the position of 'king-maker'. The ruler of that province only maintained authority with the support of the Company's troops. For the Company to withdraw that support at any time during the eighteenth century would only have left the field wide open to the French or Dutch or Portuguese. However, struggles between native factions (with their natural harmful effect on trade), coupled with disastrous droughts and famines, brought the Company's affairs to a low ebb in the early seventeen-seventies.

Warren Hastings, another former writer in the Company, was to rescue the Company's fortunes and, at the same time, to build up a strong British India. This, he felt, was inevitable; the Company must assume responsibility for and govern the native population, 'people whom as our subjects we are bound to protect'.[2] He set about judicial reform and saw that taxes were fairly assessed and collected. Lord North's *Regulating Act* of 1773 provided for a Governor-General of Bengal and Warren Hastings was the first to be appointed to that office.

Despite many setbacks and much criticism from England, he was able to carry out a number of far-reaching administrative reforms. Moreover, at a time when Britain was losing the War of Independence with her American colonies and was under attack from the French in other parts of the world, Warren Hastings was able to save the British settlements in India from the combined attacks of the Mahrattas, Hyder Ali and the French. He was indeed the founder of the British Empire in India. He converted the somewhat haphazard interference in native affairs by the East India Company into a system of responsible government which was able to maintain peace and order. That it was morally wrong to inflict British rule, unbidden, on the Indian people was argued at the time by such politicians as Burke. It has been recognised since by the granting of independence to India and Pakistan under the *Indian Independence Act*, 1947. At the time, however, it was easy to argue that the British needed to rule the Indians for their own good. Whatever the merits of the argument – and it is possible to establish a substantial case for either side – Pitt's *India Act* of 1784 laid down the system of dual control of India by both the Company and the British Government which was to last until 1858. The Act stated: 'To pursue schemes of conquest and extension of dominion in India are measures repugnant to the wish, the honour, and the policy of this nation.' Although the Company strove to implement this declaration, their efforts were in vain. Successive Governors-General after 1784 were chosen from men of high distinction. Except for Sir John Shore and Sir George Barlow, no Company servants were appointed to the Governor-Generalship. The political prestige of this new type of Governor-General allowed him to carry through legislation and reforms that would not be within its powers when the Company alone administered affairs in India. Unfortunately, under this new system, the free social intercourse between Indians and British was discouraged. Lord Cornwallis, who succeeded Warren Hastings as Governor-General in 1786, excluded all Indians and Eurasians from the higher posts in government service. If this appears harsh towards the native Indian and would seem to imply an intolerable arrogance among the British ruling class, it must in fairness be pointed out that research by modern *Indian* scholars confirms that 'the mental and moral condition . . . (of Indians in the late eighteenth/early nineteenth centuries) . . . was marked by inertia and stagnation',[3] that the people were 'generally licentious',[4] that 'honesty and truthfulness could hardly be found among them'.[5]

Such was also the opinion of the Indian character generally held by British settlers when Carey landed in Calcutta in 1793.

He had left behind him a country with an only slowly emerging democratic system of politics, with outrageous penal laws and much social injustice. The poor in England were poor indeed – but at least they had their champions. There was a stirring of thought throughout the western world – in America, in France, in England – that was challenging the old accepted order and that was to give hope and, indeed, positive progress to the poor and under-privileged. Carey arrived in a country with no democracy at all and where the poor suffered deprivation unimaginable in the west. Malnutrition and general debilitation brought about physical, mental and even moral inertia. Money-lenders were the most flourishing section of the community. The rigid caste system (which separated one group of people from another from birth to the grave without any possibility of change through education, marriage or by any other means) imposed a fatalistic acceptance of poverty as being beyond any chance or hope of improvement. It was this aspect of Hinduism – that men are very *un*equal in the sight of god and man – that was to present a far greater challenge to the missionaries than mere 'worship of heathen gods'. Hinduism was not merely a form of worship; it was a way of life, an attitude of mind.

Carey and Thomas were by no means the first missionaries to attempt to introduce the gospel to India. Indeed, there is a strong tradition that the gospel was brought at first hand by one who knew and worked with the Master – St. Thomas, the doubting disciple. Jesuit missionaries followed the Portuguese traders until the middle of the eighteenth century but these, with a few notable exceptions, were religious fanatics who, by their 'intolerance, persecution, racial arrogance and forcible conversions . . . left a deplorable legacy for the future of Christianity in India'.[6] Jesuits had visited Bengal at the turn of the sixteenth/seventeenth centuries and a French Carmelite had even set up a station at Serampore on the opposite side of the Hooghli from Calcutta in the year of Carey's birth. But there had been no protestant missionaries until the eighteenth century – Danish missionaries first in Tranquebar towards the southern tip of India; and a Swede, John Kiernander, who worked in and near Calcutta from 1758 until his death in 1786. There had also been a Moravian mission in Bengal but neither of these appeared to have left any mark on the Bengal that Carey and Thomas found only a few years later. What European missionaries had failed to realise was that the specifically western-european form of Christianity they were propagating was not necessarily suited to the Indian mind. If they were to make any headway in India, they needed to produce an Indian form of Christianity. For this, as Carey had already with so much foresight suggested in his *Enquiry*, it would be necessary to encourage and train indigenous missionaries.

On 9th November, 1793, while the *Kron Princessa Maria* lay in the Balasore Roads at the mouth of the Hooghli River, waiting for a pilot to take them up the dangerous channel to Calcutta, Carey wrote in his *Journal*: 'We have not yet been ashore; but on Monday we intend, God willing, to go. O may my heart be prepared for our work, and the kingdom of Christ be set up among the poor Hindus!'

So long had he awaited this hour; so hard had he worked at the study of Bengali on the voyage out; so much prayer had been expended for the success of his venture; so high were his expectations – yet the first six months in India were little short of disaster.

The first few days, however, seemed full of promise. On the occasion when Carey made the entry in his *Journal* just quoted, he and Thomas had been watching two small native fishing boats that had put out to the Danish Indiaman in the hope of selling some of their catch. Thomas hailed the men in their own tongue. Carey watched and listened, struggling to identify in the voluble speech some of the words he had been learning on the voyage. Thomas asked the fishermen if they possessed any of the *Shastras*, the sacred books of the Hindu religion.

'We are poor men,' they replied. 'Those who have many

cowries (i.e. are rich) read the *shastras*, but we do not know them.'[7]

This reply, when translated for his benefit, confirmed in Carey the urgent need to translate the Scriptures into the Hindu tongue and to have them available in such an inexpensive form that they could be put into the hands of even the poorest enquirer.

He was equally impressed at the courteous hearing given by Indians when, upon landing, Thomas immediately began to preach in the market-place to anyone who would stop and listen. Full of hope and enthusiasm, Carey wrote: 'I feel something of what Paul felt when he beheld Athens, and "his spirit was stirred within him". I see one of the finest countries in the world, full of industrious inhabitants; yet three-fifths of it are an uncultivated jungle, abandoned to wild beasts and serpents. If the gospel flourishes here, "the wilderness will in every respect become a fruitful field".'[8]

When they reached Calcutta, sixty miles up the Hooghli, however, Carey's problems began. They spent three weeks in that city selling the various items – pen knives, scissors and other small trade goods – they had brought out from England to provide capital for their immediate needs. Unfortunately, due to a glut on the market, the sum realised was nowhere near enough to meet their expenses, nor was it anywhere approaching the optimistic amount Thomas had forecast in England. They took up residence at first in the house that Mrs. Thomas and her daughter were already occupying. It was a big house, with several servants, and the ever-mounting expenses, Carey wrote, 'filled my mind with anxiety and wretchedness'.[9] He found the members of the European community generous and hospitable but enjoying a standard and style of living he could neither hope nor wish to emulate. Their generosity embarrassed him; their hedonism worried him. 'This is a snare to dear Mr. Thomas,' he wrote on 26th December, 1793.

In the hope of reducing expenses, the whole household moved out to Bandel, a village thirty miles up the Hooghli River from Calcutta, but it was hardly a suitable centre for missionary work. 'A missionary,' Carey had written in his *Enquiry* 'must be one of the companions and equals of the people to whom he is sent.' Bandel was too much a European dormitory for Calcutta. However, he and Thomas did go out to various villages scattered through the delta to speak and preach to the natives. It was always to be Carey's practice to seek to spread the Word through conversation with natives. They were received with polite interest but made no conversions. There was a suggestion that they should settle at Nuddea which was a centre of eastern learning, but that plan also fell through.

A constant source of anxiety was that Thomas's creditors had caught up with him again and he was in constant fear of being arrested. He decided, therefore, that the only way to quieten his creditors was to resume his profession as a doctor in Calcutta where he could soon build up a considerable practice. Carey did not hold out any great hopes that this would solve Thomas's financial problems. 'Mr. T. is a very good man,' he wrote to Rev. John Sutcliff at Olney, with the sharpened sense of reality that nearly a year in Thomas's company had brought him, 'but only fit to live at sea, where his daily business is before him, and daily provision made for him. I own, I fear that his present undertaking will be hurtful rather than useful to him. The fickleness of his mind makes him very unfit for such an undertaking.' A disillusioned assessment, perhaps, but in the very next sentence, Carey adds loyally 'I love him, and we live in the greatest harmony.'[10] Despite his loyalty to Thomas, Carey was beginning to wish he had paid less heed to his companion's somewhat sanguine predictions and had relied more on his own judgment.

Captain Christmas of the *Kron Princessa Maria*, who seems to have taken a keen interest in the welfare of the missionary party, sent word that there was a vacancy for a superintendent at the Company's Botanical Garden. Carey hurried back to Calcutta to apply for the position for which, with his great interest in plants, he would have been eminently suited – only to find that it had already been filled by Dr. Roxburgh of Madras.

It will be remembered that in his *Enquiry* Carey had suggested that new missionaries should endeavour to make themselves self-sufficient by farming. Being assured that he could settle on waste land in Calcutta belonging to the East India Company, he fetched the family back from Bandel.

Once again, his hopes were frustrated; there was no free land available. The family were practically destitute and would have been homeless had it not been for the generosity of a Bengali money-lender who allowed them to occupy his garden-house at Manicktullo – today a crowded part of north-east Calcutta but then a marshy, malarial area, the haunt of gangs of robbers. Under-nourished and ill-housed, Mrs. Carey and the two older boys succumbed to bad attacks of dysentery which left them weak and depressed. Their wretchedness during these weeks brought bitter recriminations. 'My wife, and sister too, who do not see the importance of the mission as I do, are continually exclaiming against me,' Carey wrote miserably in his *Journal*[11] 'and as for Mr. T., they think it very hard indeed that he should live in a city, in an affluent manner, and they be forced to go into a wilderness, and live without many of what they call the necessaries of life, bread in particular.'

It is impossible not to feel some sympathy for the women, sick, exhausted with constant uncertainty, bewildered by their new surroundings, friendless, and burdened by the care of providing for the constant needs of four young children. Carey's dedication to his vision must have seemed like unfeeling stubbornness to them. Despite their reproaches, he did cling to his vision:

> If my family were but hearty in the work, I should find a great burden removed, but the carnal discourse of the passage, and the pomp and grandeur of Europeans here, have intoxicated their minds, so as to make them unhappy in one of the finest countries in the world, and lonely in the midst of a hundred thousand people. These are burdens and afflictions to me; but I bless God that I faint not; and when my soul can drink her fill at the word of God, I forget all. . . .[12]

The women would indeed be 'lonely in the midst of a hundred thousand people' for they had as yet no means of communication with them. Carey, on the other hand, was making steady progress with his study of Bengali. Out of their slender means, he paid 20 rupees per month (£2.50) for the services of a 'munshi' or native teacher. Ram Boshoo was a former convert of Thomas's who had lapsed during Thomas's visit to England. This munshi was to guide Carey to the first prospect of a settled home. He had an uncle who held a position of authority in Debhatta, a village some forty miles or so east of Calcutta. Near this village, in the jungle area known as the Sundarbuns, Carey was offered some land rent-free for three years and thereafter for a small rental. The land would need clearing, a house would have to be built but, with God's help, they could scratch a living somehow and gradually become self-sufficient. Ram Boshoo would accompany them and put them in touch with his uncle.

First, however, they must have money for the journey, and to purchase tools and seed.

Carey went confidently to Thomas who had till now been handling all the financial arrangements. To his utter dismay, he was told that all the money was expended; indeed, Thomas was already once again heavily in debt. 'I am in a strange land, alone, no christian friend, a large family, and nothing to supply their wants.'[13] What despair must have been in Carey's heart when he wrote those words! 'I blame Mr. T. for leading me into such expense at first,' he continues. Then, generously, '. . . and I blame myself for being led. . .'[14]

A few days later he writes that his wife has 'relapsed into her affliction, and is much worse than she was before'.[15] This is the first mention of the disturbed mental condition which would eventually cloud Dorothy's mind completely. As one trouble after another was heaped on the young missionary's shoulders, it is difficult not to compare him with Job and his trials.

> . . . My temporal troubles remain just as they were. I have a place, but cannot remove my family to it for want of money. Mr. T. has now begun to set his face another way. . . Now he is buying and selling, and living at the rate of I know not how much, I suppose 250 or 300 rupees per month, has twelve servants and this day is talking of keeping his coach. I have remonstrated with him in vain, and I am almost afraid that he intends to throw up the mission. . . Now all my friends are but one; I rejoice, however, that he is all-sufficient, and can supply all my wants, spiritual and temporal. . . But why is my soul disquieted within me? . . . every thing is known to God, and God cares for the mission. . .[16]

Carey pours out his agony of mind into his *Journal*. One day, as above, he is full of reproach for Thomas. The following day he chides himself for his lack of charity. Though he is sometimes 'spiritually barren',[17] 'full of perplexity about temporal things', 'at an awful distance from God',[18] there is more often in the entries a dogged faith that 'I am in my work, and that is the work of God'.[19] Despite anxieties over money and fruitless visits to acquaintances in the hope of obtaining a loan, he yet finds time to attempt to preach at small gatherings of enquirers – no doubt mustered by Ram Boshoo – and to work at correcting Thomas's part translation into Bengali of the Book of Genesis. He worries over how to render 'whales' into the Bengali tongue, such creatures being unknown in that part of the world. He cheers himself by reading over again a copy of Andrew Fuller's 'charge' when he and Thomas were set aside for missionary work. 'O what a portion is God,' he writes 'and what a shame that I am not always satisfied with him!'[20]

By 4th February, 1794, by dint of borrowing money from a native money-lender at an exorbitant twelve per cent, Carey managed to procure a boat and supplies. Piling in their few precious possessions, the sad little party set out: Carey, Ram Boshoo, Dorothy – wandering in mind and still weak with dysentery – her sister Catherine and the four little boys.

The Sundarbuns was, and still is, a wide area of jungle and swamp criss-crossed with river channels, some of them very wide, making up the vast delta where the rivers Ganges and Brahmaputra debouch into the Bay of Bengal. Dense thickets of palms and low trees line the rivers right to the water's edge. It was, according to Carey's account, an area swarming 'with tigers, lepards, rhinoceroses (*sic*), deer, buffaloes, &c. . . I thought I heard the roar of a tiger in the night, but am uncertain . . . no one dares to go on shore, so as to venture a hundred yards from the boat.'[21]

The journey of forty miles took three days. Early in the morning of 6th February, as they approached Debhatta on the east bank of the River Jubona, and when they were down to their very last day's supply of food, they noticed a fine, verandahed house on the river bank. It appeared to be English-built for it was constructed of brick. Ram Boshoo confirmed that an English gentleman lived there, a Mr. Charles Short who was in charge of the East India Company's salt warehouse at Debhatta. Carey decided that their straits were such that he must call on his fellow-countryman for help.

It would be interesting to know what Mr. Short's feelings were when he went to greet the visitors his servant told him were approaching. A small group were walking up from the river in the early morning mist – not representatives on Company business, not friends from Calcutta, but *women*, and English women at that, and *children*!

With a hospitality that had been noticeably absent when Carey had walked five miles in full sun to beg for help from a certain reverend gentleman in Calcutta, Mr. Short invited the travellers into his home. Carey was completely frank. He told him of his proposed work in India and of the desperate plight in which he now found himself. If Mr. Short, being an unbeliever, felt little sympathy for Carey's mission, he nonetheless displayed truly Christian charity in the warmth of his welcome. They could stay with him as long as they wished, he insisted, half a year if need be; certainly until Carey had built his house.

Though embarrassed to be dependent on a man so indifferent to religion, Carey had really no choice but to accept the offer. His wife was desperately in need of rest and care, as was Felix. All of them required food and shelter. At least it gave Carey an opportunity to review his situation. It also afforded an opportunity for Charles Short and Kitty Plackett to fall in love and, eventually, to marry – but that is another story.

Two days later, Carey took possession of an area of promising land at Kalutala, across the river Jubona from Debhatta. He estimated that the sale of the timber he felled as he cleared his land would bring in enough to support the family. Food in the native villages nearby was cheap; game abounded in the forest and the river swarmed with fish. He threw himself with energy into carving a home out of the wilderness. Daily he rowed across the Jubona from Mr. Short's splendid residence to fell trees and to make a clearing for his own little house. This was to be built of bamboo, on stilts to raise it above the mud, and roofed with matting. He turned over a small patch of garden and surrounded it with an earthen embankment topped by a fence as protection against wild animals. (Twenty men of the salt-works had been attacked and killed by tigers during the previous twelve months.) During the time he laboured there, many families who had fled the district for fear of the tigers were persuaded to return. This Carey attributed to the efforts of his munshi who, so Carey wrote to Andrew Fuller on 15th February, 1794, had convinced them that the new English settler would be a father to them and would protect them from wild beasts!

Although Carey's hands were busy, his heart was heavy within him. Progress was so slow – with his house, with his studies, with the task he had come to India to perform. At times he confessed to apathy – 'a guilty calm is spread over my soul'.[22] At other times he counts the wasted days:

> . . .When I first left England, my hope of the conversion of the heathen was very strong; but, among so many obstacles, it would entirely die away, unless upheld by God. Nothing to exercise it, but plenty to obstruct it, for now a year and nineteen days, which is the space since I left my dear charge at Leicester. Since that I have had hurrying up and down; a five months' imprisonment with carnal men on board the ship; five more learning the language; my Moonshi not understanding English sufficiently to interpret my preaching; my colleague separated from me; long delays and few opportunities for social worship . . . no earthly thing to depend upon, or earthly comfort, except food and raiment. Well; I have God, and his word is sure. . .[23]

There is an aching loneliness about the entries in his *Journal* at this time. 'O that I had . . . an earthly friend to whom I could unbosom my soul!'[24] How often he must have wished that his wife could have been to him a loving support, a companion with whom he could share his hopes and his uncertainties. But there was nothing there to bring him comfort – only a sickly woman whose frail flame of reason was beginning to flicker and fail. He makes little reference to her condition except to speak of her as being 'so ill'.[25] Whenever he makes some small progress, he records it gratefully:

> I think the hope of soon acquiring the language puts fresh life into my soul; for a long time my mouth has been shut, and my days have been beclouded with heaviness; but now I begin to be something like a traveller who has been almost beaten out in a violent storm, and who, with all his clothes about him dripping wet, sees the sky begin to clear. . .[26]

He was more prophetic than he knew. His probationary

trials were almost over. Just as, eighteen months before, Thomas had come into his life and shown him God's opening for him in India, so again that now somewhat tarnished guardian angel was to lead him along a path that God had smoothed for him.

Perhaps Carey needed a wilderness experience to temper his faith. 'I have God, and his word is sure . . . and though the superstitions of the heathen were a million times worse than they are, if I were deserted by all, and persecuted by all, yet my hope, fixed on that sure word, will rise superior to all obstructions . . . I shall come out of all trials as gold purified by fire. . .'[27]

Carey never did occupy the bamboo hut in the jungle. Before it was completed, he was on his way to Malda, nearly two hundred and fifty miles to the north.

6

Manufacturer and Missionary

May, 1794–April, 1795

The death of a young English merchant and his wife in a boating accident on the dangerous channel of the River Hooghli one dark night in January 1794 would seem an unlikely base from which to start the forward progress of missionary work in India, but that was indeed the case.[1]

The husband who drowned was a Mr. Robert Udney whose brother, George, was Commercial Resident at Malda in the Province of Dinadjpur. A Commercial Resident was a civil servant who was responsible by means of loans to contractors for encouraging agriculture and industry in the area under his administration. He was, however, also allowed to trade privately. The then Governor-General, Sir John Shore, deliberately sanctioned this practice because he felt that best results were achieved when the interests of individuals and of the East India Company went hand in hand. Unlike some 'Residents', Mr. George Udney was a man of integrity.

During his earlier stay in India, Thomas had known the Udney brothers and their mother and had received financial help from them but, as with so many of his acquaintances, he had given offence and had become estranged from them. Despite his tactless nature and his chronic inability to handle money, Thomas was a generous and good-hearted man. On hearing of the tragedy, he immediately wrote to his old friends to express his sympathy. He was invited to Malda and there the differences between them were set aside. It happened that Mr. Udney was erecting two new indigo factories and offered the management of the one at Moypauldiggy to Thomas. It took but little persuasion for him to offer the management of the other factory to Carey.

'This appearing to be a remarkable opening in divine providence, for our comfortable support,' wrote Carey in his *Journal*, 'I accepted it'.[2]

Once again, frustrating weeks had to be spent in making arrangements for the journey but at last, at three o'clock on the morning of 23rd May, the family set out.

Practically the whole of Bengal (which province is the size of France) is a vast alluvial plain. There is no high ground at all and the area is subject to constant flooding. Thus, transport – more especially so in Carey's time – is by water. For just over three weeks – the time it took them to make the three hundred mile journey – a boat was their home. Kitty Plackett stayed behind at Debhatta to marry Mr. Short but Ram Boshoo accompanied them.

On the journey north, Carey essayed to preach to the natives at the various places where they tied up in the evening. He discovered a complication in that high-caste Indians spoke Bengali and low-caste, Hindustani. 'I understand a little of both, and hope to be master of both.'[3]

Carey does not describe the type of craft they used but it was probably one of the shallow-draught country boats with great square sails made of beaten bark such as are still used today in Bangladesh. Perhaps he poled his way up the Rivers Jubona and Isamuty for he speaks of 'procuring sails, making ropes, &c. for our boats' on 7th June, by which time he had reached Bassetpore and the main stream of the River Ganges.

The journey was painfully slow. The sluggish rivers meandered across the level plains so that they '. . . laboured two days to make about four miles in a straight line. I thought that our course was very much like the christian life, sometimes going forward and often apparently backward. . .'[4]

It says much for Carey's enterprise that he, a man from the heart of England with absolutely no experience of boats until his journey to India, should set about learning to handle a river-craft in this way. The river at Bassetpore was eight or nine miles wide and full of shallows. On several occasions they ran aground on sandbanks – 'a very unpleasant state'.[5]

It was the hottest season of the year, building up in humidity towards the onset of the monsoon. They were pestered by mosquitoes but managed to keep in good health, apart from Dorothy who was in a 'very weak state'.[6] Just how Carey coped with the journey beggars the imagination. Jabez was only just one year old, Peter five, William six and Felix nine. With their mother in a state of collapse, all the care of the little boys must have devolved upon their father. No wonder he writes (though with creditable under-statement): 'Travelling, in general, I have always found unfriendly to the progress of the divine life in my soul; but travelling with a family more particularly so. . .'[7]

On 15th June, they arrived at Malda where Carey felt an immediate sense of relief to meet Mr. Udney and his mother and to be reunited with Thomas. '. . . I feel now as if released from a prison, and enjoying the sweets of christian fellowship again . . .'.[8]

To his great satisfaction, William learned that his salary at the indigo factory was to be 200 rupees per month (£25), plus commission on all indigo sold. There was a large, brick-built two-storey house to live in. Riches indeed! Typically, he wrote immediately to the Society in England to assure them that there was now no need for them to send him any more money for his support. His new job would render him self-sufficient so that the money that would have been assigned for his support could now finance the sending out of another missionary.

The factory over which Carey took charge was at Mudnabatti in the district of Dinadjpur, some thirty-two miles north of Malda. The journey there took nearly three days up the River Tangan though whenever he needed to make the return journey to Malda, the current brought him down in fifteen hours. It was a fairly isolated station, with no other Europeans living there.

> We have no fear of beasts, though there are many buffaloes, hogs, and tigers in our neighbourhood. Tigers seldom attack men, but commit dreadful devastation among cattle. . . Serpents are numerous; and some so mortal that the patient never survives two hours, and often dies in five minutes; but they give us no concern, or very little. Crocodiles no man minds: I have one in a pond about ten yards from my door, yet sleep with the door open every night. . .[9]

At the factory, Carey had ninety employees under him of whom he commented hopefully: 'these will furnish a congregation immediately'.[10] He flung himself with his usual determination and enthusiasm into learning the work of indigo manufacture. Within days he had discovered and put a stop to a private money-making 'racket' among the overseers which was souring labour relations at the factory. Despite his love for the people of this new land and his most sincere desire to win them for Christ, it is manifest from his *Journal* that he found their character bewildering and disappointing.

> Many (Hindus) say that the gospel is the word of truth; but they abound so much in flattery and encomiums . . . that little can be said respecting their sincerity. The very common sins of lying and avarice are so universal also, that no European who has not witnessed it can form an idea of their various appearances: they will stoop to any thing whatsoever to get a few cowries, and lie on every occasion.[11]

Similarly, he found the rigid caste system one of the greatest barriers to conversion. 'Perhaps this is one of the strongest chains with which the devil ever bound the children of men. This is my comfort, that God can break it.'[12]

One day, a young boy belonging to the lowest caste came to the house begging for food. Ram Boshoo, knowing that Carey needed a servant, offered him employment – but the lad refused *lest he should lose caste by working for an Englishman*! Indeed, it would require great courage for any Indian to embrace Christianity for in so doing he would automatically lose caste and be rejected by his own people. Carey hoped that, having the management of the indigo factory, he would be able to offer secure employment to any such outcastes.

There was also a large Mahommedan population ('their zeal . . . is very great') and Carey described their curiosity, not having seen white people before, as to 'which was Saib, and which was Bibby Saib, that is, which was I, and which my wife.'[13]

Their arrival in Mudnabatti coincided with their first real experience of the monsoon. It was a busy time preparing for the season of indigo making, due to begin towards the end of July. Moreover, Carey had to visit several other factories to learn the process. All this activity in the heat made him 'very much fatigued'[14] and 'obliged to be rather more cautious'.[15]

For a man who had to earn his own living but who wished at

the same time to have ample free time for missionary work and translation, there could scarcely be a more suitable occupation than the management of an indigo factory. In the first place, the appointment would qualify him for a five-year 'licence' or work permit, making his presence in British India legal. Then the actual processing of the indigo plant only demanded about three months' intensive work a year during the rainy season, leaving the remaining nine months virtually free for other activity. Those three months, however, required careful superintendence for which Carey, with his conscientious application to detail and scientific approach, was eminently suited.

Indigofera Tinctoria is a shrub with reddish-yellow flowers which belongs to the *leguminosae* family. The plant has been grown in India for thousands of years on account of the deep blue dye it yields although, strangely, no indication of the colour is found in the plant while growing. The seeds are sown in March, kept carefully weeded, and harvested in early July, by which time the plants have grown to a height of about five feet. The cut indigo would be brought to Carey's works where it was soaked in huge vats of water in which native workers waded waist-deep. They would beat the indigo with flat paddles until it released the glucosidal solid from which the blue/green colour was obtained. The water, now coloured blue by the particles in suspension, was drained off into vats at a lower level where the granulations could settle and ferment. The liquid was allowed to evaporate and the remaining solid dried into cakes for distribution and sale. If the manufacture was carried out carefully and successfully, the yield could be highly profitable.

However, there were problems other than the actual process of manufacture to cope with – the constant battle against ignorance and superstition.

The evening before his factory was to commence production, Carey was approached by his workmen to make a placatory gift to Kally. This was the Hindu goddess of destruction, represented by a hideous, four-armed figure with protruding tongue. She stood on a dead man and wore human skulls on her girdle like beads slotted on a string. Carey was appalled and took the opportunity of preaching on the sin of idolatry. His words fell on deaf ears and the next day he was mortified to learn that the workmen had sacrificed a kid to the goddess on his behalf.

He was, of course, in an invidious position. Should anything go wrong – the monsoon fail, the river swell into flood, disease be rampant, the indigo harvest be poor – all could be blamed on his foolhardy neglect to propitiate Kally or any other of the many Hindu gods. No doubt such forebodings were voiced when Carey became gravely ill with 'fever' in September, 1794. His *Journal* had recorded as early as August: 'It is indeed an awful time here with us now, scarcely a day but some are seized with fevers,' but he had attributed these to the flooded fields. The dank ground mists or 'vapours' of the swampy countryside of Bengal were at that time considered responsible for every undiagnosed malady. William Hickey wrote in his *Memoirs* in September 1791: 'I have sent for Doctor Hare, who said (the fever) arose entirely from the dampness of the night air. . .' In Carey's case, it seems possible that he was stricken with malaria for he writes that Mr. Udney brought 'a bottle of bark'[16] (presumably cinchona bark or quinine). He recovered only slowly from the attack. Other members of the family were in poor health also. Dorothy and Felix had been suffering from dysentery for *eight months*, and at the end of September, the Careys' third son, Peter, contracted the disease and died. He was only five years old, a bright little lad already fluent in Bengali.

As if his loss was not grief enough, the distracted parents could find no-one willing to make a coffin or to dig the child's grave lest they should lose caste, despite the fact that carpenters and labourers were employed at the factory. Eventually, four Mussulmen (Moslems) were prevailed upon to dig the grave but for even this simple act of service they were ostracised by their village. Although the Moslem religion laid down no regulations about caste, Indian Moslems had adopted the Hindu ways and considered themselves a separate caste. Even with a grave dug, it looked as if William and Dorothy would themselves have to carry the corpse to its place of burial. Hindus would feel defiled to bury a corpse, for their custom was either to burn their dead or throw them into the river to be devoured by birds and fishes. Moslems did bury their dead but would only concern themselves with members of their own family, and even then felt polluted. However, at the last moment, the most menial of Carey's servants and a boy who had already lost caste agreed to perform this last service for little Peter. With great courage, Carey and Thomas later sent for the village headman and ordered him to sit down and eat with the four outcast Mussulmen in front of the whole village. The headman demurred, whereat the missionaries threatened to place the whole matter before the judge in Dinadjpur. At this, the headman gave in and ate and drank with the moslems in full view of the village, thus restoring their status.

The shock of this family tragedy seems to have brought about the final break in Dorothy Carey's frail hold on reason and, after this date, there is very rarely any mention of her either in William's own *Journal* or in the letters and diaries of his colleagues except as his 'domestic affliction'. This conspiracy of silence at first appears harsh and unfeeling until it is remembered what was the general attitude towards mental sickness at the time.

Until the end of the eighteenth century and even later, the mentally afflicted were treated with no understanding of their condition and often with great brutality. Madness was frequently regarded as possession by an evil spirit. Improved treatment came not through doctors but through the work of reformers, men of the same breed as John Howard, who revolted against the cruelty and neglect which the insane had to suffer. There had been for centuries hospitals like Bethlehem (Bedlam) in London where the insane could be segregated, but it is a travesty of the word to call them 'asylums'. The unhappy patients were at the mercy of ignorant warders. They were kept in cages or loaded with chains and, if troublesome, were beaten and tormented. They were left in filth, and the population came to laugh and gape at them. Even the great were not exempt from such brutalities. When King George III was suffering from the attacks of madness that periodically affected him, he was confined in a strait jacket and on more than one occasion knocked down by his keepers. Not until 1827 was a commission set up by Parliament to enquire into the condition of mental asylums. Even in the first quarter of the twentieth century, mental disturbance was regarded as 'madness' by large sections of the public and the sufferer of such affliction was an object of shame and disgrace to his family rather than sympathy. Mental hospitals were frequently known as 'loony bins' and their unfortunate inmates were feared as much as those of eighteenth-century Bedlam.

One odd incident is recorded which suggests that Dorothy had some form of persecution mania. Early in 1795, she apparently wrote a letter to Thomas making accusations against her husband and had it secretly delivered to Moypauldiggy where he was in charge of the indigo factory. Fortunately, Thomas, being medically qualified and, in his tolerance and understanding, way ahead of his time, viewed the letter merely as the aberration of a sick woman. He wrote sympathetically to Carey:

> You must endeavour to consider it a disease. The eyes and ears of many are upon you, to whom your conduct is unimpeachable with respect to all her charges; but if you show resentment, they have ears, and others have tongues set on fire. Were I in your case, I should be violent; but blessed be God, who suits our burdens to our backs. . .[17]

William also was in low spirits – not only due to Peter's death and his own illness but from the lack of any news from England.

> I was much disappointed on the arrival of the Nancy, packet, by the return of which I send this, at not receiving one European letter. Surely you have not forgotten us. . .[18]

> Much engaged in writing, having begun to write letters to Europe; but having received none, I feel that hope deferred makes the heart sick. . .[19]

He had been moving around so much since his arrival in India and had quite frequently been away from centres of white settlers that probably he was unaware of the violence of the war now raging between France and England. During 1794, two out of every three ships leaving Calcutta were said to be captured by French privateers.[20] Carey could not know that his own letters home were delayed. The first communication from him to reach England did not arrive until 29th July, 1794 – fourteen months after his departure. It says much for the devotion of those 'holding the ropes' at home that they did not flag in their prayers for the missionary enterprise.

After the season's indigo had been harvested and the manufacture of the dye completed, Mr. Udney urged Carey to take a holiday. His illness had left him weak and in need of a change. Accordingly, in late October 1794, accompanied by his family and Mr. Thomas and using Mr. Udney's boat, Carey went north towards the border of Bhutan. It was the beginning of the driest, coolest part of the Indian year. Thomas hunted for wild buffaloes and leopards; Carey studied the language and customs of the people and sought out new plants. Throughout his years in India, his main recreation was to be the study and cataloguing of plants but it was, even from the beginning, much more than a hobby.

Carey had the supervision of an area about twenty miles square in which were, he tells us, about two hundred 'villages' – probably then, as now, mounds of earth holding the bamboo homes of the natives above the normal monsoon flood level. He would travel from village to village checking on the growth of the indigo crop.

> My manner of travelling is with two small boats; one serves me to live in, and the other for cooking my food. I carry all my furniture and food with me from place to place – viz. a chair, a table, a bed, and a lamp. I walk from village to village, but repair to my boat for lodging and eating. . . .[21]

As he travelled from one primitive community to another, Carey could see the need for better methods of agriculture, for the tools and implements taken for granted in the rich farming country of Northamptonshire.

> . . . I wish you also to send me a few instruments of husbandry, viz. scythes, sickles, plough-wheels, and such things, *he wrote to the Society*[22], and a yearly assortment of all garden and flowering seeds, and seeds of fruit-trees, that you can possibly procure . . . and the seeds of all sorts of field and forest-trees, &c . . . as it will be a lasting advantage to this country; and I shall have it in my power to do this for what I now call my own country. . .

He experimented to discover what European plants would thrive in the more extreme climate of Bengal. He was the first of the Baptist Missionary Society's 'farming evangelists', concerned to show that the goodness of God bestows not only salvation of the soul but also rich blessing from the fruits of the earth.

But, as in farming it is necessary to submit to the slow seasons of nature, so also in Carey's missionary work, his progress seemed imperceptible and disheartening.

He doggedly continued with his work at the factory and with his work of translation. He studied Bengali and preached in that language whenever the opportunity afforded. He and Thomas set up two schools where they took Indian boys as boarders, teaching them Sanskrit, Persian, Bible study, science and mathematics. The most modern aspect of their missionary work was the medical care offered to the natives. The humble villages in the neighbourhood had no access to doctors, hospitals or medicines so that anything the missionaries could provide helped to ease the pain and suffering that are always closely associated with poverty and ignorance. 'Brother Thomas has been the instrument of saving numbers of lives,' Carey wrote.[23] 'His house is constantly surrounded with the afflicted; and the cures wrought by him would have gained any physician or surgeon in Europe the most extensive reputation. We ought to be furnished yearly with at least half a hundredweight of Jesuits' bark.'[24]

Mudnabatti proved a very unhealthy place but, despite constant bouts of fever and consequent attacks of depression, he kept his faith. It is obvious from his *Journal* that the occasional visits to Malda and Moypauldiggy and his meetings with the Udneys and other Europeans served as a tonic.

> . . . At Moypauldiggy, somewhat better, but very weak. We had some profitable discourse, and spent some time in prayer with each other. It is good to enjoy the communion of saints; and its value can scarcely be estimated unless in a situation like mine, where I am surrounded by Pagans and Mahommedans, and have no other to converse with. . .[25]

He writes of Mudnabatti '. . . here we have only poor and illiterate people . . .'[26] but of Malda, 'was much refreshed and relieved by the conversation of Christian friends.'[27] 'Spent this time at Malda in very agreeable society. Preached on Christmas day, and twice on Lord's day, the 28th; and I think I may say with truth, that the whole of this time was a time of real refreshing to my soul, which had long been in a barren and languid state.'[28]

He constantly castigates himself for want of spirituality. 'O that this day could be consigned to oblivion! What a mixture of impatience, carelessness, forgetfulness of God, pride and peevishness have I felt! God forgive me!'[29] Yet his very steadfastness in the cause of his Master belies his self-reproach. The lack of visible success obviously depressed him. He longed to cheer the Society at home with news of conversions but had as yet none to report. He yearned to deliver his new people from the 'sensuality, ignorance and superstition' in which they were 'drowned'.[30] Yet what could he expect? A missionary necessarily leads a lonely life in the midst of pagans. Carey was one solitary Christian, with an as yet imperfect command of the language, in a community of several hundred – even thousands – of Hindus and Moslems, and he was endeavouring to break the traditions of centuries. The whole rhythm of the Indian year was geared to its religious festivals: the offerings to the sun of plantains and sweetmeats which he described in January, 1795; the swinging on flesh-hooks or *Churruk Poojah* as an act of penance on the last three days of the Hindu year; the sacrifices to Kally, the goddess of destruction; the *Obitar* or incarnation of Krishnu which Carey had witnessed at Debhatta in March, 1794; the festival of the sun, called *Soorjyo* or *Deebahar*, in May, to mention but a few.

As a result, at this stage of his missionary career, Carey tended to preach against what he considered the detrimental features of Hinduism and Islam. Later (and with greater impact) he learned instead to emphasise the positive aspects of Christianity. Nonetheless, even though he disapproved of, was at times even revolted by the idolatrous practices of the Indians, he is yet curious about their ritual and significance. He does not seek to condemn them out of hand but seeks to offer an alternative. Thus, in describing the worship of the sun[31] he related how he preached from Revelations 1:16 ('His countenance was as the sun shining in his strength') and told his hearers of the glories of the Lord of the sun, as creator, governor and saviour. At times, even, he was prepared to concede that there was much that was good both in the *Shastras* and in the *Koran*[32] but that they omitted the element of forgiveness. Of course, it early became apparent to him that he was not preaching to the 'simple savage' of his *Enquiry* but to people of an ancient civilisation and equally ancient religion. The brahmins he encountered and argued with were educated men. At Mudnabatti, however, he was still serving his missionary apprenticeship. Though he wrote optimistic reports home to the Society in England, he was to admit much later than during his first seven years in India his 'mind was often almost dried up by discouragement and want of success'. Feeling 'spiritless . . . (he) went to work like a soldier who only expects to be defeated.'[33]

This was written with hindsight. During the early years at Mudnabatti, although at times his loneliness and despair pluck the heartstrings, his *Journal* repeatedly contains statements of faith. Perhaps at times he wrote them down to reassure himself. It is impossible to tell how many times he had to stifle doubts as to whether he was indeed resting in God's will. If he did have doubts, he seems to have managed to conceal them even from himself. His *Journal* reveals a stubborn faith. Despite all setbacks and discouragements and failures, he clings to the remembered passion of his address to the Baptist Association Meeting at Nottingham in May, 1792. He confidently expects 'great things from God' and will thereby be able to achieve great things in His name.

> . . . This is indeed the valley of the shadow of death to me, except that my soul is much more insensible than John Bunyan's Pilgrim. O! what would I give for a kind sympathetic friend, such as I had in England, to whom I might open my heart! But I rejoice that I am here notwithstanding; and God is here, who not only can have compassion, but is able to save to the uttermost.[34]

7

'Attempt great things . . .'

May, 1795–January, 1798

In May, 1795 – two years after he had sailed for India from Dover – Carey received the first parcel and letters from England. There was news of his father and sisters; information that his brother had gained promotion in the army. The Leicester church, which Carey had so often remembered with affection in his *Journal*, was prospering. Morris and Pearce wrote with loving concern. In addition, there was the first of many letters from his friend, Andrew Fuller, pastor of Kettering Baptist Church and now, in addition, Secretary to the Baptist Missionary Society.

Fuller's letters are a delight for the student of this period. He records that he sits at his desk writing letters 'eleven or twelve hours a day' – letters that are full of domestic details about his wife, his children, his own health; letters that trace the development of the Baptist Missionary Society; letters that allude to matters of historical significance such as Wilberforce's campaigns in Parliament or the progress of the war with France.

> Kettering.
> Mar. 25 – May 25, 1794
>
> . . . Publick affairs wear a dark aspect to a political eye. . . A dark cloud hangs over us. We expect the French will shortly attempt to invade us. They have been making great preparations for it for several months. Great numbers are going to America. Dr. Priestley & 80 or 90 families are going this month. . .
>
> Robespierre is about head cock of the walk at this time. . . Thousands court his favour while he seems to court no man's, but is more frequently employed like a bull with his tail, in whisking the flies from off his back. . .

Surprisingly, the former Leicester radical and enthusiast for the Revolution evinced little interest on paper in the news from Europe. Carey's mind had become focussed with singleness of purpose on the great mission of evangelising the heathen. 'I am not concerned about politics,' he wrote in a reply. 'I see the Calcutta papers and I think that as the people of Europe have fallen out, so they must fall in. But the religious state of the world is very important. . .'[1]

By December, 1795 he was able to report the establishment of a baptist church in Malda, albeit with only four members – himself, Thomas, a Mr. Long (baptised by Thomas) and Carey's own first baptism in India, a young Englishman by the name of Powell. However, there were living in the district Company officials, military personnel and factory managers like himself, together with their families. He could hope to draw a congregation from among these. Indeed, a large part of Carey's mission inevitably was to the British in India as well as to the native population. Much of the British society in India was raffish. The employees of the Company were not always of the best character; it was a practice to pack off to India sons who had fallen into disgrace for one reason or another and, having reached India, there was little apart from gambling, drinking and womanising with which to pass their considerable leisure time. The climate was too hot for much in the way of sport and there was little in the way of cultural activity, particularly in the smaller European centres. As far as Carey's mission to Indians was concerned, he could by now 'preach an hour with tolerable freedom',[2] though he found the scope of his preaching limited by the extremely small vocabulary of his hearers. The poor of Bengal, whose whole concern was how to ease their hunger or meet the demands of their rapacious landlords, had no time or thought for words that expressed love, repentance, salvation and other such abstracts. 'Every idea is expressed either by quaint phrases or tedious circumlocutions,'[3] Carey lamented. He held regular services at which, in addition to hymns and prayers and an address, he would encourage his munshi to read a chapter of the Bible in Bengali. If he made no actual converts among the natives at this time, nonetheless he attracted large congregations which never failed to give him a courteous hearing. At least he was able to claim that 'the name of Jesus Christ is no longer strange in this neighbourhood'.[4]

The work of translation of the Bible was going forward steadily. By October, 1795 Carey could report that he had completed the translation of Genesis and Exodus, Matthew, Mark and parts of James and John. For writing, Carey found the Bengali language rich, beautiful and expressive. His method of work was thorough. He would go through his translation with his pundit who would comment on style and syntax, while Carey had a care to the faithfulness of the rendering. '. . . If I, like David,' he wrote 'only am the instrument of gathering materials, and another build the house, I trust my joy will not be the less'.[5] In this, he foresaw his later achievement, for it was supremely as a translator, as a supplier to others of the tools for missionary work, that Carey must be remembered and praised. The number of actual conversions directly attributable to him is pathetically small; the number *in*directly attributable to him must be legion. Even with his preaching, who could say for certain that the seed fell on barren ground? A seed may lie in the earth for several years before conditions are right for it to germinate and flower. But his translations reached thousand upon thousand of people who never had the opportunity of hearing him speak.

It soon became apparent to Carey that a study of Bengali alone would not be sufficient to enable him to complete his work of translation. Accordingly he set to work to master Sanskrit, the mother language of Bengali, and by April of 1796 he was sufficiently fluent in that tongue to be comparing the *Mahabarata*, one of the two great Vedic epics, with Homer's *Iliad*. In order to be able to read fluently in the language, he translated a Sanskrit grammar and dictionary into English, and compiled his own Sanskrit/Bengali/English dictionary.

The second batch of letters from England reached India at the beginning of October, 1795. Apart from those and the earlier letters received in May and one parcel of stationery and shoes, no money, no items requested, nor anything else had reached the missionaries. Only slowly did it register how damaging was the effect of the war in Europe. Carey had asked for books, seeds, medicines, but none of these had arrived. In these circumstances, it filled him with indignation to be criticised in one of the letters that did reach him for 'engaging in affairs of trade'. It was felt, the letter said, that such activity might divert his attention from the main purpose of propagating the gospel. What Carey's critics could not know owing to the delay in the mails, and what Carey himself did not appreciate that they could not know, was that without 'trade', he and his family must surely have perished.

> I am astonished, *he wrote with dignity*, to find an indigo manufacturer called a merchant, which is just like calling a journeyman tailor a merchant. . . We receive wages adequate to the maintenance of our families; and now our buildings are over, I think no line of life could afford us more leisure or opportunity for doing good. To vindicate my own spirit or conduct, I should be very averse; it is a constant maxim with me, that if my conduct will not vindicate itself, it is not worth vindicating; but we really thought we were acting in conformity with the universal wishes of the society. Whether we are indolent or laborious, or whether 'the spirit of the missionary is swallowed up in the pursuits of the merchant' it becomes not me to say, but our labours will speak for us. I only say that, after my family's obtaining a bare allowance, my whole income, and some months much more, goes for the purposes of the gospel, in supporting persons to assist in the translation of the bible, write copies, teach school, and the like. . . I mention . . . (this) . . . to show that the love of money has not prompted me to pursue the plan that I have engaged in. I am indeed poor, and shall always be so till the bible is published in Bengali and Hindosthani, and the people want no further instruction.[6]

Unfortunately for Carey, his colleague Thomas had, as usual, been indiscreet and had caused rumours to spread throughout the Society in England. In an over-sanguine letter to his sister, he had invited his relatives to join him in India promising them that they could soon enjoy an income of £1,000 a year.[7] The reality was far from the case. Extra heavy rains in 1795 brought intensive flooding. The normally narrow Tangan river on whose banks Carey's works were situated swelled to a width of three or four miles. A sad result of this was that there was no profit to share from the indigo factory. Carey and Thomas had hoped to have as much as £300 between them to spend on printing their translation of such of the scriptures as had been completed – but there was no surplus. Indeed, Thomas was again having to borrow to quieten his creditors. 'One good season would enable me to pay all my debts and furnish me with overplus,' he wrote home with Micawber-like confidence on 13th January, 1796. He must have been at once an endearing and infuriating colleague for Carey. The one so volatile; the other dogged, even dour. The one full of charming unreliability; the other with the careful prudence of his peasant background.

> You see in Mr. Carey and myself some differences in taste, manner, &c.; *wrote Thomas to the Society with delightful understatement*, and there are many differences between us which you do not see. Do not be alarmed, for our very noses are not alike, but our hearts are one. . . We never differ but we agree to differ. . .[8]

His letter overflowed with confidence and enthusiasm, though perhaps his closing sentence would be as unnerving to his readers in England as the very real danger it dismissed had so worried Carey: 'I praise God, I am out of gaol; and I should have praised him more, perhaps, if I had been in it.'[9] The early apostles had at least only been imprisoned for proclaiming their faith – never for their unpaid debts!

Once the trickle of letters between England and India had become a steady flow, the burden of Carey's aloneness was considerably eased. 'You very encouragingly tell us not to faint, if we see no fruit yet,' Carey wrote gratefully to Fuller on 17th June, 1796, and then was able to pour out his troubles. He had had to dismiss his munshi, Ram Boshoo, for adultery – all the greater grief because Carey had hoped that working daily alongside the missionaries would have strengthened his adherence to Christian principles. He was a most intelligent and helpful translator, too.

Carey was grieved at the continued misunderstanding in England over their engaging in business. Yet it was becoming daily more apparent that some form of official 'employment' was essential if the missionaries were to be allowed to stay in India. In January 1796 he reported that magistrates in India were now required to make returns of all Europeans in their area; those British not in the service of King or Company were only allowed a limited stay in the country. Carey's employment as indigo manufacturer met this condition. He was incensed at the innuendoes against Thomas and loyally defended him. 'Mr. T. and I are men, and fallible; but we can only desert the work of preaching the word of life to the Hindus with our lives and are determined, through grace, to hold on, though our discouragements were a thousand times greater than they are.'[10]

He begged the Society to send out more men. The task facing them in India was enormous and he was well aware of the ever-present danger inherent in the endemic diseases of the country. 'We may die soon, and if we have no successors in the work, it will be a lamentable circumstance, and very much retard the spread of the gospel.'[11] He also mentioned the need for *women* missionaries to reach Indian women in purdah – again, a most advanced piece of thinking.

He tried to make the people at home understand the sheer enormity of the Indian problem. 'Only imagine England to be in the situation of Bengal; *without public roads*, inns, or other convenience for travel; without a post, save for the letters of the nobility; without the boon of printing; and absorbed in the monkish superstition of the eleventh century – that in this situation *two or three men* arrive from Greenland to evangelise the English, and settle at Newcastle – that they are under the necessity to labour for their living, and to spend much time translating the Scriptures, and you will be able to form some idea of our case.'[12]

The indigo factory continued to have problems. With each year that passed, it became more apparent that the Mudnabatti factory was wrongly sited; it was too liable to flooding, with consequent loss of production. Swinging from one extreme to another, the floods of 1795 were followed by a severe drought in 1796. These two bad years, added to the failure of a business venture of Mr. Udney's in Calcutta and the seizure of one of his ships by the French, meant that Carey's employer had no longer any spare capital to prop up the ailing factory. In mid-November, 1796, Carey wrote to Andrew Fuller of his fears that the factory might have to be abandoned. However, he was not dismayed. If need be, he was prepared to set up on his own: '. . . the experience obtained here I look upon as the very thing which will tend to support the mission. I now know all the methods of agriculture that are in use. I know the tricks of the natives, and the nature of the lowest rate of housekeeping in this country.'[13]

Even from the disappointed hopes of Mudnabatti did Carey begin to build for the future. In that same letter to Andrew Fuller, he expounded the scheme that was so soon to be put into practice at Serampore:

> I will now propose to you, what I would recommend to the Society. . . Seven or eight families can be maintained for nearly the same expense as one, if this method be pursued. . . We ought to be seven or eight families together; and it is absolutely necessary for the wives of missionaries to be as hearty in the work as their husbands. Our families should be considered nurseries for the mission; and among us should be a person capable of teaching school, so as to educate our children. I recommend all living together, in a number of little straw houses . . . and of having nothing of our own, but all the general stock . . . all should be considered equal, and all come under the same regulations.[14]

With all the practical attention to detail that went into his *Enquiry*, he proceeded to expand on his scheme, even down to costing it. But throughout ran the warning 'Pray be very careful what stamp missionaries' wives are of'.

Reading this detailed scheme arouses speculation about the condition of Carey's own family at this time. How were his four surviving sons being educated? (Another son, Jonathan, had been born in Mudnabatti after the death of Peter.) Did the older boys attend Carey's *chowpari* for native youths? Who looked after the home? Was Dorothy any longer capable of any duties about the house? Carey makes no reference to her in his *Journal* though a letter to Andrew Fuller on 17th June, 1796 concludes: 'We are well in health, except that my poor wife is in a very distressing state of mind: not maniacal, it is true, but afflicted with the species of insanity described by Dr. Arnold under the name of "ideal insanity".' It has not been possible to obtain any definition of 'ideal insanity' but, as the word 'ideal' at this time could denote 'fancied, imaginary, existing only in an idea', it is possible that 'ideal insanity' meant that the patient suffered from delusions. 'Ideal sights and sounds' wrote H. Spencer in 1862 'are in the insane . . . classed with real sights and sounds.'[15]

Some help from England did reach him. Late in 1796 a young missionary named John Fountain came out from England to join Carey and Thomas. His arrival took Carey by surprise but was nonetheless welcome. Fountain came originally from Rutland but had been helping the Society's India House counsellor, Mr. James Savage, at a Mission in Shoe Lane, off Fleet Street, London. His undoubted enthusiasm made up for his lack of training for work in the mission field. (Indeed, there was virtually no missionary training for anybody at that time.) In Carey's letters home, he had mentioned the local farming community so that Fountain 'had pleased himself with the hope of sitting in a farmer's chimney corner, and getting a basin of milk, and such hospitality as may be experienced in the house of an English farmer. But alas! he found that our farmers were not distinguishable from other people, and that houses in Bengal have no chimneys; that we are never asked to any one's house, and if we were, that there is nothing in them. . .'[16]

But if John Fountain was disappointed not to find a cosy English farm kitchen in India, he was impressed by the work that Carey was doing. His letters to England must have given further encouragement to the Society, for they described with enthusiasm the regular preaching of the gospel by Carey and Thomas (though the letters underlined the need for more missionaries); the enormous success of Thomas's medical mission; the staggering progress Carey had made with his translation of the scriptures. The New Testament was complete apart from the last few chapters of the Book of Revelation; the Old Testament was translated as far as the Book of Numbers.

Printing of the scriptures had by now become a matter of urgency. 'I am sure the work of God must prevail,' Carey wrote to Andrew Fuller on 23rd March, 1797 in a letter expressing his concern at the lack of converts. '. . . I know there are only two real obstacles in any part of the earth, viz., a want of the Bible, and the depravity of the human heart.' It was becoming increasingly clear that it would take too long to send the manuscript home to be printed. Moreover, Carey would have to send home drawings of the characters needed to be cast into type. Better to send out the money to purchase a printing-press in India or, if need be, send one out from England. But above all, could the Society find a printer who was prepared to offer his services to the work of God? Did

Carey remember William Ward whom he had met briefly in 1793?

However, as replies to his letters were so long delayed, Carey pressed ahead with his enquiries about getting his printing done in India or setting up his own press. By January, 1798 he reported that a letter foundry had been set up in Calcutta and that, backed by a promise of financial help from Mr. Udney, he was looking into the question of a press in Mudnabatti. A year later he had acquired a press for Rs.400 (£50)* and had had it set up in his home.

In March, 1797, Carey and Thomas made a missionary journey into Bhutan, the province that lay between Bengal and Thibet. It must have required great courage, for the people there were unacquainted with any English travellers. Carey wrote of his hopes of learning the language, but his vivid and descriptive letter is noteworthy more as being one of the rare occasions on which he allows himself to display any sense of humour. Yet he must surely have had a lighter side to his character than is generally apparent. No man could have retained the affection of four growing boys – as he undoubtedly did – without being on occasion able to laugh. The letter, written to Andrew Fuller from Mudnabatti on 23rd March, 1797 is too long to reproduce in full but the following extracts give an indication of its flavour:

> . . . Mr. Thomas and myself are just arrived at home from an excursion to Bootan. . . I will relate a little of our expedition. . .
>
> We went to a place called Gopalgunge, and waited on a Bootea officer, called the Jinkof; he received us very kindly, and we presented him with a few articles with which he was much pleased. . . He made us a present of some pieces of bacon about a foot long, but which were so stale as to be smelt at a great distance. After that, he treated us with tea, which they call runga. The teapot is a large bamboo, with a hole perforated through one of its knots on the inside, which is the spout; the tea is made into cakes with some composition, and is, when used, mixed with boiling water, ghee (butter melted down and then preserved for use) and salt. We tried in vain to swallow it,

* For the purposes of easy calculation, 1 rupee is taken as being the equivalent of 2s. 6d. (12½p). Carey's letter to Andrew Fuller from Serampore of 5th February, 1800 gives the exchange rate as 2s. 8d. per rupee (about 13p).

though the Bootea drank very copiously of it. His kindness, however, was very conspicuous, and he drank our rum more than we wished him. The Booteas are greatly addicted to drinking spirits, and pride themselves in drinking much, though drunkenness is reckoned a shame among them. However, all will intoxicate themselves if they can get English spirits; they are taught to drink spirits as soon as they can talk; and in all their houses you see large pitchers about as large as a small bucket, full of Bengal arrack, which they drink as we should water. . .

From Gopalgunge we went to Bote Haut . . . to see the Soobah, who is the greatest officer, that is, a kind of viceroy below the hills. . . The Jinkof himself went with us. The procession was the most comical and singular that could be imagined. . . We were preceded by a band of Bengal music, if such it can be called; we were six horsemen, and servants, people to carry our baggage, tents, &c . . . and spectators. We had near a hundred attendants on foot. On one horse was the Jinkof, led by two men, notwithstanding which he was sometimes first, sometimes last, and sometimes turning round, his horse being ungovernable: every mile or two he was stopping to drink spirits. A Hindu on another horse was much like him, except drinking; and we had enough to do to keep our horses out of their way, to effect which, we were always wheeling to the right or left. . .

The genuine politeness and gentleman-like behaviour of the Soobah exceeded every thing that can be imagined, and his generosity was astonishing. He insisted on supplying all our people with every thing they wanted; and if we did but cast our eyes to any object in the room, he immediately presented us with one of the same sort. . .

In eating, the Soobah imitated our manners so quickly and exactly, that though he had never seen a European before, yet he appeared as free as if he had spent his life with them. We ate his food, though I confess the thoughts of the Jinkof's bacon made me eat rather sparingly. . .

We found that he had determined to give all the country a testimony of his friendship for us in a public manner; and the next day was fixed on to perform the ceremony in our tent, on the market-place. . . Having chewed betel for the first time in our lives, we embraced three times in the eastern manner, and then shook hands in the English manner; after which, he made us a present of a piece of rich debang, wrought with gold, each a Bootan blanket, and the tail of an animal called the cheer cow. . .

> In the morning, the Soobah came with his usual friendship, and brought more presents, which we received, and took our leave. He sent us away with every honour he could heap upon us; as a band of music before us, guides to show us the way, &c.; in short, the whole of his conduct towards us was unvariedly as generous, polite, and friendly as I have ever witnessed. . .

One reason for the trip to Bhutan may well have been to investigate the possibility of setting up a missionary base there. Carey hinted at this in the long letter above-quoted which he wrote immediately after his return from his northern journey. Carey had no long-term security at Mudnabatti. Although he and Thomas had licences from the Company which secured their future for five years (and those would run out in two years' time), they were unable to procure such a licence for John Fountain. As long as they remained in East India Company territory, they lacked security and any missionary work carried out was done at risk, in defiance of the Company's policy. Bhutan was outside the dominion of the East India Company. (In the event, it was dismissed as a possibility as it was felt that the Company's influence could affect missionaries even there.) Yet a settled base Carey felt they must have. They needed more missionaries. The fields were white to harvest. '. . .This mission should be strengthened as much as possible, as its situation is such as may put it in our power, eventually, to spread the gospel through the greatest part of Asia.'[17]

Andrew Fuller's replies underline the difficulties of sending help. There is the problem of finding the right candidates. He can find no 'active and amiable women' to go out to India.[18] There are the difficulties of communication: 'The war makes conveyance very uncertain'.[19] There is the unsettled position at home in England: 'Things at present look dark with us as a nation.'[20]

It is interesting to note the growing self-confidence of Carey's letters from India. Some of this must have come from his growing maturity, particularly as his experience widened with the running of his factory and the supervision of native labour. Some also, perhaps, arose from his mixing in a society of a much higher social level than he could ever have aspired to in England and enjoying conversation with educated men. For example, when he made his monthly visit to Dinadjpur and preached in the local church in January, 1798 he had three English Assize judges among his congregation and dined with them afterwards. It would be inevitable that in the small European communities away from such large urban centres as Calcutta, the white settlers would tend to congregate together. Indeed, perhaps only away from England would a man of Carey's lowly origins have had such an opportunity. It says much for his charm and personality that he was accepted, particularly in an age when class distinctions were so clearly defined. Moreover, his purpose in India had become known by the mid-nineties. Copies of the Society's *Periodical Accounts* circulated throughout England, giving news of Carey's and Thomas's progress. The reports in due course were sent to India from England by readers who had relatives and friends working in Bengal. It speaks well of Carey's character also, that those same judges with whom he lunched at Dinadjpur did not, even though knowing of his missionary enterprise, feel constrained to take measures against his activity. In fact, he was able to make at least one convert among their number – Mr. Cunningham, the Registrar of Dinadjpur. Another convert was a Mr. Fernandez, a Portuguese, who was to prove a loyal servant of the Mission. He built, at his own expense, a small church in Dinadjpur to be used for the preaching of the gospel either to natives or to Europeans. Later, he opened a school in Dinadjpur along the same lines as Carey's at Mudnabatti. By 1799 Carey could speak of 'congregations' of Europeans both in Malda and Dinadjpur.

In such small ways Carey made progress. And progress, too, with his agricultural interests. His seeds and implements had arrived in 'tolerable preservation'[21] and he was in communication with Dr. Roxburgh of the Botanic Gardens in Calcutta. Through their exchange of knowledge, he hoped to make the 'investment of vegetables more valuable'.[22] He was later to lecture to the Asiatic Society on the state of agriculture in Dinadjpur. He also collected and collated information on birds, beasts, fishes and reptiles; and he studied the mythology of India.

If this sounds as if life in Mudnabatti was a placid, dilettante existence, such was far from being the case.

It seemed as if, just as he had built up for himself a position of respect in his small area of British India, so the indiscretions of John Fountain would undermine it. Fountain seemed determined to challenge authority. Fuller wrote sternly to Carey:

> . . . If Mr. Fountain be so infatuated with political folly, as not to be able to write a letter to England without sneering sarcasms upon Govts., cursing their monopolies, expressing his hope of revolution work going on &c &c I must say once for all, it is my judgment that the Society, much as they esteem him in other respects, *will be under the necessity of publickly disowning him. . .*[23]

Fuller was right to express concern. It was known that letters were opened and read several times during their long journeys to and from India. England stood alone against a hostile Europe dominated by the forces of Napoleon Bonaparte. Any hint of sympathy with France could arouse almost hysterical reaction in England. Fuller was well aware that Carey had had radical sympathies when he was at Leicester. Indeed, as mentioned earlier, he had even been so impetuous as to refuse to drink the King's health during his brief stay aboard the *Oxford* in the spring of 1793.[24] It would be tragic if his earlier radical views should damage his present work.

> . . . His (Fountain's) Journal is so full of such folly, *wrote Fuller, returning to the subject in a later letter to Carey*, as, if it had been stopped and opened as some things are, must have utterly overset the Mission. He mentions *you* too in his Journal as talking with him in the same way. . .[25]

Although there is no concrete evidence that Carey and Fountain held anti-Establishment discussions, it is not unlikely that such conversations took place. Carey had only been six years away from England, and the contrasts he saw all around him between wealth and privilege on the one hand and appalling poverty on the other, particularly among the Indians themselves, would no doubt reinforce his views.

Perhaps the warning in Fuller's letter was timely. Carey's letters from India in these early years occasionally display flashes of impatience which Fuller soothes with gentle chiding. There is no doubt that experience taught Carey a discretion which was to ripen through his years in India into the tact and wisdom of an elder statesman.

A further disappointment was that Carey lost the support of Thomas. Towards the end of 1797 he seems to have abandoned both the indigo business and, for a while, the Mission. He first of all resumed his medical practice and then went into the 'sugar trade' (a euphemism for the distillation of rum). He was ever seeking new ways of keeping ahead of his creditors.

What with Fountain's radicalism and Thomas's debts, it is a wonder that the infant Mission in India survived. Only Carey's dogged faith kept it going. He was lonely; he was disappointed; but he never dreamed of giving up.

'Mr. Thomas is gone far away,' he wrote to Fuller on 9th January, 1798, 'and my domestic troubles are sometimes almost too heavy for me. I am distressed, yet supported, and I trust not totally dead in the things of God.'

8

Growing Confidence

1798–1799

By the beginning of 1798, Carey had to abandon his *Journal* for want of time. 'The translating the scripture, and correcting former translations, constantly occupies all my candle-light, and often all my afternoons.'[1]

The translation of the Bible was almost complete and was as accurate as Carey could at that time make it. How much he took Andrew Fuller's gentle admonitions to heart is unknown. Fuller had written to him:

> . . . You desire us to keep to your spelling in what we print. We will endeavour to do so but you do not always spell alike. Sometimes you write Moonshee, & sometimes Munshi, and sometimes Moonshi. If the trumpet give uncertain sound, who can prepare for the battle? – You must allow me again to remind you of your punctuation. I never knew a person of so much knowledge as you profess of other languages, write English so bad. You huddle half a dozen periods into one. Where your sentence ends you very commonly make only a semicolon instead of a period. If your Bengal N.T. sh[d] be thus pointed I sh[d] tremble for its fate. . .[2]

Probably the criticism did not worry Carey over-much. There is an air of confidence about him in his mid-thirties. The conscientious but unsuccessful shoemaker, the penniless pastor, the frustrated idealist of Northamptonshire are replaced by a dedicated man of maturity and poise. Perhaps the very fact that Thomas had left him to his own resources made him more self-reliant. His summary to the Missionary Society of his progress to date, written on 10th January, 1799 is clear, business-like and confident. He reviews his ministry among both natives and Europeans; he describes the progress of his school, now increased to forty scholars; he gives practical advice regarding transport and equipment for intending missionaries and endeavours to make clear the difference in status between a licence-holder and a non-licence-holder in the East India Company's territories:

> We (i.e. licence-holders) have no need to conceal our real work at any other time, or on any other occasion; and were I to be in company with Lord Mornington, I should not hesitate to tell him that I am a missionary. . .

It was indeed the case that, *un*officially, missionary work was tolerated. When missionaries came to the Governor-General's notice *officially*, however, his attitude was of necessity very different. Perhaps Andrew Fuller gained from this letter a mistaken impression of the relationship between Carey and the new, magnificent Governor-General for a few months later Carey writes with one of his rare touches of humour:

> The visit which you propose for us to make to the governor-general, Lord Mornington, though proposed in the utmost simplicity of your heart, yet excited a little risibility in us. I wish I could make you understand a little about legal settlements, &c; but you must first drop your English ideas, and get Indian ones.[3]

Richard Colley Wellesley, Earl of Mornington, later Marquis Wellesley, became Governor-General of Bengal in 1798 at the early age of thirty-seven. He was undoubtedly outstanding among British rulers in India, not only in his bold grasp of political facts but also in the magnificent style of his administration. 'A very few days after Sir John Shore left Calcutta,' wrote William Hickey, 'Lord Mornington arrived there in the *Virginie* frigate, at once bursting forth like a constellation in all his pomp and splendour among us. . .'[4]

During his seven-year rule in India, recognising that any balance of power between native states was impossible, Wellesley firmly established British rule over practically the whole of India. With the help of his brilliant younger brother Arthur Wellesley (later to be created Duke of Wellington) he waged relentless war against the forces of anarchy and misrule. He crushed the power of Mysore, struck boldly at the Mahrattas and succeeded to some extent in ameliorating the miseries heaped on India's hapless millions by their incompetent native governments. In addition, he prosecuted vigorously a campaign against French influence in the courts and camps of native rulers – what he called 'the French state erected by M. Perron on the banks of the Jumna'. He was to improve the layout of Calcutta, build new roads and a splendid new Government House. He would take a keen interest in the education of young British Indian Civil Servants. But all that was in the future. For the moment, he is the new, awe-inspiring Governor-General into whose orbit Carey could hardly have expected ever to find himself drawn – although that time was to come with surprising swiftness.

One further incident during the Mudnabatti years must be recorded as it made a searing impression on Carey and was to have far-reaching consequences. On a visit to Calcutta, early in 1799, to get types cast for printing the Bible, Carey witnessed *sati*, the Hindu practice of widow-burning, which he described at length in a letter to Andrew Fuller. His account is so vivid that it is worth quoting in full:

> As I was returning from Calcutta I saw the Sahamaranam, or, a woman burning herself with the corpse of her husband, for the first time in my life. We were near the village of Noya Serai, or, as Rennell calls it in his chart of the Hoogli river, Niaverai. Being evening, we got out of the boat to walk, when we saw a number of people assembled on the river-side. I asked them what they were met for, and they told me to burn the body of a dead man. I inquired if his wife would die with him; they answered Yes, and pointed to the woman. She was standing by the pile, which was made of large billets of wood, about two and a half feet high, four feet long, and two wide, on the top of which lay the dead body of her husband. Her nearest relation stood by her, and near her was a small basket of sweetmeats called Thioy. I asked them if this was the woman's choice, or if she were brought to it by any improper influence? They answered that it was perfectly voluntary. I talked till reasoning was of no use, and then began to exclaim with all my might against what they were doing, telling them that it was a shocking murder. They told me it was a great act of holiness, and added in a very surly manner, that if I did not like to see it I might go further off, and desired me to go. I told them that I would not go, that I was determined to stay and see the murder, and that I should certainly bear witness of it at the tribunal of God.
>
> I exhorted the woman not to throw away her life; to fear nothing, for no evil would follow her refusal to burn. But she in

the most calm manner mounted the pile, and danced on it with her hands extended, as if in the utmost tranquillity of spirit. Previous to her mounting the pile the relation, whose office it was to set fire to the pile, led her six times round it, at two intervals – that is, thrice at each circumambulation. As she went round she scattered the sweetmeat above mentioned among the people, who picked it up and ate it as a very holy thing. This being ended, and she having mounted the pile and danced as above mentioned (N.B. – The dancing only appeared to be to show *us* her contempt of death, and prove to us that her dying was voluntary), she lay down by the corpse, and put one arm under its neck and the other over it, when a quantity of dry cocoa-leaves and other substances were heaped over them to a considerable height, and then Ghee, or melted preserved butter, poured on the top. Two bamboos were then put over them and held fast down, and fire put to the pile, which immediately blazed very fiercely, owing to the dry and combustible materials of which it was composed.

No sooner was the fire kindled than all the people set up a great shout – Hurree-Bol, Hurree-Bol, which is a common shout of joy, and an invocation of Hurree, or Seeb. It was impossible to have heard the woman had she groaned, or even cried aloud, on account of the mad noise of the people, and it was impossible for her to stir or struggle on account of the bamboos which were held down on her like the levers of a press. We made much objection to their using these bamboos, and insisted that it was using force to prevent the woman from getting up when the fire burned her. But they declared that it was only done to keep the pile from falling down.

We could not bear to see more, but left them, exclaiming loudly against the murder, and full of horror at what we had seen.[5]

Thereafter, Carey never ceased to campaign against this barbarous and inhuman practice.

The apprentice years were coming to a close. Just as his translation work was completed, circumstances arose necessitating his removal from Mudnabatti. The prosperity of the factory had always been uncertain due to the liability of the district to floods. A severe inundation during 1799 brought Mr. Udney such heavy financial loss that he decided to close the factory down, terminating Carey's contract with him from 31st December, 1799. Fortunately, Carey had some time earlier prudently invested some of his own savings in part payment for a small indigo factory at Kidderpore twelve miles distant. It was on slightly higher ground than Mudnabatti and less liable to flooding. Cary had the idea in mind that it could be worked in the future by his sons (Felix was already almost fourteen) or, if more missionaries arrived from England, that it could provide them with a base. Now it could become a refuge for Carey and his own family. At the same time he received the long-awaited promise that additional colleagues were on their way to join him, among them the printer, William Ward, whom he had met in 1793. Immediately, he set about erecting houses and buildings to accommodate them and the printing press he hoped Ward would operate.

It was amazing that after nearly seven years in India he was able to organise so well, to show such apparently unflagging energy. The average expectation of life of a young East India Company writer at this time has been compared with that of the subaltern in France during World War I – six months at the outside. Indeed, poor William Grant, one of the new missionaries, was to be dead within three weeks of his arrival in Bengal. Amoebic dysentery and infective hepatitis, malaria, cholera – these were all endemic diseases of India. Moreover, the life-style, feeding habits and clothing of the average English settler were most unsuitable for the climate. Many continued to wear the elaborate wigs and heavy clothing that were fashionable in Europe. It is known that Carey ceased to wear a wig on reaching India and, although the only portrait of the period – that by Robert Home painted in 1812 – shows him wearing European dress, it is apparent from a letter that the missionaries did at some time wear a version of eastern dress.[6] Carey, surprisingly, was able to tolerate the climate – despite that as a boy heat had brought on attacks of itching – though he admits to finding the rainy season trying. He adapted his routine to suit the conditions, rising early and resting during the heat of the day. Perhaps, also, he was better fed in India than when he was struggling against penury to support his family in England. This would give him greater resistance to disease. However, his natural frugality and care to use every spare rupee for the building up of his missionary work would save him from self-indulgence. It is clear from his letters that he suffered from recurring bouts of malaria, the bane of so many settlers in tropical climates. He also complains of a certain *malaise* which may well have had a medical cause that could today be cured:

> . . . I have something of a lethargic disease cleaving to my body. I feel no pain, or decay of strength, but an abundant inclination to sleep, attended with a great sense of weariness, even when I have not walked a mile. I know that this country requires more sleep than a colder one: and a sleep in the afternoon especially in the hot season, relieves me more than anything. . .[7]

So the century drew to a close. Carey had worked his seven years' apprenticeship as Jacob did before him. If he achieved no conversions among the natives up to this time, he had at least made the name of Christ known throughout Bengal. His purpose in India had become known also to the European community and, such was the respect in which he was already held, that no-one sought to prevent him from furthering it. Indeed, that same Judge Parr with whom he lunched at Dinadjpur helped him to raise money for his school. His witness to the European community had had its effect:

> If you knew how many Europeans had heard the gospel from our lips, who never would have heard it had we not come, *Fountain wrote to Andrew Fuller*, you would be far from thinking the society's money thrown away. Military officers, judges, collectors, &c., have repeatedly joined us in worship, both at Malda and Dinagepore.[8]

It was time for Carey to move on, for northern Bengal had not any sufficiently large or important population centres for Christianity to spread rapidly.

On 27th October, 1799 he writes from Kidderpore that John Fountain had gone down to Calcutta to meet the new missionaries from England and to bring them to Kidderpore. However, God had other plans.

9

Serampore

October 1799–October 1800

Carey was only expecting two new missionaries to join him but, in the event, a large party arrived: William Ward, printer and former editor of the *Hull Advertiser* whom Carey had met in 1793; Mr. and Mrs. William Grant and their two children; Mr. and Mrs. Daniel Brunsden; a Miss M. Tidd who had come out to India to marry John Fountain; and Joshua Marshman, a part-time minister and master of a charity school in Bristol, who brought his wife, Hannah, and their three children.

Despite Carey's advice in letters home that intending missionaries should be sure to obtain work permits, none of the party had been able to obtain permission to reside in British India. However, they travelled in an American vessel, the *Criterion*. It is an interesting fact that 25th May, 1799, the day on which this new missionary party left England was the same day on which Napoleon, in evacuating Jaffa, abandoned his dream of marching on to conquer India. Before leaving England, the party had obtained a letter of introduction to Colonel Bie, Governor of the small Danish settlement of Serampore, fourteen miles north of Calcutta on the western bank of the River Hooghli. The party proceeded there direct, arriving on 13th October, 1799, intending to journey on from there to Kidderpore to join Carey. However, to their dismay, the British authorities refused the captain of their American ship permission to trade unless he handed over the new arrivals to the police in Calcutta or undertook to return them to Europe.

This apparently high-handed behaviour was due to a printing error in the *Calcutta Gazette* which had reported the arrival of '*papist* missionaries' at Serampore in mistake for '*baptist*'. The news caused alarm in Government circles. Were the newcomers really French spies, taking advantage of Serampore as foreign territory to infiltrate into the Indian sub-continent? There were constant reminders that Britain was in the throes of the Revolutionary War. French ships in the Indian ocean were an ever-present threat to the Company's shipping. Indeed, the *Criterion*, on her return voyage, was engaged by a French privateer and lost her first officer and one sailor.[1] Moreover, Britain was at war also with Holland whose fleet, based in the East Indies, would ever be ready to avenge the loss of Ceylon to the British four years earlier. Of course, upon investigation, it soon became apparent that the new arrivals in Serampore were not French spies at all but English missionaries – but the harm had been done. Their presence had been brought officially to the notice of the Governor-General who could not ignore their calling or their lack of a licence to work in British India. Accordingly, they were refused permission to proceed to Kidderpore, despite appeals by Carey to Dr. Roxburgh and to Rev. Brown in Calcutta to use their influence with the authorities. The party from England could thus have been considerably embarrassed had not Colonel Bie offered them a permanent home in the Danish settlement of Serampore. Indeed, this Christian man asked them to set up a mission there.

It was not a decision that could be taken lightly, particularly as Carey had invested all his money on behalf of the Mission in the property at Kidderpore. Once again, Colonel Bie provided the means of solving the problem. He issued a Danish passport to William Ward, allowing him to travel to North Bengal with John Fountain to discuss what action to take. In any event, the new arrivals would wish to rest after their long journey. Tragedy had struck the party with the death of William Grant less than three weeks after their arrival.

'At length I saw Carey!' wrote William Ward of his first meeting in India with the missionary who had prompted his own call to service. 'He is less altered than I expected: has rather more flesh than when in England, and, blessed be God! he is *a young man still*.'[2] Carey was now thirty-eight.

There was much to be said in favour of setting up a Mission in Serampore. On Danish territory, the missionaries would be free of any restrictions on their teaching and printing. Moreover, they would be in a more densely populated area than Kidderpore and would therefore have a large audience. Against this had to be set the financial loss to Carey of abandoning his investment at Kidderpore and the cost of moving his family and effects to the new station. The cost of living in Serampore would be considerably higher than he was enjoying up-country and the style of living would need to be more formal. All the work he had undertaken in North Bengal – now beginning to show promise with conversions among the Europeans and a growing school – would have to be abandoned. Moreover, Carey considered Serampore 'the city of refuge for all who are in debt and afraid of their creditors, on which account a degree of disgrace is attached to an inhabitant thereof. And, indeed, the natives appear to me to be some of the vilest of the vile.'[3] However, if it was God's will that he should go to Serampore, he would not let material considerations or personal prejudice hold him back.

It would be wrong to say that he was not anxious. A letter dated 21st December, 1799 to Andrew Fuller sets out the frightening financial commitments to be faced in starting up the new Mission. But he is ever practical and clear-headed. He weighs up the respective costs of renting and building, provides estimates of running expenses and anticipated income from the proposed schools and printing-press, suggests shrewdly that the Society would be well-advised to invest its capital in India where interest rates were considerably higher than in England. This man who talks in thousands of pounds is a far cry from the humble shoe-maker struggling to make both ends meet on £30 a year. He has already purchased a printing press, type and paper, and proposes going ahead with the printing of one thousand copies of the whole Bible in Bengali.

He arrived in Serampore with his family on 10th January, 1800. Whatever doubts Carey had about the town's reputation, all accounts agree that it was healthful, clean and beautiful, notable for its fine trees. The 'bank is adorned with a thick robe of drooping bamboos, overtopped by stately palms and feathery cocoa-nuts'.[4]

Carey was anxious to put the Serampore Mission on a permanent footing. He was aware that the home supporters of his missionary work could well be growing restless at his lack of tangible results. Suppose the public withdrew its support? What would happen when those enthusiastic 'ropeholders', Fuller, Ryland and Sutcliff, were no more? Would the supply of money from England dry up completely? Hence his anxiety that the Society send out sufficient money to establish the Serampore Mission on a secure foundation at the earliest possible date. There is little indication from his letters that the money ever arrived.

It was agreed that all the members of the Mission – now totalling nineteen (ten adults and nine children) – should have all things in common as in the days of the early church. They invested all their available capital in putting down a deposit on a large property in two acres of ground 'the hall of which is large enough for a commodious chapel'.[5] There were enough outbuildings to convert to their residential and business needs. The printing press was set up and plans made for the founding of a school. 'We love our work, and will do all we can to lighten your expenses.'[6]

It was a relief at last for Carey to be able to devote himself wholly to missionary work, secure in the knowledge that he was under the protection of a friendly power. He was encouraged by the additions to his team:

> Brother Ward is the very man we wanted: *he writes to Fuller*, he enters into the work with his whole soul. I have much pleasure in him, and expect much from him. Brother Marshman is a prodigy of diligence and prudence, as is also his wife in the latter: learning the language is mere play to him; he has already acquired as much as I did in double the time. I believe all their hearts are entirely set on their work . . . and, indeed, after all the very distressing disappointments which we have met with, I entertain a hope that the day is not far distant, when light will most powerfully break forth and spread over this very dark part of the earth.[7]

It was as well that Carey's enthusiasm did not flag for there were many difficulties in the early days. They lived as a close community and, from the very beginning, entered into a voluntary agreement whereby all were equal. The wishes of the majority established the rule of the mission and all abided by that rule. Work for private benefit was forbidden. All put into the common stock whatever they earned and withdrew only sufficient for their family needs; any surplus – and over the years the surplus was considerable – went towards the expansion of the work of the Mission.

Living and working so closely together (they shared a

ommon table) could have produced strain among men and women less dedicated to the cause of Christ. 'One man of the wrong temper could make our house a hell,' wrote William Ward. Every Saturday evening, they met together for prayer and to discuss family concerns. At these meetings they would deal with any differences of opinion that had arisen during the week ('pledging themselves to love one another'[8]) and would allocate duties for the next seven days. To a certain extent, these duties settled themselves. Carey's printing-press had been set up at Serampore at the first opportunity so that the preparation of copy was of first importance. This was done by Carey and Fountain who alone, so far, were familiar with any of the languages of India. They also corrected proofs. In addition, Carey continued his translation work and planted and tended a garden. William Ward was in charge of printing, assisted by Daniel Brunsden and Felix Carey. The boy hero-worshipped Ward, who was thirty, and indeed looked on him as a second father. Ward, in his turn, was responsible for bringing Felix to a love of Christ. Joshua and Hannah Marshman were the first bread-winners for the Mission.

Money was desperately short in the early days. It took a long, long time to receive remittances from England, if indeed any were forthcoming. 'Could you not return answers to our letters by the fleet which generally leaves England soon after the arrival of that from India? Then, instead of waiting for answers a year and a half or two years, we should get them in less than one.'[9] No doubt it was an effort to raise funds for the missionary cause in England. The continuing war was causing much hardship. Many goods were in short supply and prices had risen alarmingly. Fuller writes of 'the dreadful scarcity of bread, & all the necessaries of life. . . Flour is 5/– stone! . . . Our cities and market towns abound with riots. Last year we had but little more than half a harvest, and this about 2/3rds or perhaps ¾ths; and a great part of that much injured by the wet. No hopes as I see of returning peace. The hand of the Lord seems heavy upon us . . .'.[10] One method Carey used to circumvent the shortage of money was to give bills on London in exchange for cash in India from English people who were returning to England and wanted somehow to get their money out of the country. Currency regulations were evidently restrictive even in 1800.

Relief came when the Marshmans opened their first boarding-schools for European and Anglo-Indian boys and girls. In March, 1800, the following advertisement was published:

> MISSION HOUSE, SERAMPORE – On Thursday, the 1st of May, 1800, a school will be opened at this house, which stands in a very healthy and pleasant situation by the side of the river. Letters addressed to Mr. Carey will be immediately attended to.

The cost of boarding and fees varied from £45 to £50 a year, according to whether 'Latin, Greek, Hebrew, Persian or Sanskrit lessons' were included. 'Particular attention will be paid to the correct pronunciation of the English language' the advertisement continued. They were soon besieged with pupils (for the old Portuguese schoolmaster in Serampore had recently died) and the profit from the school (amounting to £1,000 annually) became the mainstay of the Mission. Later in the year, Mrs. Marshman opened a 'school for young ladies'.

A 'shopping list' sent to the Society at this time[11] includes:

1 Electrical Machine
2 Barometers
2 Thermometers
1 Air-Pump
12 Missionary Magazines
12 Baptismal Registers
6 Gibbons Rhetoric
50 Hornsey's Grammar
24 New Testaments (well bound)
Two large barrels of good printing ink made for a hot climate
500 Quills

Medicines asked for include:

Nitre
Quassia
Rheubarb (*sic*)
Glauber Salts
Epsom ditto
Sal Volatile
'Any preparation of Hemlock & Henbane which will keep in a hot climate.'

Later, presumably as the pupils in the schools progressed, there are requests for:

6 Bonnycastle's Geometry
12 Turner's Geography
12 Dissected Maps of the World
12 Eton Latin Grammar
12 Bell's Greek Grammar
24 Cowper's Poems
12 Cicero's Orations – Latin
24 Milton's Paradise Lost
A small ship's bell and
'A clock like what are usually put up in meeting houses'[12]

It must not, however, be thought that the schools were used purely as a means of profit. A month after the fee-paying schools had been opened, a free school for Bengali boys was established and within six weeks had over forty children. There was much prejudice to overcome concerning the schools. William Ward describes how fearful were some of the children that they would be kidnapped and shipped to England.[13]

In addition to all this, the men undertook regular preaching engagements and also went out among the native population taking every opportunity to put across their message of the saving love of Christ.

The optimistic reports to the Society at home minimise the difficulties they must often have encountered. Hannah Marshman in later life told her daughter-in-law how Dr. Marshman had many times returned home covered with blood from the stones and bricks thrown at him by those who were hostile to his preaching.[14] Ward relates how a brahmin came several times to the school, cursing the name of Jesus and upsetting the children. Carey writes '. . . we were assaulted with all the insulting language that malice could invent.'[15]

Quite apart from the difficulties inherent in the work of a missionary, there were the problems peculiar to India. Hannah Marshman's letters to her friends in Bristol contain such references as:

> We found a poisonous serpent of the worst sort in John's bedroom. Soon after another in our bathing house; and since then another and another. . .

> As I was returning across to our own house, I trod on a serpent, which twisted round my leg, and gave my heel a hard smack. I shook it off, and felt no harm.[16]

William Ward wrote in his diary: 'Preaching in black cloth in this climate is a sad burden. The very papers in my pocket are dyed black.'

Illness continued to take its toll. John Fountain, who had gone up to Dinadjpur in July, died there in that first August of the new century, leaving his wife of less than a year pregnant. Dorothy Carey was so deranged that she was quite incapable of sharing in any of the domestic responsibilities.

How grateful Carey must have been for the capable and warm-hearted Hannah Marshman. She had already taken over the responsibility of Grant's orphaned children before Carey arrived at Serampore. Now she took William's lively but undisciplined sons under her wing. Though she respected Carey as a Christian and a scholar, she had no illusions as to his failings as a parent. A frank letter from her to John Ryland shows Carey as ineffective at controlling his sons as he was his class of village lads at Moulton:

> This evening a most painful task fell to me: to speak a word of reproof to Felix. . . It is necessary first to say, that owing to Brother Carey's domestic affliction, his perpetual avocations, or perhaps an easiness of the temperament not wholly free from blame, his two eldest sons were left in great measure without control; hence obstinacy and self-will took a very deep root in their minds, while he, like David, never displeased them. I have heard that it was nothing uncommon for them at table to seize a favourite dish and appropriate it to themselves, without ceremony. If the father mildly remonstrated they would throw it from them in anger and refuse to taste a morsel. The good man saw and lamented the evil but was too mild to apply an effectual remedy. . .
>
> Felix had for some months past addicted himself to so luxurious a way of eating and drinking, that at last it quite alarmed us both on his own account and for the sake of the family. In vain did his father remonstrate, in vain did Brother Ward, who loves him with peculiar affection, endeavour to restrain him by the most tender reproaches, nothing was produced except a kind of secret and obstinate determination to persist. I could not see this without almost trembling for the consequences of

> such obstinacy in a lad not yet 17. I thought that to refrain longer would be criminal. . .[17]

She did *not* refrain and, after speaking frankly to the boy about his behaviour (no 'tender reproaches' from her) she reports that he 'seemed exceedingly affected'.

The younger boys, of course, could now attend school regularly and there is no further report of any head-on clash with authority. William Carey, Junior, aged thirteen in 1800, took part of each day off from schoolwork learning to bind the books that were printed.

In addition to teaching in the school, Hannah Marshman organised the domestic side of the Mission, coping with the problems of caste among the servants as competently as she managed the catering for the now considerable number of missionaries, staff and scholars. An extract from one of her long, gossipy letters home gives some idea of the scope of the task and also of the life-style of the missionaries themselves:

> . . . No European ever dines without a dish of curry and rice. In every dinner we expend four very large dishes of boiled rice piled up on a heap; four dishes of curry, three or four joints of meat, sometimes eight or nine large fish, seven or eight dishes of vegetables from our own garden, three tureens of soup with bread. . . Our victuals are always boiled in earthen pots, except when we have rump of beef. It is all in the English way, except the curry. We have often puddings and pies made by our own cook. . . We have very good butter made twice a day; it will not keep good any longer. We have one plate of toast, six large plates of bread and butter, besides two very large dishes of the same.[18]

This is a far cry from 'living a great while together without tasting animal food' as Carey had done at Moulton. Hannah Marshman continues:

> Our dinner is all brought from the cook-room to the hall in a very large wooden chest or box with four handles, and is carried by two men in the same manner as a Bath chair. This is the universal custom of the country, and is very necessary, not so much for the sake of keeping the food warm, as for preserving it from kites and crows, which would be utterly impossible, if it were not covered, they are so numerous. As one of our servants was going to the cook-room one day, with a plate in his hand

and a large silver spoon upon it, a kite flew down and seized the spoon, carrying it off in his mouth, and we saw it no more.

There is no beer in this country, except a little that is sometimes sold out of ships and which is very dear. The common drink is water. Rum is cheap because it is made in the country. The common drink with Europeans is madeira wine.

We use no tea-pots. We make tea in two large urns. . . This is a very quick way of despatching business: though we are nearly sixty in number, yet we scarcely ever sit more than twenty minutes at breakfast or tea. . .

There is a great deal of trouble with the servants, on account of their different caste: one will not touch this thing, nor another that. A man called a Bearer, who is kept to carry the "chatta" (umbrella) over the children, rub furniture, clean shoes, and many other things, would not take a dirty plate, glass, or tea-cup, or a candle-stick off the table on any account.

Pork is an abomination to Mussulmen, they will not touch it. We keep our own pigs, and often have pork, but any one of them would sooner lose his place than he would cut a bit on a child's plate, who is too small to cut it for himself. Their attachment to their caste is so strong, that if you were to compel them to do anything contrary thereto, they would say, – "Salaam, Sahib," – or "Salaam, Babu Sahib," – i.e. your servant, sir, or your servant, Madam, and leave you immediately. . .

We hire our tailors by the month: I keep two constantly for the use of the school. They do all sorts of work, and make frocks as well as any woman. I keep one about six months in the year on my own account. He makes a muslin gown just as well as he does a coat. Our clothes are nearly all washed by men; we give a rupee and a half per hundred! We write down every article as it goes out, and read the list again when it is brought home. They keep them eight days; and as we are obliged to change every day, and our children twice, you may guess how many clothes we need.

Scarcely any of the servants in this country except females sleep in their masters' houses: they go home in the day to eat, and at night to sleep. The women are in general very dirty, and almost as unmoved as Stoics. Boiling their rice, and bathing their children is nearly all they do. . . There are some few among them who will spin a little thread, or beat a little buck-dust, but these last are very few. Our native sisters are become very decent, and keep their houses in very good order. Since we have talked to them, they spin a little thread for the dirzees or tailors.

So the pattern of the work at Serampore settled into a routine punctuated by such highlights as the pulling off the press on 17th March, 1800 of the first page of the New Testament in Bengali. On 24th April, there was a service of thanksgiving for the completion of the building works at the mission. On 20th October, Felix preached his first message at the evening service and was soon thereafter joining Ward and Brunsden in preaching to the natives. 'From being a tiger, he was transformed into a lamb under Ward's influence,'[19] wrote John Clark Marshman of Carey's eldest son.

In October also, John Thomas arrived at Serampore, having presumably abandoned his sugar-refining. Although unreliable in so many ways, his sincere desire for the propagation of the gospel among the natives of India can never be questioned. His own ventures into missionary work were, at best, sporadic but always seemed to have far-reaching results. This had been the case when he visited England in 1792/93 and fired the newly-formed Baptist Missionary Society to commence their operations in India. Similarly in January, 1794 he had renewed his friendship with the Udneys, so opening the way for Carey to spend seven years in North Bengal as an indigo manufacturer. Now, in 1800, he was to make his final and perhaps his most dramatic and direct contribution towards the 'conversion of the heathen'. Fittingly, it came not through his silver tongue or his gift for friendship but through his God-given talent of healing.

> . . . Into whatsoever city ye enter, and they receive you . . . heal the sick that are therein, and say unto them, The kingdom of God is come nigh unto you.[20]

10

A Wonderful Year

1800–1801

Early on the morning of 26th November, 1800, a Bengali carpenter named Krishna Pal went down with his children to the Ganges to bathe. He slipped on the ghat (the steps down to the river) and fell, dislocating his right shoulder. Perhaps the news had spread that an English doctor was staying at the Mission; for whatever reason, Krishna Pal sent his children there for help.

Thomas left his breakfast half-eaten and hurried to the aid of the injured man. He soon had the bones in place and made his patient as comfortable as possible. Then they talked, Thomas taking the opportunity to tell how Christ could heal not just a man's shoulder but his soul as well. Far from his words going unheeded, on this occasion they spoke to a genuine need. Krishna Pal had for some years been burdened by a sense of sin which had driven him to seek relief by joining the Kharta-bhojas, a breakaway sect from Hinduism.

The following day, Carey visited him to enquire after his injury and suggested that he came to the Mission for medicine to soothe the pain in his shoulder. This Krishna Pal did, taking with him his friend, Gokul. The pain in the shoulder eased but still he and Gokul continued to visit the Mission regularly. They would have discussions with William Ward and with Felix. The two Englishmen read and explained to the two Indians passages from the Bible which they felt would speak to their need.

It could not have been easy at any time to explain to simple and superstitious people that the God of the Christians could die, yet still live. Gokul, in particular, was at first very confused over John 3, v. 16: 'For God so loved the world, that he gave his only begotten Son, that whosoever believeth in him *should not perish, but have everlasting life*.' He took the verse at its literal meaning and urged his neighbours to embrace Christ so that they could become immortal! It required much patient explanation by the missionaries before he understood the strange and wonderful implications of Jesus' words.

Gradually the two Indians grew in conviction until, on 22nd December, they affirmed their belief that Jesus died to save sinners. Thomas welcomed them into the faith. 'I call you brother,' he said to each in turn. 'Come, let us eat together in love.' This was indeed a momentous occasion – the two Indians breaking caste to sit down at the luncheon table with the missionaries, their wives and children.

The Mission servants soon spread the news that Krishna Pal and Gokul had 'become Europeans' – an action that was regarded with horror by their fellow countrymen. Their rage took a vicious form and the two men were attacked on their way home. The following day brought further intimidation. It so happened that some years before, as was the Hindu custom, Krishna Pal had married his daughter to a young man in Calcutta, although as yet the couple had not met. It was a child marriage. The time for handing her over to her husband had arrived but, as the daughter was considering becoming a Christian (as were also her mother and three sisters) Krishna Pal hesitated to insist on her going. The girl herself expressed revulsion at the idea of living with heathens. All this gave the mob the excuse for further violence. They dragged Krishna Pal and his luckless wife and daughter before a judge who had them imprisoned for breaching the contract of marriage.

Marshman and Carey hurried to the Governor to intercede for the family, explaining how Krishna Pal and his family had asked for baptism and how, in the circumstances, the Hindu marriage seemed unendurable. Governor Bie was more than sympathetic – he not only ordered their release, he upheld the daughter's right to remain with her father for the time being. Further, he provided a sepoy guard on their house lest the mob should attempt to kill them. (Eventually the girl had to go to her husband, it being held that conversion to Christianity could not dissolve a marriage legally entered into. Carey was able to console the girl with the thought that her going to a heathen family afforded her the opportunity of witnessing for Christ and perhaps of gaining converts from among her husband's family – but that was some months later.)

On 28th December, with great courage, Krishna Pal submitted to the ordinance of baptism. At the last moment, not surprisingly in view of the violence with which they had been threatened, the courage of his womenfolk failed; also of Gokul whose wife and mother had left his home because he professed a belief in Christ. But one was enough.

> What man of you, having an hundred sheep, if he lose one of them, doth not leave the ninety and nine in the wilderness and go after that which is lost, until he find it?
>
> And when he hath found it, he layeth it on his shoulders, rejoicing.
>
> And when he cometh home, he calleth together his friends and neighbours, saying unto them, Rejoice with me; for I have found my sheep which was lost.[1]

Ward wrote rapturously in his diary: 'The chain of the caste is broken; who shall mend it?' It was a day of great joy for Carey. Not only did he baptise his first native Indian – after seven long years of hope deferred – but also his son Felix. 'Yesterday,' he wrote in a compendious letter to John Sutcliff that covered events from 27th November to 29th December, 1800, 'I had the happiness to desecrate the Gunga (Ganges) by baptising the first Hindoo, viz. Krishna, and my son Felix. . .'

The river Ganges ran past the front gate of the Mission. There was a big crowd of both Europeans and natives to watch the ceremony. Ward preached in English and Carey in Bengali and a hymn was sung in Bengali also. It was ever Carey's practice (as he had set out so many years before in his *Enquiry*) to endeavour so to master the language of his flock 'as to be able to convey any sentiments we wish to their understandings.'

Sadly, Thomas was not able to be present, even though he had been the means of bringing Krishna Pal to Christ. It was sad that he was unable to savour the joy of achieving a conversion after so many years of disappointment. Apparently, however, he also had been subject to intermittent bouts of mental breakdown during the past year or so. He became raving and violent on the day of the baptism and had to be confined for his own safety in the schoolhouse. His companions declared that the excitement had proved too much for his over-wrought temperament. The following day he was committed to the lunatic asylum in Calcutta. Although later released, he never fully recovered his reason.

Among the European witnesses of the baptisms were Governor Bie and the Lady Charlotte Rumohr. Colonel Bie was moved to tears by the significance of the occasion. Lady Rumohr clasped Krishna Pal's hand and held it for some moments, as if trying to express through touch the welcome into the Christian faith that she could not express in Bengali.

The first mention of Charlotte Emilia Rumohr by Carey appears on 28th November in the long letter to John Sutcliff above-quoted. He had been introduced to her by the Governor with a view to his giving her lessons in English. She is described sometimes as 'German' and at other times as 'Danish'. This was due to what the late Professor Keith Feiling called 'the weary tangled matter of Schleswig-Holstein, the two duchies part-Dane and part-German, bound to Denmark by the same royal dynasty, to each other by ancient history and, in the case of Holstein, to the German federation by law'.[2]

She was the wealthy invalid daughter of the Chevalier de Rumohr and his wife, the Countess of Alfeldt. One of her sisters was married to the King of Denmark's Chamberlain. Charlotte had never been strong, even as a child, but became disabled at the age of fifteen. This was the result of a disastrous fire at the family home. Her warning on that occasion roused the castle but she herself was badly injured in the flames, losing both her voice and the use of her legs. Since that time, she had travelled widely all over Europe in search of a cure but without success. A friend of her father, a Director of the Danish East India Company, suggested that the warmth of India might help her condition. He gave her letters of introduction to his brother who was Governor of the Danish settlement at Tranquebar on the south-eastern coast of India. However, the ship had brought her first to Serampore a few months before her meeting with Carey and there she had remained. After their first meeting, he reports that 'her speech is restored, and she can walk a little'.[3]

To a man whose only experience of women to date had been his mentally disturbed and unlettered wife, or the virtuous and thrifty wives of his fellow-missionaries, this petite, elegant, cultured woman must have been a revelation and a stimulus. Dorothy Carey had long since ceased to be a companion. Now she was not only deranged, she was dangerous. 'Mrs. Carey is obliged to be constantly confined; she has long gotten worse and worse, but fear both of my own life and hers, and the desire of the police of the place, obliged me to agree to her confinement.'[4] 'Poor Mrs. C. is rather worse than better; a very distressing object indeed. This affliction is heavy. O may I bear it like a christian, and may it be of benefit to me!'[5] In marked contrast, Charlotte Rumohr was well-read and fluent in most European languages. In addition, she was an earnest seeker after Christ. When she arrived in India, she had been a sceptic, repudiating the 'barren orthodoxy of the Lutheranism in which she had been brought up'.[6] However, hearing the missionaries at Serampore caused her to change her views. She bought a house on the river front, adjoining the Mission, and joined the missionaries in their public worship. Hence her presence on the bank of the Ganges on that most auspicious day in December, 1800.

> We have toiled so long, and have met with many discouragements; *wrote Carey* but, at last, the Lord has appeared for us. . . I feel much concerned that they (the new converts) may act worthy of their vocation, and also, that they may be able to teach others. I think it becomes us to make the most of every one whome the Lord gives us.[7]

Carey was indeed fortunate in his first convert. Krishna Pal was to become the first native missionary to Calcutta and then to Assam, and he became the first Bengali hymn-writer.*

Already, as can be seen from the above-quoted paragraph from a letter to John Sutcliff, Carey is looking ahead to further expansion of his work. He was never idle in doing good. This letter, which expresses such joy at the gathering momentum of events, continues with equal enthusiasm to embrace his other interests:

> . . . We are sending an assortment of Hindu gods to the Bristol Museum, and some other curiosities to different friends. Do send a few tulips, daffodils, snowdrops, lilies, and seeds of other things, by Dolton, when he returns, desiring him

* A translation by Joshua Marshman of one of Krishna Pal's hymns is still in use (*The Baptist Hymn Book*, No. 213).

> not to put them in the hold. Send the roots in a net or basket, to be hung up any where out of the reach of salt water, and the seeds in a separate small box. . .

So the first year of the Serampore Mission came to a glorious end and the second started with the baptism of yet more converts: Rasoo and Jeymooni (Krishna Pal's wife and sister-in-law) and Annada, a widow. Later in the year, Gokul and his wife, Kamal, were also baptised. Carey's every thought was now fixed on India. Except in so far as it interfered with the mails, the European conflict seemed far away. He does report the loss of the *Queen* off the coast of South America 'with whatever letters had been sent from England'[8] and the daring capture of the *Kent* by Surcouff in the mouth of the Hooghli river. (Her captain and several of the crew lost their lives in the engagement). However, the war could not be ignored. Russia, Sweden, Prussia and Denmark had recently revived the Armed Neutrality of the North (the Maritime Confederacy). They asserted that it was to withstand Britain's claim to the right of search of vessels at sea. The United Kingdom (as it had become on 1st January, 1801 by Ireland joining the Union) considered the Northern League a French instrument to destroy the Baltic supplies on which the British navy depended. The Confederacy's resistance did not last long. Nelson's defeat of the Danish fleet at the Battle of Copenhagen in April, 1801 crushed opposition in the west. In India, the British bloodlessly but firmly took over the Danish settlement of Serampore on 8th May.

Seeing that Marshman, Ward and Brunsdon were the same three missionaries whose return to England had been ordered so peremptorily by the British authorities less than eighteen months earlier, it could have been expected that their position would once again be under threat. Such, however, was not to be the case.

On 5th March, 1801, the first complete bound New Testament in Bengali had been published, though extracts such as individual Gospels, had been coming off the press earlier. In Serampore, a bound copy was placed reverently on the Communion table. On its arrival in England, a copy was presented to King George III. Even though the translation was far from perfect, it displayed a grasp of Bengali unusual in an Englishman. It is surely not mere coincidence that the appearance of the New Testament in March was followed only a month later by Carey's being approached to become a teacher of Bengali and Sanskrit at Fort William College.

This institution was the creation of the Governor-General, Lord Wellesley. Once he felt that a measure of peace had been restored to India, he turned his considerable talents from war to administrative reform. The quality of the civil servants of the East India Company, with a few exceptions, was at 'the lowest depths of ignorance and vice'.[9] There was no training for the young men coming out from England in the responsibilities that lay before them. Whereas in its early days the East India Company had been concerned solely with trade, now it administered an empire. The new recruits to the Company, usually between fifteen and eighteen years of age, had rarely completed their English education before being sent overseas, let alone having any grasp of the languages, customs, politics or economics of their adopted country.

Lord Wellesley decided to found an institution along the lines of the Oxford and Cambridge colleges where the new recruits to the Indian service could acquire a comprehensive knowledge of Indian language and culture. Hence Fort William College which opened towards the end of 1800 with a hundred students from the three Presidencies of Calcutta, Bombay and Madras. They were given free food and lodging and a salary of Rs. 300 per month (£37.50).

The project met with a great deal of opposition. The Court of Directors of the Company felt it was too expensive, that the education provided was beyond what was necessary. However, Wellesley had the power and the personality to override their opposition.

> If the Court of Directors should abolish this Institution *he wrote* it is my fixed and unalterable resolution to propose to Parliament, immediately after my return to England, a law for its restitution. For I *know* it to be absolutely requisite for the good government of these possessions. So convinced am I of its necessity, that I am determined to devote the remainder of my political life (if needs be) to establishing it, as the greatest benefit which can be imparted to India's public service, and as the best security for the welfare of our Indian subjects.[10]

Lord Wellesley himself approved Carey's appointment in the full knowledge that he was a missionary – though he first established that he was 'well affected to the state'.[11] The appointment for the moment could only be as 'teacher', not 'professor', of Bengali and Sanskrit as Carey was a Dissenter. He celebrated his new position by presenting a copy of the Bengali New Testament to Lord Wellesley. It was 'graciously received'.[12]

It was a bold and imaginative appointment to put Carey, self-taught and lacking any academic qualifications, in charge of students many of whom were from aristocratic backgrounds and from the best schools in England. Two of his first students had been at Eton.

'For my own part, I am almost sunk under the prospect, having never known college discipline,' Carey wrote to Dr. Ryland, now Principal of Bristol Baptist College. 'My ignorance of the way of conducting collegiate exercises is a great weight upon my mind. . . Give me your advice about the best manner of conducting myself in this station, and . . . pray much for me. . .'[13]

Carey did not accept the appointment without detailed discussion with his colleagues. However, they were enthusiastic that he should take it up.

The immediate benefit was financial. Carey's salary at the College was Rs. 500 per month (about £65). This was a princely sum which, along with the profits from the Marshmans' schools, enabled the Serampore team gradually to extend their work and open up stations in other parts of India.

The second benefit was that the Mission, through Carey's appointment, had almost a Government 'seal of approval'. As long as Lord Wellesley was Governor-General, the Mission generally and the Serampore Press in particular enjoyed considerable prestige.

A third benefit was the assistance Carey could now obtain in his study of Indian languages and in his work of translation. Many learned teachers from all over India congregated in the College in Calcutta. This was to give impetus to a further ambition of Carey to translate the Bible into every language of Asia.

Further, the appointment gave Carey the opportunity to widen the scope of his translations into Eastern languages. He discovered that there were no books available to his students to assist in the study of Bengali or Sanskrit. Undeterred, he set about providing them. He compiled textbooks, grammars and dictionaries. In all, he produced six grammars (of Bengali, Sanskrit, Marathi, Panjabi, Telugu and Kanarese, and with John Clark Marshman, one of Bhutia). He wrote his *Colloquies*, a lively picture of the manners and notions of the people of Bengal. Ram Boshoo (now gathered back into the fold and appointed a pundit at the College) wrote a history of Raja Pratapaditya, one of the ancient Indian princes and hero of the Sundarbuns. The other pundits also produced books. All these were printed by the Serampore press and provided the beginning of modern Bengali literature.

The trickle of success that had attended Carey's work in India since 1793 now became a flood. At forty, he was at the peak of his powers.

Henceforward, Carey spent as much time in Calcutta as he did in Serampore. Each Monday evening towards sunset he was rowed down the winding river to Calcutta; each Friday evening he made the return journey to Serampore.

Calcutta at this time was already a vast cosmopolitan port, some three or four miles by one mile in extent. The River Hooghli which bounded the city on the western side was half a mile wide at this point, enabling shipping from all parts of the world to anchor there in its deep harbour. It was a great centre for trade, being the outlet for the products of Bengal, Oudh and the more remote western provinces, which were brought to the city down the vast waterways of northern India. The population of Calcutta was multi-racial. Europeans, 'Portuguese' and some Chinese occupied the area adjoining the river, while the remainder of the city was occupied by an Indian population of both Hindu and Moslem religion. (The term 'Portuguese' at this time did not mean merely people of Portuguese nationality; it was the name given commonly to Eurasians, those with an Indian mother but a European father who might well be English, French, Dutch or Danish.) The European quarter had gracious houses and there were two protestant churches, one of which (St. John's) with its spire and pediment and classical columns, would have been at home in Wren's rebuilt London.

To the south of the city and joining Calcutta to Fort William was the Esplanade, an extensive plain adjoining the river for a mile and a half, with beautiful trees shading walks and roads where it was the custom of society towards sunset 'to take an airing, driving to the race-course, where the carriages all drew up and a general chat took place'.[14] Adjoining the Esplanade was the magnificent new Government House, the Raj Bhavan, erected by Lord Wellesley between 1799 and 1803 as 'a palace suitable to his magnificent ideas, and such a one as would be proper for the residence of the British Governor-General of India'.[15] This superb edifice, which resembled Kedleston Hall in Derbyshire, was approached by four colossal gates emblazoned with the Royal Arms. It had over sixty rooms and public halls, verandahs, porticos and a sumptuous Throne Room.

Fort William itself lay to the south of Calcutta where its guns could command any approach by sea to the city of Calcutta itself. It was begun in 1757, immediately after the Battle of Plassey, and though it took almost twenty-five years and an estimated 20 lakhs of rupees (lakh = 100,000), it was considered one of the finest forts in the world and virtually impregnable.

Fort William *College* was in Calcutta itself. It did not have its own purpose-built premises. Lord Wellesley proposed to build a worthy home for his university at Garden Reach, an elegant stretch of the frontage to the River Hooghli a few miles south of the city. Here gentlemen of the highest rank in the Company's service had splendid houses in a cooler and more refreshing environment than central Calcutta. At first, however, the College was accommodated in a number of houses rented by the Government on the south side of Tank (later Dalhousie) Square in the centre of the city. Student accommodation was in the old Writers' Building on the opposite side of the square. The college had an assembly hall, library, lecture-rooms for the study of Arabic, Persian and Sanskrit, Bengali, Hindustani, Tamil and modern European languages. In addition, there were lectures in Hindu and Moslem law, government regulations, political economy, chemistry, geography, mathematics, philosophy and the arts (though later some of this syllabus was pared down). It was indeed an imaginative scheme, not only enabling new servants of the East India Company to learn something of the languages and manners of the East, but also enabling the authorities to weigh up the character and capabilities of the students before making appointments.

Carey was fascinated by the colourful scene that Calcutta presented. On his first visit in 1793, his view was no doubt jaundiced by penury and by anxiety over the welfare of his family. Moreover, in the words of his map of Moulton days, 'all are pagans'. Now the 'pagans', after nearly ten years of work amongst them, had sorted themselves into Moslems and Hindus, into rich and poor, into high-caste and low-caste, into members of the many different peoples who went to make up the vast population of India. He saw the long-legged 'adjutant' cranes which acted as scavengers in Calcutta's busy streets, he saw the flocks of kites and parakeets. A letter to his sisters of 2nd December, 1802 – so much more descriptive than his early letters – describes the bustle and colour of the Calcutta scene: the primitive covered bullock carts hiding children or secluded females; the luxurious palanquins (a sort of sedan chair) attended by servants; the bamboo carts of the poorer natives, with broken-down horses; the elegant phaetons of the Europeans.

But he was shocked by the dissolute habits of Europeans in Calcutta, so graphically described in William Hickey's *Memoirs*, with the 'fevered cosmopolitanism',[16] the drinking and feasting, the lack of sabbath observance. 'The utmost profligacy of manners prevails both among natives and others. Europeans have their work carried on, their assemblies and routs, on the Lord's-day the same as on another day; and a man, when he arrives in India, shows what he would have been in England if there had been no restraint,' he wrote sadly to his sisters.[17]

Letters to England at this time report a steady trickle of conversions. 'Baptised three natives and my son William';[18] 'our number of baptised natives is now twenty-five'; 'we have hope of one or two more'.[19] Though the totals were minute against India's teeming millions, they must have seemed a rich harvest after the seven lean years in Mudnabatti.

Yet the whole enterprise was still balanced on a knife-edge. The numbers of the missionaries were few. How long could they survive the killing conditions of Bengal? Grant had died, Fountain had died. In 1801, Daniel Brunsdon succumbed to a liver complaint and shortly afterwards, Thomas died 'of an ague'. The high mortality rate was an ever-present threat to the work in India and a constant burden in Carey's letters home:

> Should the Society send out any more missionaries, I would propose to them to have their eye upon some one who would be capable and willing to step into the school in case of the death of brother Marshman. . .[20]

> I have outlived four of my brethren, Mr. Grant, Mr. Fountain, Mr. Brunsdon, and last of all, Mr. Thomas, who died on October 13th last. I know not why so fruitless a tree is preserved; but the Lord is too wise to err.[21]

Strong self-criticism and a deep consciousness of sin were common among intensely religious men of this period but Carey did himself less than justice to call himself a 'fruitless tree'. More suitable would it be to call his first forty years a time of 'pruning' for in 1801 his most fruitful years lay ahead of him.

> I am the true vine, and my Father is the husbandman.
> Every branch in me that beareth not fruit he taketh away: and every branch that beareth fruit, he purgeth it, that it may bring forth more fruit.[22]

11

Conflict with Government

1802–1807

On 27th May, 1802, the Treaty of Amiens brought the Revolutionary War with France to an end. It was, in fact, to be no more than a breathing space before the next conflict; almost exactly a year later, Britain and France launched into what have since become known as the Napoleonic Wars. However, the Treaty did result in the handing back of Serampore to Denmark. At the time, it seemed an event of little significance for, under Lord Wellesley's unofficial patronage, the work of the Mission flourished. Lord Wellesley celebrated the Peace with 'a most splendid entertainment'.[1]

Carey was particularly gratified when, in late 1801 or early 1802, he was asked by the Governor-General to enquire into the frequency, nature, and reasons for infanticide at the island of Saugor near the mouth of the Ganges. As with *sati*, this 'dreadful Practice'[2] had long been a burden on Carey's heart. As early as 1794 he had seen near Malda the remains of an infant devoured by white ants after being exposed as a sacrifice. At Saugor, children were thrown into the river to be devoured by alligators, in fulfilment of vows their mothers had made: if they were blessed with two children, one would be sacrificed to the holy Ganges. According to Ward, who helped with the enquiry, a hundred children were sacrificed each year.

Carey wrote a general 'memorial on Murders committed under the pretence of religion' so that he could also include evidence of the widespread practice of *sati*. Following the report, Lord Wellesley passed a Regulation in 1802 prohibiting infanticide. He would have banned *sati* as well but on that subject he had much more prejudice to overcome than over infanticide. Opposition from Hindus was strong. Europeans, rather than risk upsetting the Hindus, took a weak line.

Accordingly, Wellesley did not succeed in getting through any measures against it before his term of office was over.

There was similar bitter hostility to the new converts to Christianity. Although their numbers among the natives increased, so also did the prejudice against them. The new Christians were persecuted by their fellows; some were even murdered. In 1803, a Kulin Brahmin (i.e. one of purest blood) believed and was baptised. He then married one of Krishna Pal's daughters (despite her being the daughter of a carpenter – a notable triumph over the caste system). This young couple were pelted with dung in Calcutta. Converts learned early in their Christian career what it was to 'take up the cross'. Nonetheless, in spite of opposition and in spite of the backsliding of some of the converts, the work of the Mission grew and prospered.

At all times, a most effective tool of missionary work was its exponents' own personal example. In November, 1803, when Gokul died, his coffin was carried to its grave by three Europeans and three Indians. Marshman and Carey's elder sons, Felix and William, were the Europeans. The Indians were Krishna Pal (Gokul's friend and the Mission's first Indian convert); Peeru, their first convert from Mohammedanism, and a Christian Brahmin. 'The crowd was much struck,' wrote Marshman 'by the reverent love Christians show, even in death, to one another.'[3]

The Lady Rumohr was baptised by Carey in June 1803 and devoted her considerable talents to work among the blind and the lame. She also supported the schools, in particular one for Indian girls at Cutwa (modern Katwa). This town lay about two hundred miles north of Calcutta and was the first of a series of mission stations set up in India by the Serampore team. At first John Chamberlain was put in charge. He had arrived from England in 1803. Unfortunately, despite his sincerity, he was not a success as a missionary. From the beginning he was 'almost always engaged in acrimonious disputes with his colleagues, Indians and government officials'.[4] Money to finance the expansion into other stations came from the Marshman schools and from Carey's salary at Fort William College. Of the £1,000 a year profits from the schools, the Marshmans only kept back £35 for their own needs. All but £40 of Carey's salary was handed over to Mission funds.[5]

Large sums were needed also for the printing press. As the work of the press expanded, more employees had to be taken on. Eventually, thirty pundits were employed to help with the work of translation. There were also printers, punch-cutters, type-setters and so on. The capacity of the missionaries to be self-sufficient was remarkable. When type was difficult or impossible to obtain, they located a former Indian blacksmith named Panchanan who had been instructed in the art of punch-cutting by Sir Charles Wilkins (originator of the first fount of Bengali type). Panchanan trained others with the result that the Serampore press not only produced all its own type, in whatever tongue was required, but sold it as well. As early as 1805 Carey reported that they were making their own printers' ink to avoid having to import it.[6] By 1809 they even had their own paper mill (run on steam from 1820 onwards). From the very beginning, the press was busy printing Christian literature. As its reputation grew and capability expanded, commercial printing was undertaken both to subsidise other missionary undertakings and also to provide work for the growing number of Indian Christians whose conversion precluded them from other jobs.

In 1803, Carey began to revise his Bengali New Testament, realising that his first effort was too English in style and idiom, and in the use and order of its words. But already, he had a wider vision. 'If we are given another fifteen years,' he wrote to Andrew Fuller 'we hope to translate and print the Bible in all the chief languages of Hindustani. We have fixed our eyes on this goal. The zeal of the Lord of hosts shall perform this'.[7]

In this ambition, he was greatly encouraged by an approach from the newly-founded British & Foreign Bible Society (which was Anglican) to join with them in promoting and securing Bible translation. Though this cooperation later foundered, with the Anglican clergy concerned seeking virtually to take over the control of the Serampore Mission affairs, it did – at least in 1804 – give Carey further impetus in his translation work. As his studies proceeded, particularly through teaching Sanskrit at the College, he arrived at the conclusion that it was necessary to translate the Bible into Sanskrit first of all. As this was the root of all the Indian tongues, the pundits would find it easier to make their first-draft translations from Sanskrit into other Indian languages. His Sanskrit New Testament was published in 1808.

Carey's mastery of Sanskrit was sufficiently distinguished for him to be appointed moderator in 1804 of the annual 'Oriental disputations' in that language by prize students of the College. This glittering occasion was held on 20th September at Government House in 'the southern room on the marble floor'. It was attended by the élite of both European and Indian society. The Chief Justice, the judges of the Supreme Court, the members of the Supreme Council, of the College Council, military officers, a Persian envoy from Baghdad, and distinguished men of letters were present. The Governor-General's soldier brother, Arthur Wellesley, attended also, fresh from the peace negotiations that followed his Mahratta Wars of the previous year. (These had extended the dominion of the British to the Himalayas in the north and had taken in all the Indian seaboard on the east.)

After the disputation was over, Carey himself delivered an oration in Sanskrit, praising the Governor-General's foresight in founding the college. Carey had the courage – temerity, even – to declare publicly in this oration his missionary purpose and his hope that his teaching of Indian languages would 'enlarge the bounds of Oriental literature . . . and diffuse the spirit of Christian principles throughout the nations of Asia. . .'[8] It was a testimony that could well have given offence, particularly as Hindu and Moslem princes were present in the audience. However, Lord Wellesley wrote that he was 'much pleased with Mr. Carey's truly original and excellent speech'. He added that he esteemed 'such a testimony from such a man a greater honour than the applauses of courts and parliament'.[9]

What was it about Carey that earned him the respect and friendship of such a man as Wellesley? Was it his patent goodness? Or had he developed qualities of personality and character that gave him a certain charisma? Nothing in the accounts of his friends and colleagues suggests personal magnetism but everyone speaks of him with affection and respect.

Carey dined at Government House in February 1805. On this occasion, Lord Wellesley questioned him keenly about the Mission (about which, it seemed, he was already well-informed) and 'expressed his satisfaction with the whole'.[10] He also sent Carey copies of inscriptions and documents in obscure dialects for him to translate. Through Government channels, Wellesley subscribed liberally to the Serampore publications. For example, the Government gave £800 for a hundred copies of Carey's Sanskrit Grammar.[11]

This period of security for the Mission was not to last long. In the summer of 1805, Wellesley was abruptly and ignominiously dismissed and the elderly and ailing Lord Cornwallis was sent to India to replace him. Wellesley left for England in August. His high-handed methods had made him many enemies. In particular, his contempt for the Court of Governors of the East India Company caused them to be his bitter opponents for the next thirty years. Although his military operations had secured the whole of the Indian subcontinent for the British, they had increased the Company's debts from £17 million in 1797 to £31 million in 1806. The balance of trade deficit was enormous because the export trade from India was virtually at a standstill. Pitt declared that the Governor-General 'had acted most imprudently and illegally, and that he could not be suffered to remain in government'.[12]

Fortunately, the College continued as before and Carey was able to lay before its Council and the Asiatic Society a project which he considered would help to make Indian culture better understood in Europe. This was to publish a series of Indian classics with text, English translation and notes. He and his fellow missionaries were allowed Rs. 300 monthly (£37.50) to carry out the work. A start was made by Carey and Marshman together on the epic poem, *Ramayana*. Little wonder, with this extra work on top of his collegiate duties and regular preaching three times a week, that Carey had little time for letter-writing. 'The truth is, that every letter I write is at the expense of a chapter of the bible, which would have been translated in that time,' he wrote to Sutcliff.[13]

Lord Cornwallis died on 5th October, 1805, before he had even had a chance to carry out the financial retrenchments that were felt to be necessary. Until a new appointment could be made, his Deputy, Sir George Barlow, became acting Governor-General. He was a senior member of Council but a man of unpopular manners. William Hickey, dipping his pen in vitriol, wrote:

> A grievous change was experienced upon the succession of Sir George Barlow to the situation (so different a man in every respect) Lord Wellesley had so recently filled, the one all dignity and possessed of the most shining talents, the other a compound of meanness and pride without a particle of genius. Sir George Barlow was the son of a silk mercer in King Street, Covent Garden, and nature had intended him for nothing more elevated in Society than a measurer of lute strings from behind a counter: although that fickle jade, Madam Fortune, with her usual unsteadiness, threw him into so much more exalted a sphere. His manner in society was cold, distant and formal. I do not believe he had a single friend in the world, nor one individual person about whom he cared or in whose welfare he felt at all interested.[14]

Though obviously full of unkind prejudice, Hickey's criticism was true in part for Barlow was a man of only mediocre ability. However, he was a conscientious Governor, loyally carrying out the policies of his superiors and effecting drastic economies in his administration. The contrast after his predecessor's flamboyant style must have been marked. Everything Wellesley had done, whether it was building or town-planning or entertainment, had been done on a grand scale. For example, shortly before his dismissal, 'a separate peace having been effected with the Mahrattas, Lord Wellesley gave a splendid entertainment to the whole Settlement. Magnificent fireworks under the direction and management of a French engineer were played off, the artillery upon the ramparts of Fort William being discharged all round the fort three different times, which altogether produced a very grand effect.'[15]

But if Sir George Barlow could not lend his patronage to the Mission in tangible form as had his predecessor, at least he gave it his tacit support. 'He is friendly to the undertaking,' Carey wrote, 'but a clause in the Charter, it is said, obliges him to take no steps either directly or indirectly to convert the natives.'[16] However, Barlow approved of the Biblical translations and did not oppose the invitation of subscriptions towards 'the translation of the scriptures into all the languages of the east'.[17] In July, 1806, the subscriptions had already totalled £3,000 which would indicate that not all Europeans in India were opposed to missionary activity.

Although Barlow could not officially sanction the opening of branch stations of the Mission, he did not oppose the extensions. This was a relief, for Carey was ever anxious not 'to conceal a single step that we took from Government'.[18] Yet there were still instances where local magistrates insisted on the strict letter of the law. For example, William Carey, Junior, and William Moore (a new missionary who came out in 1803) were distributing books to an eager crowd in Dacca when they were stopped by order of the local court.

Dacca was one of the centres where the Serampore team hoped to set up a station. By 1806, they already had missions in Calcutta itself, in Dinadjpur, Cutwa and Jessore. They left southern India to Danish and Dutch missionaries and to the London Missionary Society (formed in 1795) with whom they maintained a cordial correspondence. In northern India, however, they planned to have stations two hundred miles apart, each one to be served by a missionary and an Indian pastor or evangelist. Each station was to be self-supporting so that it was necessary that each new missionary coming out to India should have the capacity to earn. Of course, many more missionaries would be needed. In 1806, Carey wrote to the Society asking for forty more men to be sent out. He was also in regular touch with Baptist churches in America, despite that there was still ill-feeling between Britain and its former colonies. John Williams of New York and Thomas Baldwin of Boston corresponded with him from the beginning of 1800 and sent him frequent help. Staughton (the 'anon' of the collection in Mrs. Beeby Wallis's back parlour in 1792) emigrated to the United States and became Secretary and, later, President of the American Baptist Missionary Convention. He also kept in touch. In time, the Baptist mission stations would extend westwards along the Ganges and Jumna valleys as far as Delhi, and in the east to the border with Burma.

It seemed as if, at last, the bonds that had kept missionary work in check were broken. Carey was full of enthusiasm and vision:

> . . . The Cape of Good Hope is now in the hands of the English. (It had been recaptured from the Dutch at the beginning of 1806.) Should it continue so, would it not be possible to

have a general association of all denominations of christians from the four quarters of the world, kept there once in about ten years? I earnestly recommend this plan. Let the first meeting be in the year 1810, or 1812, at furthest. I have no doubt but it would be attended with very important effects. We could understand one another better; and more entirely enter into one another's views by two hours' conversation, than by two or three years' epistolary correspondence.[19]

(Fuller was to dismiss this suggestion as impracticable – he called it 'Carey's pleasing dream' – and it was to be a hundred years before missionaries met on such a scale, at the first International Mission Conference in Edinburgh in 1910.)

Carey was busy also with innumerable projects, as the following time-table for Thursday, 12th June, 1806, indicates:

> I rose this day at a quarter before six, read a chapter in the Hebrew Bible, and spent the time till seven in private addresses to God and then attended family prayer with the servants in Bengalee. While tea was pouring out, I read a little in Persian with a Moonshi who was waiting when I left my bed room. Read also before breakfast a portion of the Scriptures in Hindoosthanee. The moment breakfast was over sat down to the translation of the Ramayuna from Sangskrit, with a Pundit . . . continued this translation till ten o'clock, at which time I went to College (Fort William), and attended the duties there (teaching Bengali, Sanskrit, and Marathi) till between one and two o'clock – When I returned home I examined a proof sheet of the Bengalee translation of Jeremiah, which took till dinner time. . . After dinner translated with the assistance of the chief Pundit of the College, greatest part of the 8th Chap. of Matthew, into Sangskrit – this employed me till six o'clock, after six sat down with a Tilingua Pundit . . . to learn that Language. Mr. Thomas (son of the Rev. Tho. Thomas of London) called in the evening; I began to collect a few previous thoughts into the form of a Sermon, at Seven o'clock, and preached in English at half past seven . . . the Congregation was gone by nine o'clock. I then sat down to write to you, after this I conclude the Evening by reading a Chapter in the Greek testament, and commending myself to God. I have never more time in a day than this, though the exercises vary.[20]

All this after thirteen years in the debilitating climate of Bengal!

If the time allowed for preparing his sermon seems short, this was because (according to Eustace Carey's account in his *Memoir*) Carey 'never *wrote* a sermon in his life. . . He had gone through the sacred books so often, and with so much critical attention, and in so many languages, that there was scarcely a passage with . . . which he was not perfectly familiar.'

Despite the busy schedule, Eustace Carey records that his uncle never showed any resentment if his programme was interrupted. For whatever time was necessary, he would give his visitor his undivided attention. Immediately the visitor left, Carey would immediately be able to resume his work as if there had been no interruption. He obviously had tremendous powers of concentration.

The 'Calcutta Chapel' referred to in the time-table was presumably either the one opened in Bow Bazaar on 1st July, 1806 or that in Lall Bazaar on 1st January, 1809. The former was in the hall of an undertaker; the latter was in an area where were numerous taverns and brothels frequented by seamen of a dozen nations. Until the chapels were built, Carey and his colleagues would preach in the open air or in private houses. They did this regularly from 1803 onwards.

By the time Carey moved to Serampore, he had changed in his approach from attacking the shortcomings of the Hindu religion, finding it more effective to concentrate on the story of the death and resurrection of Christ. His sermons were always simple. According to J. H. Reilly who, as a boy, heard him preach, Carey would 'emphasise important parts with a sharp drop of the forefinger of the right hand – its whole length – on to the book or table.' During the singing of hymns, he stamped his foot vigorously to set the time.[21]

All these high hopes for spreading the Word of God on a wide scale were dashed by a sudden about-turn in Sir George Barlow's attitude. During Wellesley's administration, four new Baptist missionaries (John Biss, John Chamberlain, Richard Mardon and William Moore) had entered Bengal without any hindrance. However, when William Robinson and John Chater arrived from England in August, 1806 to supplement the Mission, they were immediately ordered to leave the country. Carey protested to the magistrates in Calcutta and was informed by them that the Governor-General desired 'that he would not interfere with the prejudices of the natives by preaching to them, instructing them, or distributing books and pamphlets among them; . . . and that . . . (they) . . . would not permit the converted natives to go into the country to spread christianity among the people . . .'.[22]

The reason for this *volte face* was the Vellore Mutiny which had occurred in the previous June. Vellore was a military station in the Madras presidency, occupied both by British troops and two native regiments. The mutiny, in which a number of British officers were massacred, was by the native troops, known as Sepoys. Although it is now accepted that the mutiny was due to 'imprudent orders of Government directing the Seapoys to rub off Vishnoo's marks from their foreheads & to wear a Turban with leather on it',[23] at the time many took the opportunity of attributing it to the Baptists' proposals for the translation of the Bible and/or to the planned increase in the number of Anglican chaplains in India.

Over the first of Sir George Barlow's requirements (i.e. not to preach or distribute books and pamphlets to natives) the Serampore missionaries decided to 'yield a little to the present storm, it may soon blow over'.[24] Outright defiance of the Governor-General could have resulted in demands for the closing down of the Mission (though, for the time being at least, it was under Danish protection). As for the second demand, that converted natives were not to evangelise, this was impossible for the missionaries to carry out, even had they wished to do so.

'We are much in the situation in which the apostles were when commanded "not to teach nor preach any more in his name",' wrote the Missionaries. 'They . . . replied, "Whether it be right in the sight of God to obey you rather than God, judge ye".'[25]

Even before news of the mutiny reached England, Sir George Barlow's restrictions were eased; and an official letter from the Danish Governor of Serampore no doubt contributed to the suspension of the deportation orders on Chater and Robinson. Moreover, as with so many stumbling-blocks that strewed their way, the Serampore missionaries were able to use the restrictions as stepping-stones to further outreach. If they were forbidden to expand in Bengal, they would spread their effort into Burma. Mardon and Chater agreed to begin the work there.

Was there also an opening even further east, into China? It seemed significant that there should arrive at Serampore at this time Johannes Lasser, an Armenian born in Macao, who was fluent in Chinese. He began to teach the language to Joshua Marshman and his son, and also to Jabez Carey, still only thirteen years of age. At the same time, Burman and Chinese nationals were employed at the Serampore press to work on translation and to cut wood blocks of the Chinese characters.

In the midst of all the controversy over the Mission, Carey was elevated to the full stature of 'Professor' of Bengali, Sanskrit and Marathi at Fort William College, with a consequent increase in salary to £1,500 per annum. No wonder he was able to record of all these events: 'It is the Lord's doing, and marvellous in our eyes.'[26]

However, the repercussions of the Vellore incident rumbled on. In England, more than in Calcutta, the mutiny was attributed to missionary activities. The Government of the day and the Directors of the East India Company were much influenced by anti-missionary letters from India. Rancorous pamphlets from the pens of Thomas Twining, Major John Scott-Waring and Major-General Charles 'Hindoo' Stewart not only attacked the idea of allowing missionaries into India but defended Hinduism in glowing terms and extolled the morality of Indians! A 'minute' of 1806 on the subject of missionaries by William Fullarton Elphinstone, Chairman of the Court of Directors, gives some indication of the wild misunderstanding that obtained in England concerning the state of affairs in India:

> . . . The operations of the Missionaries, even admitting them to be well meant, which I very much doubt, & the numerous Translations of the religious books of the Christians, have alarmed the Sepoys, or rather have furnished a pretence for Emissaries & evil disposed Persons to alarm them, with the Idea, that the Company intends to make them all Christians.
>
> I shall not enter into the private characters of the Missionaries, one or two of them, or their Agents, before they became Apostles, were Indigo Makers in Mr. Udny's service. Instead of fermenting a Weed, which is finished in 24 hours,

> they are employed in fermenting the Whole Country & their handy work will last for years.
>
> I believe they all of them reside at Serampore . . . from this Place, there is constant Intercourse, either direct, or by way of Tranqubar, with the Isles of France. . . They must know everything that passes in Calcutta, & all the News of the Country. From them, the French residing at Serampore, can get every Species of Information. . .[27]

It had indeed been wise of Fuller in 1800 to urge Carey and Chamberlain to be discreet in their letters home.

The war with France was going badly for Britain. Napoleon's armies seemed invincible. Such accusations as the above, that the Baptist missionaries were French spies, could well have resulted in their expulsion had there not been powerful voices in England raised in their defence. The 'Clapham Sect' led by William Wilberforce, M.P. declared Barlow's measures a most 'shocking Violation of all Religious Liberty'.[28] Lord Wellesley declared that the idea of missionaries being in any way responsible for the Vellore Mutiny was impossible. Charles Grant, Deputy-Chairman of the Directors of the East India Company, protested to Lord Bentinck, former Governor of Madras. Andrew Fuller prepared a written defence of the missionary position and sent it to the President of the Board of Control and the Directors of the Company. Missionary supporters, including Lord Spencer, the Home Secretary, pressed the missionaries' case with Lord Minto who in the early summer of 1807 left England to replace Sir George Barlow as Governor-General.

Soon after Lord Minto's arrival, he invited Carey to breakfast with him. Carey was encouraged by this to think that the way was opening to new and cordial relations with government. Unfortunately, this was not to be the case. A crisis arose out of the issue from the Serampore press of a tract in Persian entitled *An Address to Mussulmands with an Appendix Containing Some Account of Mahomet*. This came to be known as the Persian Pamphlet. It contained a violent attack on the Mahommedan religion and on the person of its prophet. Carey was taken aback when confronted with the pamphlet; abuse was not a weapon of which he approved. The fault lay with Ward who had handed a perfectly harmless tract to a pundit for translation into Persian. The pundit had added offensive passages of his own which Ward had failed to notice. Apologies were not sufficient. Lord Minto, who was fearful of a repeat of the Vellore affair, had genuine reason to be afraid that similar excesses might have been overlooked in other tracts and that the religious susceptibilities of more of the native population might be offended. He wrote to Governor Krefting of Serampore demanding that the press 'should be placed under the immediate controle of this Government'.[29]

Once again, the missionaries could be grateful for the protection of the Danish Government. Governor Krefting replied that the surrender of the press would be 'highly prejudicial'[30] to the Danish settlement as all his official printing was executed there. Moreover, he was under orders from his king to protect the missionaries. It was as well that Governor Krefting took his stand at this time for in February of the next year, 1808, following an alliance between Denmark and France, Serampore was again seized by the British and held until the end of the Napoleonic Wars in 1815. Thereafter, it remained Danish territory until 1845 when the British Government purchased it, along with Tranquebar and Balasore, for the sum of 12½ lakhs of rupees (£186,250).[31]

Meantime, the Serampore missionaries applied for an audience with Lord Minto. On their undertaking to submit all their publications to the Government for approval, the restrictions against their operations were lifted. Carey, indeed, considered their situation better than before because pamphlets passed by the Government could be circulated without hindrance. 'The storm,' Carey said, 'is gone over.'[32] An invitation for him and Marshman to dine with Lord Minto at his residence at Barrackpore later in October brought promise of fairer weather to come.

As Carey wrote to his sisters in January, 1808: 'The last year has been one of the most eventful of my whole life.'[33] Among its joys had been the granting to him in March of a Doctorate of Divinity by Brown University in America, an academic distinction which would give more authority to his position at the college. Even more gratifying was the ordination of his eldest son, Felix, at the age of twenty-one. He was to join John Chater as a missionary to Burma. The Bible was by now translated into and printed in Sanskrit, Bengali,

Mahratta, Orissa, Hindustani, Gujerati, Chinese, Sikh, Telugu, Kurnata, Burmese and Persian. Among the year's anxieties had been the 'hard struggle'[34] with government. Carey adds 'God has exalted himself above the wrath of his enemies. . . I do not recollect any occasion on which I have felt so much; nor do I recollect any circumstance in which so full an answer was granted to prayer in so short a time.'[35]

12

Indian Idyll

1808–1811

On 8th December, 1807, Dorothy Carey died of a fever. Her case had been hopeless for many years. Even Carey, reporting her death to Andrew Fuller on 14th January, 1808, uses the word 'maniacal'. Ever since the move to Serampore, however, she had been loyally cared for by the other Mission wives. 'The affectionate attention which the sisters paid to her made a deep impression on my mind,' William wrote to his sisters in the same month. Her death must surely have been a relief to everyone near her. William Ward comes closest to admitting this when he writes in his diary:

> *Tuesday. Dec. 8, 1807.* This evening Mrs. Carey died of the fever under which she has languished some time. Her death was a very easy one; but there was no appearance of returning reason, nor any thing that could cast a dawn of hope or light on her state.

Dorothy had been deranged for twelve years. How much her breakdown was influenced by poor housing, inadequate diet and a constant struggle against penury in the early years of her marriage can never be established. Likewise, it is impossible to assess how much her inadequacy contributed to the family's being caught and held in the poverty trap for so many years. While Dorothy deserves sympathy for being dragged unwillingly half way across the globe in her husband's wake, it is nonetheless a source of wonder and admiration that Carey achieved so much without the support – indeed, with the positive handicap – of his mentally sick wife. It is all the more remarkable that their sons, despite their poor start in life, inherited to a large degree their father's intelligence and industry.

'It will serve to give some idea of the strength and energy of

Dr. Carey's character,' wrote John Clark Marshman, 'that the arduous Biblical and literary labours in which he had been engaged since his arrival at Serampore, were prosecuted while an insane wife, frequently wrought up to a state of most distressing excitement, was in the next room but one to his study.'[1]

Quite apart from Carey's utter dedication to the missionary purpose, it is possible that he immersed himself in hard work to compensate for the tragedy of his marriage. His weekdays in Calcutta must have constituted a relief from the ever-present agony and reproach of a deranged wife. If, indeed, it was a reproach. There is no indication in his letters or journals of any guilty fear that her translation from Northamptonshire to India had hastened her decline. The wishes of a wife did not hold much importance at that time. The place of a wife, along with her children, was at her husband's side wherever he might go. The tombstones in the graveyards of India bear witness to how many wives followed their menfolk only to their early deaths.

> I went to the old Cemetery in Park Street – a depressing-looking place, full of huge monuments, obelisks, vases, pillared buildings, etc. etc. put up to officers, governors, commanders and their wives and dating from 1760 to 1800 or thereabouts. . . It was sad to see how many young men and women were buried there. 20, 26, 33, were common ages. I did not see one older than 54.[2]

John Chamberlain was to lose all three of his children within nine months between midsummer 1811 and March 1812; and the first two months of 1812 would carry off Mrs. Mardon and her youngest child, Joshua Marshman's baby son, one of William Ward's daughters (he had married Fountain's widow), a woman servant of Hannah Marshman and a young boy boarder at the Marshman school. It says something for the care that William Carey bestowed on his wife that she survived so long. She was within a few weeks of her fifty-second birthday when she died.

In less than six months after Dorothy's death, Carey announced his intention of marrying the Lady Rumohr. The news caused dismay at Serampore. Whether this was because Carey's intention seemed to indicate unseemly haste, or whether it was considered that Charlotte Rumohr's health would prove an undue burden is not clear. As far as the former reason is concerned, Carey could surely not have been accused of lack of respect for his late wife. His had proved a tragic union and can have been a marriage in name only for many years. Feelings must have run high, however, for Carey's colleagues sent him a 'round robin' of protest. 'How did my whole body tremble when I was called upon to sign the letter!' wrote Hannah Marshman. It seems quite out of character that any of the missionaries should have used this form of communication. A rule of their community, as recorded by William Ward in his *Journal*, was that Saturday evening should be 'devoted to adjusting differences'.[3] On this occasion, it would appear that embarrassment made the missionaries abandon the rule. Eventually, opposition to the marriage was withdrawn and on 9th May, 1808, Carey and Charlotte were married by Joshua Marshman at the bride's house adjoining the Mission. They were both forty-six years of age.

The Governor-General, writing light-heartedly to his wife of the event, describes Carey as a 'learned & very pious' man marrying a Danish countess 'whom he had converted from a Christian to a Baptist' by 'very near drowning her in the ceremony of baptism . . . performed in that sect'![4]

On the material level, the marriage was of assistance to the Mission because Charlotte gave her house to become part of the Mission property and, over the years, used all her money to support its work. Her contribution on another level must have been incalculable. Her union with Carey was indeed a 'marriage of true minds'. She matched him in spirituality and in intellect and, with her fluency in languages, was able to understand and discuss with him the problems of his translation work. Quite apart from any intellectual attraction between them, they were deeply in love. Fragments of letters from Charlotte to William that have survived are tender and charming and deeply loving:

> My Dearest Love – I feel very much in parting with thee, and feel much in being so far from thee. . .
>
> . . . I hope you will not think I am writing too often. . . I cannot help longing for you. . .

> . . . I thank thee most affectionately, my dearest love, for thy kind letter. . . I am much with you in my thoughts. . .
>
> . . . I find so much pleasure in writing to you, my love, that I cannot help doing it. I was nearly disconcerted by Mrs. – laughing at my writing so often; but then, I thought, I feel so much pleasure in receiving your letters that I hope you may do the same. . .[5]

Thus, for the first time, Carey could enjoy the companionship and support of an equal and devoted partner. Moreover, her breeding could not fail to influence William and help his own self-confidence. The growing respect in which he was held in Bengal (even by people who did not agree with his purpose), his status as Professor at Fort William College, his membership of the Asiatic Society brought him into contact socially with the élite of Calcutta society. Although he seems to have combined a fine intellect with a becoming modesty, a certain social grace was necessary also if he was to be equally at ease in Government House as in his own Mission. It points to some extraordinary quality of character in Carey that, in such a class-conscious age, he was able, despite his lowly origins, to be accepted at all levels of society – although (according to his nephew Eustace Carey's account) he never found general conversation easy and he retained his 'rustic manner' and 'inharmonious voice' to the end of his days.

Carey had repeatedly warned the Society at home that it was 'absolutely necessary for the wives of missionaries to be as hearty in the work as their husbands'.[6] Now at last his own work was encouraged rather than criticised. Charlotte learned Bengali so that she could help native Christian families. It is not without significance that Carey's best and most prolific period of work coincided with that of the greatest happiness in his life.

Contemporaries describe how Charlotte was always cheerful, despite her physical frailty. She went out every day at dawn and again in the evening to enjoy the river breeze, drawn along the mall in her little carriage accompanied by a bearer. Or she would sit in the garden her husband had created and where he had built a bower for prayer and meditation.

Charlotte seems to have been equally beloved by William's

children. Jabez was fifteen at the time of his father's re-marriage and Jonathan was about thirteen. Both spoke of her as 'dear mother'; William Junior, years later, wrote of 'her great affection and very motherly care'. Felix, of course, was in Burma when the wedding took place. He had, tragically, lost his own wife that year. William, who was twenty, married at about the same time as his father. He had been ordained and worked first of all at Dinadjpur as an assistant to Fernandez, the Portuguese who was one of Carey's first converts at Mudnabatti. Later William was posted to Sadamahal, a more remote station with no Europeans for miles. The place was dangerous both from the activities of the gangs of violent robbers known as dacoits and from the presence of wild animals. William was gored by a buffalo and wrote to his father asking if he could return to Serampore. Carey's high sense of duty comes through his reply in which he refuses William's request and offers Cutwa or Dacca as alternative postings:

> I ought, however, to say that I think there is much guilt in your fears. You and Mary will be a thousand times more safe in committing yourselves to God in the way of duty than in neglecting obvious duty to take care of yourselves. . .[7]

Commitment. Duty. Those words embody Carey's attitude to his mission. Even in the glow of his new-found happiness, he did not slacken in the tasks he had set as his goal. The biggest labour on hand was the revision of his second Bengali version of the Bible. He completed this on 26th June, 1809.

It appeared that his idyllic time with Charlotte was to end all too soon for on 27th June he was smitten by a severe illness and his life was despaired of. Charlotte nursed him devotedly. The fever lasted two weeks during which time he raged in delirium against war and against the Pope. A military surgeon was called to attend to him but the sight of his red uniform touched off another tirade against armies. There seemed little hope that he would pull through. After all, sixteen years in India was something like a miracle of survival. Thomas had died after only eight years, Fountain after five, Brunsdon in less than two, Grant after only a month. But the miracle did happen.

'Carey has just been raised from the dead, and the machine

goes on a little longer,' Ward was able to write to Andrew Fuller. 'But we cannot expect these resurrections oft repeated.'[8]

Ward urged the Society to send out more missionaries who could be trained to take over the work from himself and Carey and Marshman. 'What would you think if the safety of the whole Baptist interest in England depended on yourself, Ryland, and Sutcliff?' he demanded. 'Would you not tremble for the Ark?'[9]

In India, however, the 'Ark' was for the time being on an even keel. There were no more crises with Government, thanks to the sensible arrangement of submitting the output of the press for official approval. Whether under the influence of his wife, or whether as a natural development from his interest in Indian life and culture, Carey began to widen the scope of his translation work. In 1811, he published his *Itihasmala* or *Garland of Stories*, translations into English of charming and amusing Hindu legends somewhat after the style of Aesop's *Fables*. The stories show how Carey was beginning to understand the Indian mind. Two brief extracts illustrate their flavour:

> A yogi told a Brahmin that he was on his way to meet God. 'Then tell Him,' cried the Brahmin, 'of the wretched poverty of my wife, my son, and myself, and implore His deliverance.' Which the yogi promised and did. And God said, 'If each shall wish, immediately after bathing, their desires shall be granted.' Upon hearing from the yogi this good news, the wife hasted to bathe and to wish for youth and beauty, rich adornment and raiment. And these were hers by an instant transformation. So fair and affluent she looked that she was coveted by a Mohammedan, who had her seized and set beside him in his carriage. At this calamity, the son ran to his bath and wished that his mother might change into a pig; for then the mohammedan would spurn and thrust her from beside him. Which also came to pass. The Brahmin, in anguish, bathed and wished, 'Oh, let us be as we were!' and thereafter murmured at his poverty no more.

> A devout Brahmin asked an alms at the house of a cobbler. The cobbler's mayna cried crossly, 'Be off, you hypocrite! you thief!' Timid and vexed, the Brahmin moved away. At a sage's he next begged. 'Come in, man of God, come in,' said the sage's

> mayna. 'This house is blessed by your presence.' Then the Brahmin told how he had been insulted by the bird of the cobbler. 'And yet,' said the mayna, 'we are from one nest. Only he has learned to talk like his master; I like mine.'

In 1921, Sir Rabindranath Tagore told S. Pearce Carey that his great-grandfather 'was the pioneer of revived interest in the Vernaculars' of India.[10] Carey encouraged his pundits to write texts in Bengali for use by his students, and encouraged his students to translate the great European classics into Bengali. Some of these are referred to in his reports on his students, conserved among the Minutes and Correspondence of the College Council. There are references to student debts and to their expensive entertainments. They are taken to task for shooting at crows with pistols and catapulting passers-by in Tank Square. Carey remonstrates with a student named Kennedy for boxing his pundit's ears. He commends one Henry Sargent for translating four books of the *Aeneid* into Bengali and two other students for doing the same with *The Tempest* and *Telemachus*. It is recorded that 'Udney (presumably a relative of Carey's benefactor at Mudnabatti) should study more and worry less'; and that 'Barton has been distinguished by marked aversion to study, a neglect of preparation, and an endeavour to escape before lectures are concluded.' As Carey had developed in authority throughout his years in India, so, apparently, had his ability to discipline his pupils.

One of his students gave an account of his manner of teaching:

> I heard C's lectures on botany. He would go first into the garden and pluck some leaves and flowers, and bring them to the class-room. He spoke quietly, but without hesitation, and very interestingly. His notes were on a slip of paper about three inches wide. . . He would tell us many anecdotes of his Mudnabatti years.[11]

Outside India, the struggle with Napoleon dragged on. Fuller had written from England'. . . your dear friend Cunninghame (the former Registrar at Dinadjpur) . . . has now the command of a Volunteer Corps, as we are almost all soldiers, & the attempt at Invasion is reckoned to be on the point of execution. . .'[12] Arthur Wellesley prosecuted the war in the Spanish Peninsula and was created Viscount Wellington after the defeat of the French at Talavera. At the same time his brother, Lord Wellesley, the former Governor-General, became Foreign Secretary in Spencer Perceval's administration in England. From there he was able to authorise what he had hoped to achieve from Calcutta – strong naval expeditions against the French frigates and privateers that had inflicted so much damage on British shipping. Mauritius was captured, thus flushing the enemy out of the base from which they used to menace the sea-lanes to India. With the capture of most of the East Indies from the Dutch, the Indian Ocean once again became safe for the East India Company's clippers.

It seemed that in Carey's personal life, as in the wider world, events were entering a period of stability. It proved to be no more than the quiet before the storm. On 11th March, 1812, disaster struck.

13

Phoenix Rising

1812–1813

On the evening of 11th March, 1812, William Ward was working late at his desk. It was about six o'clock. The staff had all left – native typefounders, compositors, pressmen, binders, writers. Suddenly, Ward became aware of smoke seeping into his office. He hurried through into the long printing-room next door to find the cause. Smoke billowed thickly at the far end. He ran down the long room, past the silent presses and plunged into where the smoke was thickest. His way was blocked by flames and the smoke was suffocating. The paper store was ablaze.

Stopping only to close all doors and windows, he raised the alarm with Marshman and the resident Serampore staff. Despite the danger, Ward and Marshman climbed onto the roof of the paper-store itself and poured bucket after bucket of water onto the fiercely burning fire below. All water had to be carried by hand but they kept up a continuous supply. One man who tried to enter the building was overcome by the heat and fumes and had to be dragged to safety. For four hours they fought the blaze. Gradually the flames lessened. Although the paper still smouldered, it seemed as though the blaze was at last under control.

Ward left the group of fire-fighters and hurried back to his office to begin to remove the most valuable papers. In his absence, someone opened a window. The consequent inrush of air caused the fire to flare into life. Within minutes, the whole building was engulfed in flames. Nothing could be done to save it. With every falling timber, showers of sparks flew up into the night air and a strong breeze fanned them across to the school buildings. For some hours there was concern lest those, too, should ignite. The school-children were awakened and hurriedly evacuated to a safer part of the grounds. It was an anxious and exhausting night.

By two in the morning, the fire had burnt itself out. Daylight revealed a smoking heap of ruins as all that remained of Serampore's printing enterprise. Fortunately, the other mission buildings were unscathed and no lives had been lost.

It has never been established precisely how the fire started, whether by accident or malicious design. Equally, the person who opened the window could have been stupid and ignorant or he could have been determined on destroying the missionaries' work. Joshua Marshman thought the fire might 'have originated in a coal from the Bengalee Hooka'.[1] From whatever cause, it seemed that the printing enterprise was irretrievably damaged.

How were they to break the news to Carey who was at the College in Calcutta at the time of the fire? How to tell him that all his precious manuscripts were destroyed? The draft of his great polyglot dictionary. The Sikh and Telugu grammars. Ten versions of the Bible that had been going through the press. The translation of the *Ramayana* on which he and Marshman had been working for over six years, and so many other works.

Dr. Marshman himself hurried to Calcutta on the Thursday morning to break the news in person to his colleague. That afternoon they returned to Serampore with one of the Company chaplains, Rev. Thomas Thomason and walked sadly round the smoking desolation. Tears filled Carey's eyes. 'In one short evening,' he said, 'the labours of years are consumed. How unsearchable are the ways of God! I had lately brought some things to the utmost perfection of which they seemed capable, and contemplated the missionary establishment with perhaps too much self-congratulation. The Lord has laid me low, that I may look more simply to him.'[2]

All was not entirely lost. Already, after only a few hours, Ward had sorted through the debris and had dragged out the five presses, four thousand punches and matrices and had made arrangements to carry on the printing work in a warehouse belonging to the Mission near the river. Providentially, the tenants, Messrs. Palmer & Co., had moved out only the previous Saturday. The presses and steel punches were undamaged but many of the beautiful hand-cut founts of type had been reduced to lumps of molten metal. Yet Ward determined that they would be re-cut, even though the work might take months. With the Chinese, it took over a year to reproduce the characters in type. A huge quantity of paper had been destroyed – hundreds of reams – but some at least was still usable. Surviving copies of the April, 1812 edition of *Circular Letters* (a monthly collection of reports and letters from missionary stations) show that it was printed on paper scorched along the edges.

The biggest loss was the destruction of manuscripts, most of which were Carey's. With the doggedness which characterised his whole career, he patiently set to work to make his translations all over again. This time he brought to the work even greater dedication and utter humility, for he had persuaded himself that the fire was a Judgment from God for some presumption on his part.

> The Lord has smitten us, he had a right to do so, and we deserve his corrections. I wish to submit to His sovereign will, nay, cordially to acquiesce therein, and to examine myself rigidly to see what in me has contributed to this evil.[3]

Two potentially great works, however, were lost for all time. One was his translation with Joshua Marshman of the *Ramayana*. They never again had the time to spare to spend on its translation. The other was Carey's polyglot dictionary. This ambitious work, giving the equivalent of each Sanskrit word in every language of Asia, would have been a work of supreme philological importance. Carey, although by now a Doctor of Divinity *honoris causa*, could have felt he had truly earned such a title by this single work.

As has been seen, Carey was not by training an academic. He had an outstanding gift for languages but they were self-taught. Therefore his knowledge of languages had the inherent defect that he had never been taught style and had to pick up idiom as best he could. He managed adequately with such languages as Bengali and Hindi which he spoke every day; with less familiar languages, however, scholars claim that the finer points escaped him.[4] Some of his translations, it has been asserted over the years, lacked style, tended to follow English constructions, were too literal; equally, it has been alleged that some of his translations *into* English were pompous. As far as the latter criticism is concerned, Claudius Buchanan made a comment in 1811 which is apposite: 'The very best translation must, in the lapse of ages, change with a changing language.'[5] The style of eighteenth-century and early nineteenth-century English was often ponderous, florid and heavily latinised. Carey's English is as dated to the modern reader as that of the King James's Bible but this is not a reason for censure.

With regard to the former criticism, that his translations lacked style, the wonder is not that the translations were not well-done but that they were done at all. The Serampore translations could probably be best compared for significance with the work of Wycliffe and Tyndale (though their translations of the Bible were into English only). There were errors in their translations as well but these were due to the state of knowledge at the time. Subsequent research has thrown new light on the interpretation of ancient languages. Carey was translating from Greek and Hebrew (which he knew imperfectly) *via* English into Asian languages which he had to acquire for the purposes of translation. No grammars or dictionaries were available to help him; he had to devise his own as he went along.

Carey himself, aided by his learned Indian pundits, is credited with the fantastic achievement of having translated the *entire* Bible into Bengali, Oriya, Marathi, Hindi, Assamese, and Sanskrit; and parts of it into twenty-nine other languages. That, whatever the standard of translation, points to amazing dedication and industry. When the work of the other members of the Serampore team is added, the tally of Bible translations runs to Armenian, Assamese, Bengali, Burmese, Chinese, Gujerati, Hindi, Kasmiri, Malay, Marathi, Naipali, Oriya, Panjabi, Pashto, Persian, Sanskrit, Thai, Tamil, Telugu and twenty-seven other languages or dialects. There can have been few parts of Asia where the Serampore translations could not be read and understood.

It is this breadth of vision of making God's Word available to all mankind in its own tongue that is Carey's chief glory. 'Go ye therefore, and teach all nations. . .'[6] That a man of such limited education and from such humble origins could imagine and put into operation with so few helpers an undertaking of such magnitude surely earns him the right to be described as a great man. He could so easily have said with Gideon 'Oh my Lord, wherewith shall I save Israel? Behold, my family is poor in Manasseh, and I am the least in my father's house.'[7] But William Carey already knew and had faith in what would be his Lord's reply: 'Surely, *I will be with thee*.'[8] God's transforming power as surely invested William Carey as it did Gideon, as it did the first apostles.

Once he was convinced of his missionary call, Carey put his complete faith in God to guide him and to supply all his needs. 'Expect great things from God' had been the first part of his command at the Association Meeting in Nottingham in 1792. Though the expectations were not always met in the form or at the time Carey anticipated, nonetheless, he would claim that the help did always come and to an ever-increasing extent. Thus he was able to 'achieve great things *for* God.' The blessings were not a reward for work done; they were a pre-requisite for carrying out the work.

Many scholars since Carey's time have produced more accurate, more graceful translations of the Bible into the languages of Asia but the Serampore missionaries provided the foundation on which those later translations could be built.

It is impossible to measure the results of the work of the Serampore team. At the outset, it was of necessity an act of faith which might not show fruit for many, many years. Carey and his colleagues were convinced that if once the Word of God was placed in a man's hands, the Book in itself would be sufficient to effect its work of transformation and salvation. Sadly, this hope was not realised to any measurable extent. Indeed, as far as can be ascertained, none of the thirty or more pundits who worked at Serampore helping with translation was Christian and there is no record of any of them being converted and baptised. Preaching that *expounded* the scriptures was necessary if their message was to be fully understood. To say this, however, is not to deny that the scriptures by themselves may not have had great influence, even if the readers were not converted.

Although the main output from the Serampore press was Bibles and tracts, there were other works as well: grammars, dictionaries, text books for Fort William College and for the schools, as already mentioned. In addition, they produced

Christian literature and carried out official printing first for the Danish authorities and later for the British Government in India.

In yet another aspect of translation work, Carey was ahead of his times. In order to understand Hinduism and to be able to counter its doctrines, Carey felt it was important to make available in English for missionaries and others the *Vedas*, the ancient sacred writings of the Hindu religion. As early as 1805, the Asiatic Society and the College of Fort William had been allowing the Baptists Rs. 300 monthly (£37.50) 'to assist . . . in translating and printing the Sangskrit writings, accounted sacred, or scientific.'[9] The *Ramayana*, the translation of which had been destroyed in the fire, compares with the Greek poems ascribed to Homer. Carey and Marshman had been sufficiently foresighted to appreciate the value of such works to historians for the understanding of cultural traditions. After all, the civilisation of India was more ancient than that of the West. Andrew Fuller, on the other hand, when he read of the project, declared such work 'obscene'.[10] However, as the proceeds from the commission were being used to help finance the printing of Bibles, Carey and Marshman felt no guilt on their consciences:

> It makes us smile . . . when we consider that Satan will probably here be overshot in his own bow. He certainly did not intend when he dictated those vile and destructive fables, that the publishing of them to the enlightened world, should supply a fund for circulating the oracles of Truth.[11]

Last among the achievements of the Serampore press were the books written in the Bengali vernacular. Ram Boshoo followed his *Biography of Pratapaditya* with *Lipa Mala* (*Bracelet of Writings*). Other pundits produced *The History of Raja Krishnu Chundra*, *Tota Itihasu* (*Tales of a Parrot*) and other works. Carey contributed his *Colloquies* in Bengali. Up to the advent of the Baptist missionaries, Indian vernacular literature had been largely oral in character. Sushil Kumar De, an authority on nineteenth century Bengali literature, credits Carey with raising Bengali 'from its debased condition of an unsettled dialect to the character of a regular and permanent form of speech, capable, as in the past, of becoming the refined and comprehensive vehicle of a great literature in the future'.[12] It would not be an exaggeration to say that the Serampore missionaries contributed to the renaissance of Indian literature in the nineteenth century.

Such encomiums, however, also lay in the future. Carey would not have welcomed them in 1812; he saw in the fire the chastening hand of God. 'I am fifty-one years old the seventeenth of this month,' he wrote to Andrew Fuller in August, 1812. 'I have been now almost nineteen years in the work of the mission, and seem as if I had but just gotten over the principal obstructions which blocked up the threshold of the door.'[13] It was characteristic of him, however, that he used those stumbling blocks as stepping stones to greater achievement. How truly he described his attitude to the constant setbacks to his work when he told his nephew 'I can plod. I can persevere. . .'[14]

The fire had three direct results. First of all, the missionaries redoubled their efforts and, like the phoenix of eastern mythology, a new and even more efficient press rose from the ashes of the old, printing new and more scholarly translations. Immediate financial help, to the extent of Rs. 7,000 (£875) came from such local friends as George Udney, Chaplain Thomason and from Carey's students at the college.

The second and greatest result of the fire was that the work of the Mission became publicised throughout Britain. What had been known to a few dedicated supporters now became a household word. The letters reporting the fire did not reach England until September 1812 but once they did, the response was overwhelming. Insurance in the modern sense was only just beginning to be established. Certainly the Serampore missionaries had no cover for their properties so their need was great. However, money flowed in, not just from Baptist churches but from Free Churches of all denominations, and from Anglican churches as well. The loss occasioned by the fire totalled between nine and ten thousand pounds; this vast sum was contributed in a mere two months. Edinburgh churches (Scotland was always generous) contributed £800, Bristol £400, Birmingham £320. Carey's first little church at Moulton raised £50 – as much as they had paid him during his whole five years' ministry with them. Even the tiny congregation at Hackleton, among whom Carey had worshipped when an apprentice, sent £7. William Wilberforce contributed £10 and Mrs. Beeby Wallis, in whose back parlour the Baptist Missionary Society had been founded, contributed a staggering £20. The Bible Society undertook to send out 2,000 reams of paper. Andrew Fuller travelled the length and breadth of the country to rally support. And all this at a time, 1812, when Britain was still locked in combat with France, with its disastrous effects on trade; when corn prices had risen from 43 shillings a quarter in 1792 to an unimagined height of 126 shillings a quarter in 1812; when war had again broken out between the United States and Britain over the latter's restriction of neutral commerce with the continent and insistence on the right to search American ships. The loss of 1,600 British merchant ships to American guns, besides being a humiliation, added to the scarcity and high cost of goods in England.

The third result of the fire was a demand for a likeness of William Carey. The new supporters of his work had for the most part never met him. Andrew Fuller had a portrait of Carey, painted before he left for India, but this was probably done by a hack artist rather as today a photograph might be taken. Fuller describes it as follows:

> . . . I have got bro^r Carey's likeness in my parlour: but I do not like his black coat & stiff old powdered wig.[15]

This is probably the portrait that hangs in the Library of Regent's Park College, Oxford. It is small and badly executed and not at all flattering.

Accordingly, William Ward was instructed by the Society to arrange for a portrait of suitable distinction to be painted. He engaged the services of Robert Home (1752–1834) 'then deemed the best artist in Asia'.[16] He had been a pupil in London of Angelica Kauffmann and had gone out to India in 1790. He first came to prominence with the *Select Views of Mysore* which he painted for Lord Cornwallis in 1794. He had painted the Wellesley brothers for Government House; also Sir William Jones, founder of the Asiatic Society.

The Home portrait of Carey also hangs in Regent's Park College (which is the descendant of that Stepney Baptist College in which the painting was originally hung). The colours are somewhat subdued – whether by age or intent – but the portrait is striking, It depicts Carey as a mild-faced, balding, middle-aged man in European dress seated, pen in hand, at his work of translation. It is not a brilliant painting – the eyes are too lack-lustre – but it depicts a strong face and a tranquil one, with level brows and a resolute cleft chin. The mouth is firm but surprisingly delicate, with the merest hint of a smile lifting the corner. The hands, too, are delicate for a man who began life as an artisan. He is surrounded by his books and papers. Parts of the Sanskrit version of Acts 2, v.11 ('We do hear them speak in our tongues the wonderful works of God') have been meticulously copied onto the manuscript before him. Beside him sits his pundit – a pale, slight, sharp-featured figure. 'His likeness is a very good one,' commented Carey, though his smallness of stature gives somewhat the impression that he has been deliberately reduced in scale to give more prominence to his master. This is reminiscent of the style of Egyptian paintings (though not so exaggerated) where Pharaohs were depicted as much as ten times larger than their subjects in order to emphasise their superiority. Carey would not have approved of exaggeration for this purpose.

Engravings of the portrait were circulated throughout Britain at one guinea each and the money so raised went to the work of the Society.

In the midst of the rejoicing over the generous response to the appeal for funds and the acclaim of the missionary work that the portrait signified, Andrew Fuller sounded a warning note:

> The fire has given your undertaking a celebrity which nothing else, it seems, could; a celebrity which makes me tremble. The public is now giving us their praises. Eight hundred guineas have been offered for Dr. Carey's likeness! If we inhale this incense, will not God withhold his blessing, and then where are we? Ought we not to tremble? Surely, all need more grace to go through good report than through evil. . .
>
> When the people ascribed 'ten thousands to David', it wrought envy in Saul, and proved a source of long and sore affliction. If some new trials were to follow, I should not be surprised; but, if we be kept humble and near to God, we have nothing to fear.[17]

Fuller was more prescient than he knew, though the incident which led to Serampore's 'long and sore affliction' did not at the time seem to have any particular significance.

Two new missionaries arrived at Serampore in 1812. John Lawson was a professional type-cutter whose services were quickly pressed into use following the fire. He was particularly useful in 'improving the Chinese types'. Dr. William Johns (who brought with him possibly the first missionary nurse, Miss Chaffin) not only cared for the health of the Mission members but was appointed medical officer of the town of Serampore. Neither man held a licence from the East India Company. It appeared at first that no objection would be raised to their presence. Lord Minto, the Governor-General, was (according to Carey) 'a friend to liberty . . . not . . . a persecutor'.[18] They were more fortunate than the American team of missionaries who arrived later in the year. The Judsons, the Newells, the Notts, Luther Rice and another man named Hall were all refused permission to enter India and had in consequence to settle elsewhere. Americans were not acceptable in British India owing to the state of war that existed between the two countries. '. . . There is a very strong sensation agst America in Britain,' wrote Andrew Fuller, 'as having sort (*sic*) its ruin at a time when the world was in arms agst her. American missionaries will not be admitted into British India. Is not Burmah the place for them. . .'[19] The Judsons did in fact go on to Burma; the others stayed in Mauritius.

However, a crisis arose towards the end of 1812. John Chamberlain has already been mentioned as having a natural propensity for trouble. On a visit to Agra, he incurred the displeasure of Government authorities by his virulent attacks on the Moslem and Hindu religions alike. His behaviour was considered likely to cause a breach of the peace. Despite warnings to moderate his language and to restrict his activities, Chamberlain clashed with the military commander in Agra who had him arrested and sent down to Calcutta. Although he was released almost immediately, the incident revived the suspicions harboured by Government officials against missionaries in general. The Serampore Trio were by now inviolate. They had proved their ability in various directions; they had friends in high places both in England and in India; they were also famous for their literary achievements.

'Had you been a company of illiterate men,' Fuller had written to them perceptively, 'you must ere now have been crushed.'[20] The position of Johns and Lawson was not so secure. On 5th March, 1813, they were ordered to leave for England by the next ship out of Calcutta.

It would have been thought that Johns' official position in the community would have been reason enough for him to stay. The Government themselves had appointed him medical officer at Serampore. This availed him little. A scapegoat was needed. Despite strong protests from Marshman, Johns was deported. Surprisingly, Lawson was allowed to remain – perhaps because his work on the printing of Chinese was of some use to the East India Company over its trade with China.

It was sad that the first actual, as opposed to threatened, deportation of a missionary took place at a time when public opinion in England was being mobilised to make the Company change its policy regarding missionaries. The debate on the renewal of the East India Company's Charter opened in the House of Commons on 22nd March, 1813. Wilberforce turned with redoubled vigour to the cause he had promoted unsuccessfully in 1793. 'Now the Slave Trade is abolished,' he said 'the exclusion of missionaries from India is by far the greatest of our national sins.'[21] He campaigned tirelessly to organise petitions to Parliament supporting his cause. 837 petitions were presented, representing over half a million signatures. He enlisted the aid of the churches, of the missionary societies and of the Abolitionists who had supported his campaign against slavery. Andrew Fuller flung himself into the campaign with his usual energy. Public opinion in England had been mobilised to such an extent, he wrote enthusiastically to Serampore, that the presentation of petitions 'was not a shower, but a set rain'.[22]

In Parliament, former Governors-General were called upon by both sides to support their cases. Warren Hastings, now an old man, stirred up the fears left by the Vellore Mutiny. Lord Wellesley, declaring his support of the Serampore missionaries, stated that he 'never knew of any danger arising from the missionaries' proceedings'.[23] Charles Marsh, lately of Madras and now Member of Parliament for East Retford, castigated the missionaries as 'these apostates from the loom and anvil, these renegades from the lowest handicraft employments. . .'. Wilberforce spoke of them as 'these great and good men'. He described the work of the Serampore Mission, in particular praising Carey and telling the House how he made over the whole of his salary from Fort William College (£1,500 a year) to the work of the Mission. 'By the way,' Wilberforce wrote afterwards, 'nothing ever gave me a more lively sense of the low and mercenary standard of your men of honour, than the manifest effect produced upon the House of Commons by my stating this last circumstance. It seemed to be the only thing which moved them.'[24]

Whether it was indeed the knowledge of Carey's selflessness, or the half-million petitioners, or the cumulative force of argument that impressed the House, Wilberforce won the day. The 'Charter Renewal Bill as Amended by the Committee of 28 June, 1813' included a clause stating that it was the duty of Britain 'to promote the interest and happiness' of the Indian people by taking 'such measures . . . as may tend to the introduction . . . of useful knowledge, and of religious and moral improvement' and that facilities should be afforded by law to persons wishing to go to India for that purpose.

The first person to receive a licence from the Company to work openly in India as a missionary was Carey's nephew, Eustace.

14

Backbiting and Building

1814–1820

Lord Moira succeeded Lord Minto in Bengal in 1813. He was not the first Governor-General to show friendship to the Serampore missionaries but he was certainly the first to be able, officially, to request them to extend their missionary activities. After his predecessor's expeditions of 1810 and 1811 had placed the East Indies under British control, the islands needed a Governor and Sir Stamford Raffles was appointed. As soon as news reached him of the so-called 'pious' clause in the 1813 Charter of the Company, he applied to Lord Moira for missionaries and Malay Bibles to be sent to the Moluccan island of Amboyna. This request was passed on to the Serampore Mission and in January, 1814, Carey had the joy of seeing his nineteen year old son Jabez baptised, married and ordained, all in three days, in order to take up this appointment. Felix and William, Jnr. both came home for the event.

On Felix's return to Burma, however, the vessel carrying him and his family up the Irrawaddy River to the capital, Ava, capsised in a storm. Felix's second wife and his children were drowned. In addition, a printing-press, gospels and the manuscript of Felix's Burmese dictionary were also lost. His cousin Peter (son of Carey's soldier brother Thomas) was killed about the same time in a riding accident. He had joined the Army like his father and had been delighted to be posted to India where he could meet his now-famous uncle. A month after the accident – too late to see his older brother before he died – Eustace Carey arrived from England to join the Serampore team.

It would have been thought that the relaxation of controls on missionary work would have heralded an era of renewed blessing in India but such was not to be the case. William

Johns had taken hard his expulsion from India. When he arrived back in England, he complained bitterly of his treatment at Serampore, accusing Joshua Marshman in particular of being half-hearted in his efforts to have the deportation order set aside. His criticisms came at a time when some members of the Society at home were beginning to question the lack of supervision from England of the Serampore enterprise. Andrew Fuller was both aware and afraid of this questioning. He urged his friends in India to beware of a 'speechifying committee' which would have a 'fondness for multiplying rules and resolutions'.[1] He reiterated his belief that Serampore should be self-governing '. . . for two reasons. One is, we think them better able to govern themselves than we are to govern them. Ano^r is, they are at too great a distance to wait for our direction.'[2]

Yet these questionings and anxieties stemmed directly from the success of the work in India. In the early days of the Baptist Missionary Society, the 'Home Trio' – Fuller, Sutcliff and Ryland – had been able to cope with all the work involved in fund-raising and sending out supplies. Now that operations were on so much wider a scale, they could no longer manage alone. As early as 1812, nineteen members had been added to the Committee. Most of these had no personal acquaintance whatever of any of the Serampore team. There was pressure to move the headquarters of the Mission's operations to London. As long as Fuller lived, he was able to keep control from Kettering. Sutcliff was nearby at Olney for consultation; only Ryland was at any distance – he had moved to Bristol. However, on 14th June, 1814 John Sutcliff died.

These were only distant rumblings of the storm to come. In India, Carey had more immediate problems to face. It was disappointing enough to him that his youngest son, Jonathan (now seventeen or eighteen years of age) had not yet affirmed his faith in Christ. The bitterest blow came in December 1814 when Felix resigned from his missionary work to become ambassador in Calcutta from the King of Burma. Many fathers would have rejoiced at such an appointment but Carey wrote home bitterly: 'Felix is shrivelled from a missionary into an ambassador.'

The young man was held in high esteem by the King of

Burma who supported his missionary translation work. Moreover, Felix had studied medicine for a while before going to Burma and introduced the practice of smallpox vaccination into that country – for which advance he earned the approval of the East India Company.[3] This must be one of the earliest instances of vaccination being practised in the East for it was still a somewhat controversial innovation. The English physician who introduced it, Edward Jenner (1749–1823), first performed public vaccination in 1796, using his own son as the subject.

Felix arrived in Calcutta and began to live in ambassadorial state with 'a red umbrella with an ivory top, gold betel box, gold lefeek cup, and a sword of state'.[4] He lived in such splendour, in fact, that he soon ran into debt. He had never recovered completely from the shock of losing his family. He became sick both spiritually and mentally. Possibly, even, he may have inherited from his mother some tendency to mental instability. He began to drink heavily and sank deep into debt. Eventually, his father had to draw on his own savings to quieten Felix's creditors. The strain on Carey's finances was considerable and the whole unhappy episode was a distress and humiliation for him.

There appears to have been some confusion over Felix's letters of credit as an ambassador. After seven months in Calcutta, he was recalled in disgrace to Burma. Fearful of the King's displeasure, he abandoned his position at court and fled across the border into Assam. It was a strange period of aberration in an otherwise brilliant career.

News of the ending of the long struggle of the Napoleonic Wars with the Battle of Waterloo in June 1815 must have seemed of little importance against the much more personal and shattering news of Andrew Fuller's death on 7th May, 1815. He was sixty-one. He had been a true and faithful 'rope-holder' from the first days of the Society. He was the Mission's chief apologist and had driven himself almost to the point of exhaustion during the long campaign two years earlier for the 'pious' clause in the East India Company's new Charter. He was tireless in raising money, preaching, writing letters and, above all, praying for the work at Serampore. In the administration of the Society's affairs, he wrote to William Ward, 'we have never had a speech among us from the beginning; all is prayer and brotherly consultation. . . We talk things over till we agree. . .'[5]

The last of the 'Home Trio', John Ryland, took over as Secretary to the Society after Fuller's death. Unfortunately, he was not able to exert such a firm control as his predecessor. Being President of Bristol College, he was unable to attend closely to the Society's affairs and much of his work had necessarily to be left to assistants. None of the new men could remember Carey. He had been twenty-two years in India. It was sixteen years, even, since Ward and Marshman had sailed from England. With no chance of face-to-face discussion, with letters taking months to reach their destination and their intention even then being possibly misinterpreted, the climate was suitable for the growth of the distrust and bitterness between India and England that was to sadden Carey's next fifteen years.

His first unease is expressed in a letter to Dr. Ryland dated 14th October, 1815. The Society was contemplating retrenchments in the missionary work in Java and Ceylon. Serampore opposed any reduction at all in the number of stations. Such retrenchment seemed to Carey a denial of the 'pressing demand' of 'Divine Providence'. Christ's command was 'Go ye into *all* the world and preach the gospel'.[6]

> I intreat, I implore you in England not to think of the petty shop-keeping plan of lessening the number of stations to bring them within the bounds of their present income, *he wrote*, but to hand all their attentions and exertions to the great object of increasing their Finance to meet the pressing demand. . .[7]

Ward endorsed his view that they should expand their work in the sure faith that God would provide. He insisted that the home churches should be prepared to contribute more. '. . . Make England, Scotland, Ireland and America ring with the cry of your need,' he wrote.[8]

New missionaries did come out to India. In 1816, an engineer named Randall arrived to help run the paper-mill. A schoolmaster named James Penney came out the following year. Not all new missionaries, however, fitted in with the strictly disciplined and self-denying life of the Mission. Calcutta beckoned. There was more excitement there, more European society. For example, William Yates, the shoemaker from Carey's former church at Harvey Lane, Leicester, who had arrived in 1815, demanded 'a separate house, stable and servants'.[9] Of William Moore, Carey had written '. . . indolence and a thirst for European society are his bane'.[10] This was a situation Carey had feared for some time, despite the pressing need for more assistants. He had stressed in letters home that new recruits should not expect necessarily to remain in the secure havens of Serampore or Calcutta where they could preach to European congregations. Their duty as missionaries was to preach to Indians and they must be prepared to serve at the various out-stations.[11] Moreover, at all times the decision as to where new missionaries should serve lay with the Serampore Trio.

Unfortunately, the responsibilities and functions of the home Committee had never been clearly defined. In his *Enquiry* Carey had suggested that home supporters should encourage missionaries by prayer and gifts. The foundation meeting of the Society in 1792 had appointed a home Committee but had failed to define its terms of reference. None of this mattered so long as Fuller, Sutcliff and Ryland were in charge at home, and Carey (with, later, Marshman and Ward) in India. These men knew and trusted each other. Nor did this trust encompass only the posting and duties of missionaries; it extended to the handling of money. Although scrupulous accounts were kept of the relatively small amounts of money sent out from England, the Serampore Trio had never felt an obligation to nor had they been required to account to the home Committee for the very much larger sums of money they raised in India by their own efforts.

With the death of Fuller and Sutcliff this happy, if somewhat casual relationship ceased. Johns' complaints about Serampore did not pass unremarked in England. Whispers grew into rumours, and rumours into slanders that the missionaries at Serampore were amassing private fortunes. Nothing could have been further from the truth. Apart from small sums to cover the necessities of life, everything the Trio earned was ploughed back into the Mission. When enquiries reached him as to his handling of the Mission's finances, Carey was stung into as near anger as he was ever to show in his letters from India:

> . . . Beloved Fuller, with one scowl of his brow, would have dissipated a thousand such insinuations! . . . Were I to die today, I should not leave property enough for the purchase of a coffin, and my wife would be entirely unprovided for. . .[12]

But, of course, Fuller was no longer there to scowl. There were new men in charge in England and they could scarcely be blamed for not understanding the involved finances of the Mission. Perhaps the new Committee were over-conscientious in their enquiries but if there had indeed been any misuse of funds in India, they could have been accused of negligence not to uncover it. But the Trio in Serampore were wounded that any suspicion should attach to them. They were all ageing; they had spent themselves unstintingly under most trying conditions. *They* knew their integrity. How could anyone outside question it?

When the home Committee demanded that all the property at Serampore – schools, printing-press, church, houses – should be transferred to the care of trustees (three in Serampore but eight in England) the Trio refused point blank. Instead, they drew up a declaration whereby the property was held in trust for the Baptist Missionary Society by the Trio alone and by any future trustees they themselves might appoint. In fact, this was merely giving legal form to the existing state of affairs but it caused alarm and suspicion in England. Protests passed back and forth between the home Committee and Serampore. Carey wrote a long sad letter to Ryland begging the Society through him 'not to attempt to exercise a power over us'.[13] He reminded the Society that in the quarter century he had been in India, the amount of money received from England (including money raised after the fire) would scarcely have been sufficient to pay the European staff over the period. All else – the salaries of native preachers, the schools, the land and buildings in Serampore, Calcutta, Patna, Rangoon, etc., the type-foundry, the printing-works, the paper mill, all the equipment and stock – had been paid for by the missionaries themselves out of their own earnings. They had borrowed money and worked to pay back the loans with interest. In these circumstances, they would not agree to their affairs being ruled and over-ruled by some unknown trustees in England, however worthy they might be as individuals. 'We are your Brethren . . . not your servants,' he concluded.[14]

What finally touched off the explosion in India was the arrival from England in August 1817 of Mr. and Mrs. William H. Pearce. Pearce was the son of Carey's 'beloved' friend, Samuel Pearce of Birmingham. He had been a printer with the Clarendon Press in England and was therefore eminently qualified to assist William Ward. On both counts, therefore, he would have been a welcome addition to the Serampore team. The hurt to the Serampore Trio lay in the fact that Pearce and his wife had been *directed* to reside at Serampore by the home Committee. Always up till that point, missionaries had been *invited* to stay on at Serampore after a sufficient residence had shown that they would fit in with the close-knit 'family' there. In retrospect, it seems a small matter to cause so great an upheaval but it was really only the spark needed to set alight the fuel of discontent that had already piled up.

It has been said that the greatest trial of a missionary is often another missionary. The new men at Serampore had been sent out by the post-Fuller administration and they were no doubt in sympathy with the Society's desire to exercise greater control over the pioneer missionaries. Moreover, influenced by Johns' complaints at home – particularly against Joshua Marshman – they approached Serampore in a critical frame of mind. Eustace Carey was particularly bitter. They chafed at the self-imposed disciplines of the Serampore elders. Perhaps, in fairness to the new missionaries, the 'Seniors' were somewhat autocratic. Serampore was *their* creation. They had long experience of India. It would not be surprising if their attitude was dogmatic. Moreover, all three were on the defensive. Marshman was bitterly hurt at the criticisms levelled against him. Ward was overworked and in failing health. Carey was grieved at the growing controversy that strained relations both at Serampore and with England; grieved also at the news of his father's death a few months earlier; at Felix's continued wanderings in Assam. Moreover, he was suffering as the result of an accident earlier in the year. He had been returning home in a horse-drawn buggy when the harness broke. The horse was mettlesome and seemed likely to bolt so Carey leapt from the carriage for safety. He damaged his foot in the process – an injury from which he never fully recovered for he was lame to the end of his days. All three men were feeling the strain of many years in the debilitating climate of Bengal with no home-leave or even vacation in India during their long service.

It is a profitless exercise at this distance of time to attempt to apportion blame for the break between the 'Senior' and 'Junior' missionaries. It is sufficient to state that in 1817, Yates, Lawson, Penney, Pearce and Eustace Carey (all under twenty-six years of age) left Serampore to establish an independent mission station in Calcutta. Their organisation was similar to that in Serampore except that it was subordinate to the Baptist Missionary Society. All money earned was handed over to the Society in return for a salary. They had a printing-press, church and schools, all of which they were well-qualified to run. Yates made translations, Pearce ran the press, Penney the school, Lawson the type-foundry. All of them, with Eustace Carey, were engaged in preaching in chapels and bazaars – but only on the opposite side of the Hooghli from Serampore.

The quarrel would not have been so public had they set up their mission at a distance. There was a crying need in Chittagong, in Sumatra, in Assam, in Rajputana. The highest officials in the East were now begging the Serampore missionaries to open schools and mission stations. The Governor-General, Lord Hastings, invited Carey and Marshman to dinner with him at Barrackpore to beg for schools to be opened in the newly-acquired province of Rajputana. Sir David Ochterlony, who had extended the boundaries of British India north from Bengal to the foothills of the Himalayas, wrote for assistance in the new territories over which he was Resident. Sir Stamford Raffles asked for missionaries for Sumatra. After all the years of struggling against official disapproval, it must have been a bitter disappointment to the Seniors that the long hoped-for new missionaries ignored the challenge of fresh fields and chose to work in that part of India where the ground had already been well-tilled – Calcutta. In the event, Jabez Carey (who had returned from Amboyna after its return to the Dutch at the end of the Napoleonic Wars) went to Rajputana and William Ward's son went to Sumatra.

To establish their Mission almost on Serampore's doorstep, to set up a rival church to the Lall Bazaar chapel, to draw their pupils from the same catchment area as the Marshmans, to run their printing press in competition with Serampore's own was, to say the least, 'indelicate' (to use William Ward's description). How could the Christian church hope to give an effective witness if it showed itself divided? It was all a bitter grief to Carey yet, with a restraint that does him great credit, he made no mention in his letters home of the schism (as he called it) until the break was complete and the 'Calcutta Missionary Union' was officially established. He stoutly defended Marshman, against whom most of the Juniors' criticism was levelled and laboured patiently to heal the breach. He admitted there were 'grudges and collisions'[15] and 'much pride . . . on both sides'[16] but he still hoped that the differences could be settled in a Christian manner.

The tragedy was that when news of the schism did reach England, the home Committee tended to take the part of the young missionaries who had gone out to India under their sponsorship. To most of the Committee, the Serampore Trio appeared awkward and intransigent. They had forgotten (if, indeed, they ever realised) that from the day of his appointment – in fact, until the day of his death – Carey himself received less than £600 from the Society's funds. From his earliest days in Bengal, he earned his own living and, out of the success he made of his various undertakings in India, he himself contributed something in the region of £40,000 to Baptist missionary work in India. This sum must represent at least half a million pounds in modern terms, probably considerably more. If the amount earned by Marshman and Ward be added, all of which was used to purchase land, buildings, plants, type, etc., the Serampore Trio's material contribution to missions was impressively large, quite apart from the dedicated labour they gave. All that Carey, Marshman and Ward required was to be trusted to run the mission in the way they considered best.

But there was to be no trust, no peace. The controversy continued, fuelled and re-fuelled by letters and pamphlets on both sides. It did not, however, impede the progress of the work at Serampore. If anything, the Mission seemed to be challenged to even greater effort.

In 1818, the Mission decided to launch into magazine and newspaper production. Their first venture into the field of journalism was a monthly magazine in Bengali, *Dig-Darshan* (*The Signpost*). It was primarily educational, not religious, in character. It was published for use in schools, to induce a habit of reading for pleasure, and contained articles on various aspects of history, adventure, agriculture, industry, botany, zoology and the like. In a way, it was a forerunner of the *Feed The Minds* campaign of today's Christian church. The Calcutta School Book Society alone purchased a thousand copies each month. With large print-runs, it was possible to keep the price of the magazine low and therefore within reach of even poor families. The success of *Dig-Darshan* prompted the issue of a weekly newspaper in Bengali for adult readers. *Samachar Darpan* (*News Mirror*) was, according to J. C. Marshman (later its editor) the first western-style newspaper to be printed in an oriental language.[17] There was some uncertainty at first as to whether the newspaper would give offence to the Government but instead Lord Hastings commended their endeavours 'to excite and to gratify a spirit of inquiry in the native mind by means of a newspaper'.[18]

The third Serampore periodical was the English-language monthly, *Friend of India*, which, besides publishing general news and opinion, provided a forum for discussion of the many social evils against which the missionaries continued to campaign. Three such were the still-prevalent practice of *sati*; the inhuman treatment of lepers who were frequently buried or burned alive; and the needless deaths at the *melas*, the great religious pilgrimages. A few weeks before the fire at Serampore, Carey had sent home a moving description of the Hindu indifference to the value of human life:

> While I am writing the drums employed in the worship of idols, in their great processions, are beating – *Idolatry destroys more than the sword*. Yet in a way which is scarcely perceived I reckon that 10,000 women annually burn with the bodies of their deceased husbands. The custom of half immersing persons supposed to be dying undoubtedly occasions many deaths. To enumerate all the methods of destruction would furnish an account which might exceed credibility, yet not exceed the truth. The numbers that die in their long pilgimages from want,

> or fatigue, or from dysenteries and fevers caught by lying out and want of accommodation, is very great. To mention only one idol, the famous Juggunnath of Orissa, to which 12 or 13 pilgrimages are made every year. The numbers that go thither in one of these pilgrimages is supposed to be on some occasions 600,000 and at scarcely any time less than 100,000. There cannot be less than 1,200,000 attend in the year. Now if only one in ten of these die, the mortality caused by this one idol would be 120,000 annually. But instead of one in ten *dying*, some are of the opinion that not many more than one in ten *survive*, and return to their own homes.[19]

William Ward who, with John C. Marshman, produced the periodicals, had from the beginning shown a sympathetic understanding of the Indian mind and a quick grasp of Bengali. Now, to Carey's great joy, he was joined by one of the finest Bengali scholars of the day, the ex-missionary, ex-ambassador Felix. On a visit to the Chittagong station early in 1818, Ward had established contact with Felix once again. Carey's eldest son had been travelling in Assam ever since his flight from Burma, botanising, studying the various dialects and gathering political information. During these three years of wandering, he had recovered his spiritual and mental health. Ever since his 'teens, Felix had loved William Ward like a second father so that it took little persuasion to bring him home to Serampore. In addition to working on the newspapers, he translated Bunyan's *Pilgrim's Progress* into Bengali for use in Fort William College; also *A History of British India and of England* and he wrote a treatise in Bengali on anatomy and physiology, *Vidyahara Vali*.

Bringing Felix back into the fold was the last contribution William Ward made to the work of Serampore before leaving for America and England for a much-needed period of leave. While in England, he tried to explain to the Committee the position at Serampore, to allay their fears that he and his colleagues had gained illegal control of the Mission property and that it had been bought with Society funds. But their attitude had hardened. 'Here the matter is brought to an issue,' he wrote to his colleagues. 'There is no chance of union with the Society but by acknowledging their supremacy.' This the Serampore missionaries could not bring themselves to do.

> Nothing I ever met with in my life – and I have met with many distressing things – *Carey wrote to his son, Jabez*, ever preyed so much upon my spirits as this difference.[20]

After twenty-five years in India, Carey and his colleagues could count some six hundred baptisms and a few thousand supporters. Set against India's millions, this was hardly the rapid conversion of which Carey had had such sanguine hopes when first he embarked upon his missionary venture:

> . . . Africa is but a little way from England, Madagascar but a little further. South America and all the numerous and large islands in the India and China Seas, I hope, will not be passed over. A large field opens on every side. . .[21]

Indeed, he could have applied to himself and his colleagues Andrew's despairing words to Jesus when he showed him the five barley loaves and two small fishes which were all the food available to feed a hungry multitude: 'What are they among so many?'[22] Sometimes he chafed at the slow progress. Writing to Jabez, he complained that people appeared 'as insensible as ever' to Christianity.[23] Yet he knew that God's transforming power could show how to spread their influence as surely as He divided the loaves and fishes among the five thousand. They would establish a College to train converted Indians in missionary work.

Study of Reformation history had taught them that persistent labour in education by scholarly men over many years had been necessary to rescue the peoples of western Europe from the supersititions then attaching to the Church of Rome. *Ergo*, how much more scholarship would be necessary to rescue India from darkness? How could preachers counter the centuries-old mysteries of Hinduism, the fanatical hold of Islam, if they had no knowledge themselves of the literature of these religions, let alone a sound knowledge of the Bible and of Christian precepts?

As early as January, 1795, Carey had outlined in his *Journal* a scheme for a school which he and Thomas had planned to set up in which the study of Sanskrit, Bengali and Persian was blended with Bible teaching, western science and literature. Now, the Serampore missionaries planned to extend this idea.

Already in Calcutta there was Fort William College for the

higher education of young Europeans. The Hindus, seeking to give their own young men an education of equal standard, had instituted a similar college (Vidyalaya) in Calcutta through the efforts of Rammohun Roy, with emphasis on such subjects as English and western science. Well-to-do young Moslems were catered for by their Madrassa (College) also in Calcutta.

On 15th July, 1818 Carey and Marshman issued their prospectus of a 'College for the instruction of Asiatic, Christian and other youth in Eastern literature and European science'. The prospectus made it clear that the purpose of Serampore College was evangelisation. 'If ever the Gospel stands in India', it read, 'it must be by native opposed to native in demonstrating its excellence above all other systems' and '. . . the evangelisation of the country must be accomplished through the vernacular tongues.' Serampore College would be unique, however, in that, although primarily a divinity school, it would bring higher education to Indians regardless of caste or creed; that, in addition to the western subjects, it would give instruction in Sanskrit and Arabic, so opening the door to knowledge of India's ancient literature and philosophy and to the literature of Islam. Only in this way would the Indians themselves be able to compare the new message of salvation with what had been offered before, to allow truth to grapple with error, light with darkness.

It was a natural progression from the free schools the Mission had founded for low caste and outcaste children in Mudnabatti, Serampore, Calcutta, Cutwa – indeed, wherever their presence was felt. Only if Indians were educated could they grasp for themselves the message of truth and pass it on to their fellows. Serampore did not seek to turn Indians into Europeans; rather its aim was to draw out what was best in India itself and harness that for the glory of Christ. India must produce its own evangelists and its own interpretation of the Christian message – a point made in this century by the Christian Indian mystic, Sadhu Sundar Singh.

It was all the more creditable when it is remembered that the Serampore missionaries had themselves no collegiate experience nor, indeed, was it very often the practice at that time for any Baptist ministers to receive college training. The gift of the Holy Spirit was considered to be all-sufficient for a minister's needs. Carey and his colleagues realised that if their new Christian teachers were to be able to out-argue the brahmins, they must be as well-versed in the brahmins' own learning as in their Christian studies. 'Out-Sanskrit the pundits, and then add such knowledge of the Scriptures and of Western science that, stronger than your antagonists, you may foil them with their own trusted weapons, and capture their spoil.'[24]

Moreover, Serampore College was not to be just a Baptist College but open to every Christian denomination in Asia. 'It will be time enough a hundred years hence,' they said, 'when the country is filled with knowledge and truth has triumphed over error, to think of sects and parties. Every public institution, aiming at India's betterment ought to be constructed on so broad a basis as to invite the aid of all denominations.'[25] This ecumenistic approach was in itself evidence of Carey's maturity and broadened outlook. Some of his earlier tirades against the Catholic Church do him little credit, even allowing for the prejudices of the age in which he lived. To give an example, he wrote in 1798: 'I also see in the Calcutta papers that the pope was dying, the cardinals fled, and priests marrying, last June. I hope it was true; and also that the old gentleman is dead and buried, and that no more of his seed or sort may any more exist in the earth.'[26] By 1807, his attitude had modified considerably. Writing to John Chater, he said 'If you should be introduced to Roman Catholic priests, show towards them every degree of frankness, and in a prudent manner seek their confidence, and do them good offices.'[27]

Serampore College was built to accommodate two hundred students. Not all would be potential preachers – most would be teachers, doctors, lawyers. It was not even insisted upon that all students should be Christian. The founders had the vision to see that education was to a certain extent a *prerequisite* to the spread of Christianity. Even if it did no more, such rubbing shoulders by Christian and non-Christian would break down barriers of prejudice. The only distinction between Christian and non-Christian students was that the latter were not accepted as boarders. This was for the entirely practical reason that differences of caste, social customs, diet, etc. would complicate the domestic arrangements of the College.

Building work began in 1818 on over five acres of land, part of which was given by the King of Denmark, the remainder purchased by the Mission. For the rest – for staff, equipment, books, support for poor students – they had to rely on their own resources and on help from other quarters. Lord Hastings was their first patron and gave them Rs. 1,000 (£125). Charles Grant, the former Chairman of the Court of Directors of the East India Company who had been a benefactor of the Mission in so many ways, gave them Rs. 2,000 (£250). The Government met the cost of a medical professorship. Baptists in Britain and (after a visit by William Ward) in America contributed £5,000 towards the expenses of the *theological department only*. Such strictures indicated the wisdom of the Serampore missionaries in maintaining control of their own affairs and declining to be ruled from home. Many Baptists in England and America would have preferred the college to refuse entry to non-Christian students. Indeed, William Ward was requested by the Society not to solicit money from Baptists at all but to confine his applications to those 'friends of religion who are best able to appreciate the value of *literature*.'[28]

Such a narrow-minded approach only serves to emphasise the wider vision of the Serampore missionaries as contrasted with the blinkered outlook of much of the Baptist denomination at that time both at home and in America and India. Both William Yates and Eustace Carey denounced the idea of admitting non-Christians. Eustace in particular derided the 'literary institutions' at Serampore, seeming to regard Christianity and literature as incompatible. Despite such carping criticism, however, the College continued to prosper. The imposing classical style buildings which survive to this day were completed in 1821. Such was his respect for the missionaries' enterprise that in 1820 King Frederick of Denmark awarded to each of the Serampore 'Seniors' a gold medal as a token of his approbation.

As if the College and periodicals were not sufficient new undertakings, Carey found the time and energy to further another scheme long dear to his heart. He had always had an interest in botany and over the years had experimented in his garden at Serampore with seeds, bulbs and plants sent from all parts of the world – from wherever he happened to have correspondents.

In everything to do with his garden, he was very methodical. 'Indeed,' wrote an Edinburgh student, Mr. Leslie, who visited Carey in 1824, 'he carries method into everything he does; classification is his grand hobby, and wherever anything can be classified, there you find Dr. Carey; not only does he classify and arrange the roots of plants and words, but visit his dwelling, and you find he has fitted up and classified shelves full of minerals, stones, shells, etc., and cages full of birds.'

Now, in September 1820, with the active support of the Governor-General's wife, Carey founded an Agri-Horticultural Society. In the Society's prospectus Carey wrote:

> In one of the finest countries in the world, the state of agriculture and horticulture is so abject and degraded, and the people's food so poor. . . India seems to have almost everything to learn about the clearing of jungles, the tillage of wastes, the draining of marshes, the banking of river-courses, the irrigation of large areas, the mixing of composts and of manures, the rotation of crops, the betterment of tools and transport, the breeding of stocks, the culture of new vegetables and herbs, the planting of orchards, the budding, grafting and pruning of fruit-trees, the forestation of timbers. . .

His enthusiasm and attention to detail were boundless. He hoped to attract 'Native Gentlemen' to become members and officers of the Society; also that zemindars (landlords) would be encouraged to increase their incomes through improving the land rather than increasing their rents. Lord Hastings gave them land at Barrackpore on which to try out experimental crops and arranged a Government grant of Rs. 1,000 (£125) per annum to aid the work. They began by planting coffee, cotton, tobacco, sugar-cane and cereals. It was again a far-sighted enterprise, one for which there is still a need today if the problems of feeding the starving millions of India are ever to be solved. It must have been at once a joy and a relaxation for Carey to visit the Society's trial fields and a relief from the close and tedious work of translating and teaching. 'I hope it will ultimately be of great benefit to the country,' he wrote to Dr. Ryland.[29] Though Carey's hopes for the Society proved, in the event, too optimistic, he had at least tried to do something to improve the lot of those he called his fellow-countrymen. 'My heart is wedded to India,' he wrote in 1825.[30]

Despite the distress of the breach with the Society in England, these were busy and productive years. Respected and successful in India, happy in his marriage, proud of his sons' contributions, it would be expected that Carey, now rising sixty, could pass his remaining years in peace. It was not to be. 'God has a sovereign right to dispose of us as he pleases,' Carey had written to Andrew Fuller after the fire of 1812. 'We ought to acquiesce in all that God does with us and to us.'[31] Carey was to need that trustful submission throughout the next few years.

15

Bitter Disputes

1821–1827

In 1820, old mad King George III died and his eldest son, who had been acting as Prince Regent since 1811, ascended to the throne as King George IV. The first year of his reign was disgraced by his public attempt at divorce through the *Bill of Pains and Penalties* against the Queen. The Bill dragged its way through the House of Lords with ever-decreasing majorities and was eventually abandoned. Caroline survived a few more months as Queen and died in August, 1821, unloved and unlamented.

If news of these events reached Serampore, Carey could well have contrasted his own happy marriage with the scandal of the King's. Ever since 1808, Charlotte had provided a still centre for Carey's busy and anxious life, had shared with him what Marshman called 'her blended Christian simplicity and patrician polish'. No doubt some of that grace brushed off onto her husband and enabled him the more easily to move in the Governor-General's circle across the river at Barrackpore, to command respect in the various Societies in Calcutta of which he was a member. No doubt Charlotte was also responsible for strengthening the ties with her husband's scattered family. She was in constant correspondence with them all and, according to their admiring letters about her, was able to give them the loving counsel they had never enjoyed from their mother. It appears that, contrary to expectation, her health even improved after her marriage. Charlotte describes in a letter how, during one of Carey's bouts of illness, she found the strength return to her legs so that she was able to move around again and nurse him.

However, by the end of 1820, her health deteriorated markedly. Carey would carry her in his arms to a chair outside so that she could enjoy the fragrance of the garden he had made. Her death came on 30th May, 1821, at the age of sixty.

'We had been married thirteen years and three weeks,' Carey wrote to Ryland[1] 'during all which season, I believe, we had as great a share of conjugal happiness as ever was enjoyed by mortals.' There is something particularly touching about 'thirteen years *and three weeks*'. It has the freshness of a child, as if every moment of his marriage was counted and treasured. 'Her soul was continually engaged . . . in prayer or in the reading of God's Word,' he wrote to Jabez. 'Next to that she lived for me. She never did a thing during the thirteen years we lived together without consulting me, even though she was sure of my consent. She watched every change in my countenance with the utmost solicitude, and often was full of anxiety, if she perceived the least sign of weariness, illness, grief or distress. My loss is irreparable . . . I am very lonely.'[2]

His closest friends in England were dead; his father was dead; the Marshmans' eldest daughter died shortly after Charlotte. It was years since he had seen his sisters, and their letters to him were few. William, Jnr. and Jabez were in distant stations. William Ward was in England on furlough and Hannah Marshman was there also. These separations, added to his alienation from the Society at home, must have deepened his sense of isolation. Then in August 1822, Krishna Pal died of cholera. He had been the Mission's first native convert and had worked with courage and dedication for his Saviour. Despite being mobbed and beaten for his new faith, he had remained a fervent Christian, the first of many native missionaries to go out from Serampore to minister to the needs of his own people. Later that year Felix died of a liver complaint at the age of thirty-seven. His death deprived Carey not only of a beloved son but also of a much-needed translator. William Ward returned from his four-year furlough in England and America towards the end of 1822, refreshed and eager to take his part in the running of the College and in the production of the various periodicals. He flung himself with his usual enthusiasm into the work but, tragically, for only a few months. On Wednesday evening, 5th March, 1823, he preached 'very impressively'; on Thursday, 6th March, he was in the printing office till the early afternoon; by 5 p.m. on Friday, 7th March, he was dead. Such is the speed at which cholera attacks and claims its victims. He was only fifty-four. He had always had an ability to understand young men, most notably in the case of Carey's sons, each of whom he had in turn influenced to make a decision for Christ. 'I think God has endued you with a talent for the young. . .' Fuller had written to him many years earlier. 'They naturally open their minds to you. He has given you Felix and Wm. Carey and perhaps more.'[3] William, Jnr. wrote from Cutwa: 'My heart bleeds for you all . . . Mr. Ward was very dear to me. How often has he upheld me, when my feet well-nigh slipped! He was my spiritual father. . .'

One by one, all those most dear to Carey were dying. When news arrived in 1825 that John Ryland – the last of his 'ropeholders' – had also died he realised that, apart from his sisters, there was no-one left in England to whom he mattered. 'Wherever I look,' he wrote, 'I see a blank. Were I to revisit that dear country, I should have an entirely new set of friendships to form.'[4]

New friendships had been needed in India, too. In January, 1823, Lord Hastings had finally given up the Governor-Generalship after a decade's tenure. Though Wellesley had outshone him in dignity, style and originality, Hastings had nonetheless proved an able administrator. He had completed the work of Wellesley in establishing British dominion over the whole of India and had put down decisively the revolts of the Pindaris and Mahrattas. With the resultant more settled conditions in India, the country became more prosperous. There was at last money available to establish schools for native Indians – a course in which, as has been seen, Lord Hastings enlisted the aid of Serampore. He was also responsible for the decision to protect the East India Company's China trade by allowing Sir Stamford Raffles to occupy Singapore in 1819. Hastings had been a good friend of Serampore (and Lady Hastings had been, also) and he even became patron of a Mission for Seamen which Carey opened in Calcutta.

His successor, Lord Amherst, arrived in August, 1823 and immediately had to cope with the problem of making the north-east safe against the Burmese who were over-running Assam. John Chater, who had worked as a missionary with

Felix Carey in Burma, was now in Ceylon – but if this was a cause for relief, Carey had other trials.

On 8th October, 1823, he had another bad fall. This time it was on the ghat at Serampore as he alighted from his boat. The injury to his thigh was serious enough, but in addition he developed a severe fever and once again his life was despaired of. Medical science was still crude. Carey writes of 'one hundred and ten leeches . . . applied to the thigh'.[5] Lord Amherst sent his personal surgeon out from Calcutta to advise on treatment. Carey pulled through but was unable to walk for several months and then on crutches. He was carried in a chair into his classes at Fort William and Serampore College, and into the pulpit to preach.

Shortly before this fall, William had married for a third time. His new wife was Grace Hughes, a widow of forty-five. William was sixty-two. She was gentle and affectionate and Carey told Jabez that 'her constant and unremitting care and excellent nursing took off much of the weight of my illness. . . We live in great happiness'.[6] They enjoyed a good relationship and Carey was delighted when, shortly after her marriage to him, she asked for baptism, along with her daughter by her first marriage.

Yet it seemed as if Carey was to be subject to the trials of Job in reverse. His dear ones had died, he had been smitten in his body. Now his chattels were to be taken from him. The whole of lower Bengal was overwhelmed by disastrous floods towards the end of 1823. Houses and cattle were swept away and the Mission was helpless to alleviate the suffering so caused, having suffered extensive damage to its own property. The school buildings were seriously damaged; Carey's own home was destroyed and his beautiful garden was washed away.

Whereas in 1812, Fuller had whipped up support at home and had raised within two months sufficient funds to make good the damage suffered in the fire, now there was no help forthcoming from England. Slander had stifled the generosity of Baptists at home towards the work at Serampore.

With the dogged perseverance that he displayed in the face of every discouragement, Carey set to work to restore the damage. The first mail ship out of Calcutta after the flood carried with it his orders for bulbs and seeds. To pay for these and for repairs and replacements at the Mission, he took on the additional work of translating Government Statutes into Bengali – a task which brought in £450 a year – though Carey commented wryly that translating *Ephesians* into Bengali was child's play compared with these involved legal documents! Despite financial difficulties, the Serampore mission further increased the number of their out-stations in Bengal. News flowed in of baptisms in distant stations – of a Brahmin in Delhi, of a Chinese in Sumatra and so on. 'In due season, ye shall reap, if ye faint not.'[7]

In these later years, Carey was becoming well-known not only for his work as a translator and orientalist; his distinction as a botanist was recognised in 1823 by his being elected a Fellow of the Linnaean Society of London, one of the world's most distinguished botanical societies. He was elected a member of the Geological Society and became a 'corresponding member' of the Horticultural Society of London. His favourite flowers were lilies, the members of the *Amaryllidaceae* family, and he had the honour of having one (*Careyanum*) named after him by its producer, Hon. & Rev. W. Herbert. As his students and Marshman's pupils grew up and dispersed to their various avocations, they shared Carey's enthusiasm for plants and sent him specimens from wherever they were stationed – Edward Gardiner from Nepal; W. B. Martin from Amboyna; David Scott from Assam.

In addition to his other multifarious duties, Carey was still regularly engaged in revision and correction of the various Scriptural translations coming off the Serampore press. If not much detail of these activities is given for this period, it is because the account would tend to be repetitive. Eustace Carey in his *Memoir* writes of this period: 'I have not . . . thought it expedient to publish so largely upon this . . . period of Dr. Carey's life . . . because the bulk of his correspondence is occupied with the controversy pending at the time between the Serampore missionaries and the parent institution.'

What Eustace Carey does not reveal is that he himself refuelled the dying fires of the controversy – although, in fairness to him, the breach was healed many years later and his *Memoir* of his uncle is a reverent and admiring work. Failing health had compelled him to return to England in 1825. By this time the breach in India was healed; the quarrel at home less so. Eustace's criticisms of the Serampore missionaries (particularly of Marshman who had, unfortunately, a somewhat autocratic manner) was listened to and believed in Baptist circles in England. For a time, even, Carey's own sisters turned against him. Jabez, too, briefly joined with those who accused Dr. Marshman of 'aggrandisement'. In vain did Carey point out that the Marshmans were as poor as he.

Hannah Marshman's diaries bear witness to the truth of Carey's assertions that they lived modestly:

> We lately purchased a palanquin carriage for the use of our school. But what a burden it was on my mind. . . Nor could I bear to see either of our brethren become coach-drivers; it does not become a minister of the gospel. . . My chiefest dread was lest it might prove a curse to us, and bring down God's anger upon us – being a deviation from the simplicity of our manners for the last fifteen years. But today the carriage has gone, and I desire to thank and love God, Who has mercifully delivered us from this burden. . .

That is hardly the writing of one desirous of 'personal aggrandisement'.

Carey himself on 15th July, 1819[8] wrote eleven pages of indignant and scornful refutation in answer to a letter from Rev. Dyer charging Marshman with the above-mentioned 'aggrandisement'. A few quotations will give the flavour of Carey's defence:

> . . . Some person, we know not who, told some one, we know not whom, 'that we had been often at Lord Hastings's table, but that Brother Marshman's table far exceeded his'. I have also been at Lord Hastings's table (I mean his private table), and I do therefore most positively deny the truth of the assertion. . . I suspect the informant *never was at Lord Hastings's table*, or he could have not been guilty of such misrepresentation. Lord Hastings's table costs more in one day than Brother Marshman's in ten. . .
>
> . . . Brother Marshman retains for the school a French master, a music master, and a drawing master. The expenses of these are amply repaid by the school, but Brother Marshman's children . . . have the advantage of their instructions. . . *Envy*

has not failed to charge him with having retained them all for the sake of his own children. . .

. . . I have no doubt but my collection of plants, aviary, and museum would be equally impeached as articles of luxury and lawless expenses; though, except the garden, the whole of these expenses are borne by myself. . .

. . . I disapprove as much of the conduct of our Calcutta brethren as it is possible for me to disapprove of any human actions. The evil they have done is, I fear, irreparable; and certainly the whole might have been prevented by a little frank conversation with either of us; and a hundredth part of that self-denial which I found it necessary to exercise for the first few years of the mission, would have prevented this awful rupture. I trust you will excuse my warmth of feeling upon this subject, when you consider that by this rupture that cause is weakened and disgraced, in the establishment and promotion of which I have spent the best part of my life. . .

. . . As to Brother Marshman, seriously, what do they want? . . . Would they exclude him from the mission? Judge yourself whether it is comely that a man, who has laboriously and disinterestedly served the mission so many years . . . should be arraigned and condemned without a hearing by a few young men just arrived, and one of whom had not been a month in the country before he joined the senseless outcry? Or would they have his blood? . . .

. . . As a missionary I could go in a straw hat and dine with the judge of the district, and often did so; but as a Professor in the College I cannot do so. Brother Marshman is placed in the same predicament. These circumstances impose upon us a necessity of making a different appearance to what we formerly did as *simple* missionaries; but they furnish us with opportunities of speaking to gentlemen of the first power and influence in government, upon matters of the highest importance to the great work in which we are engaged. . .

Carey complained bitterly that 'except for Mr. Burls and Ryland, no person belonging to the Committee has, since Fuller's death, written me a single letter of friendship'.[9] 'I cannot write freely to the Society's secretary,' he states on another occasion, 'because his letters resemble those of a Secretary of State.'[10]

Marshman travelled to England on furlough in 1826 and

personally attempted a reconciliation with the home Committee. The result was disastrous. Relations between the Society on the one hand and Serampore and its nineteen out-stations on the other were severed completely by a declaration signed by Mr. Dyer for the Baptist Missionary Society and by Joshua Marshman on behalf of the Serampore missionaries. The rock on which all negotiations foundered was always the same: who should have control of the Serampore monies, personnel and properties. This severance of relations was followed by three years of bitter attack on Serampore in Baptist magazines in England.

That the squabbles were between people who claimed to be Christians was the greatest grief. The troubles aged Carey more than any demands of work or climate. Letters written by visitors to Serampore during the long years of the quarrel with the home Committee give a picture of a shabby, elderly man, though still vigorous in his mind.

> Dr. C. is a very equable and cheerful old man, in countenance very like the engraving of him with his pundit. In body, however, he is now much inferior, being rather less in size, and not so robust. Nor does he wear such a fine dress as is given him in the plate. His general costume is white stockings, nankeen breeches, and white waistcoat, a round white jacket and an old black hat hardly worth a shilling.
>
> . . . his dress neat, but antiquated, . . . his countenance mild and benevolent, . . . only in conversation that the vast stores of his mind became apparent.[12]

Jesus had prayed that 'all may be one . . .'.[13] That was the ideal at which Carey had aimed from the time of the Cape of Good Hope 'pleasing dream' of 1806 to the foundation of Serampore College. At a time when there was a stronger movement in England towards religious tolerance towards all denominations than there had ever been in the church's long and turbulent history, it was tragic that the Baptist denomination should be so riven – and not over weighty matters of doctrine, but over petty details of housekeeping. 'Satan has indeed gained an advantage over us,' Carey wrote.[14]

If he could have met the Committee himself, things might have been different. Whatever bitter criticisms were spoken and written about the Serampore missionaries, Carey's name always commanded respect. But from the very beginning of his ministry in India, Carey had known that he was unlikely ever to return to England. As long ago as 1796, he had written to his friend, Andrew Fuller, 'We must not expect, I suppose, ever to see each other in this world any more. I account this my own country now, and have not the least inclination to leave it . . .'.[15] And when pressed some years later to return to his home country, Carey wrote to his friend Steadman: '. . . I should be obliged to say more than I am disposed to. So I fear my going to England would neither be useful nor comfortable . . .'.[16]

So Serampore with its subsidiary stations stood alone, confident in the rightness of its cause, confident also that it could support itself financially in the future as it had done since its foundation in 1800.

Carey had stated in a letter of 1796: 'I am not concerned about politics.'[17] However, it was impossible for him to isolate himself from politics and their consequences. 1826 brought the end of the Burmese War which had occupied the whole period of Lord Amherst's Governor-Generalship. Though the result of the war had finally gone to the British, together with the acquisition of the entire seaboard from Assam to Malaya, its prosecution had been inefficient, lacking in initiative and enormously expensive. It had cost twelve times as much as the Pindari and Maratha campaigns put together. The repercussions of that war would leave their mark on Serampore – but not just yet. For the moment Serampore's fortunes were riding high in India.

Its crowning achievement came in 1827 when the King of Denmark granted a Charter to Serampore College with authority to grant degrees in all Faculties. It was a splendid 'first' for India, a triumph for the Mission's 'consecrated cobblers',[18] a magnificent tribute to the vision of its founders. From his heart Carey could indeed say: 'Expect great things *from* God; achieve great things *for* God.'

16

Undefeated

1828–1834

Wars create as many problems as they solve. The long struggle with France that ended in 1815 had removed the threat of conquest and, in the settlement that followed, had secured for Britain the sea route to India by giving her the Cape of Good Hope and Mauritius. But though Napoleon had been defeated, the wars which had had their beginnings in revolutionary ideals about the rights of man left a legacy of radical ideas. As poverty in England followed the war, those radical ideas erupted in such demonstrations as the Derbyshire 'Insurrection' of 1817 and the tragic Peterloo Reform Meeting of 1819.

The war had left Britain exhausted and in debt, with reforms long deferred and prices driven high by depreciated currency. Unemployment was also high as men demobilised from the army and navy came home to join those made redundant by the growing mechanisation of industry and the employment of women and children in the men's places. Further financial distress was caused by the failure of nearly two hundred joint-stock banks in England during the eighteen-twenties.

Similar problems faced Lord William Bentinck when he took up office as Governor-General in 1828. There was a need for savage cuts in public expenditure to offset the wasteful extravagance of the Burmese War. He needed to save £1½ millions in civil and military services. The axe did not fall immediately, however. First of all he turned his attention to social reform. He set about breaking up the Brotherhood of Thugs, a secret society who worshipped the goddess Kali and were dedicated to robbery and murder. He attacked *sati*. In this, the Serampore missionaries' long campaign against the practice came at last to fruition. Through the columns of

Samachar Darpan and *Friend of India*, the Baptists had continued over the years to draw attention to this inhuman practice, publishing regularly such figures as they could obtain of the number of deaths. It was estimated that between 1819 and 1829, more than six thousand women were immolated in Bengal alone. The missionaries' protests reached an Indian as well as a European audience. It was argued by some that *sati* was undergone by choice on the part of the widow, but *Samachar Darpan* for 10th August, 1819 describes how one widow was three times forced back into the flames despite her efforts to escape. There were other abuses of the practice. *Sati* was not compulsory for child-widows. However, the same paper in its issue of 17th October, 1820 reported a case where relatives of a very rich man falsely declared that his eleven-year-old widow was fifteen, in order that she might burn and his fortune fall to the relatives.

Lord William Bentinck took a year to examine the question of *sati* from every angle but, having once made a decision to abolish it, he over-rode every protest and made an Order in Council on Friday, 4th December, 1829 declaring the practice both illegal and criminal.

This was one Government order that Carey could not translate too quickly into Bengali. The edict reached him on Sunday, 6th December. He even abandoned his regular preaching appointment in order to give the translation his immediate attention. It was truly a day of rejoicing, a positive achievement pointing the way from the superstitious cruelty of the Hindu religion to Christ's loving concern for humanity.

Carey needed such encouragement for, only three months earlier than this vindication of the anti-*sati* campaign, he had been attacked over his dearest project, Bible translation. The September issue of the *Asiatic Journal* had contained a savage onslaught by one Lieut/Col. Vans Kennedy. His article called the Serampore missionaries 'a set of narrow-minded, tasteless, money-making bigots' and specifically criticised Carey's Marathi New Testament as swarming 'with every fault of taste' and 'exactly fit for worms'.[1] Though a distinguished Cambridge orientalist later defended both the accuracy and readability of Carey's translation,[2] the public humiliation at the time must have been wounding. Not that he was ever deterred in his efforts by unkind criticism. His shoulders were broad enough to take it. Joshua Marshman, returning at the end of 1829 from three and a half years' furlough, comments on Carey's continuing vigour and cheerfulness. He still 'rides out four or five miles every morning . . . goes on with his work of translation day by day; gives two Divinity lectures and a Natural History one every week in the College, and takes his turn at preaching both in Bengali and English'.[3]

It was good to have his old friend and colleague back at Serampore. He could bring news that the Duke of Wellington – the brilliant soldier brother of Lord Wellesley, who had been present at the 'Disputation' at Government House in September 1804 – was now Prime Minister in England; that the Test and Corporation Acts that had so long placed restrictions on Dissenters were now repealed; that the Catholic Emancipation Act had brought further religious tolerance to England. This must have been an encouragement to a man who had spent his life fighting prejudice and oppression. He had need of cheer for 1830 – the year that brought King George IV's younger brother to the throne as William IV – was to bring perhaps the worst troubles the Mission had had to face in its thirty-year history.

Carey had always been poor, though during his middle years he had had the use of large sums of money to further his great design for India. Now even that was to be denied him. The Serampore College and Mission lost all the funds they had in India through the collapse of the European Agency Houses in Bengal.[4]

The Agency Houses were established (for the most part around 1783) for the purpose of trading and banking; for buying and selling on a commission basis; as bill-brokers, freighters, shipping and insurance agents; as moneylenders and travel agents. The Houses attracted large deposits as the rates of interest they offered were high. In 1799, Carey had suggested that the Society's funds could be invested in India with a yield of 12 per cent interest.[5] The Agencies enjoyed the confidence of the whole European community in India whose investment in indigo, mines, cotton mills and so forth was often financed by them. However, in the eighteen-twenties, trade was depressed. There was economic depression at home. The cotton trade with China declined through lack of demand. China tea was paid for with Indian opium but the price of opium in Canton dropped markedly so that the cost of tea became proportionately higher. The war with Burma caused further trade difficulties. France, now able, thanks to the conclusion of hostilities, to resume trade in India, competed in the indigo market. There was a super-abundant crop of indigo in 1829 causing a disastrous drop in the market price. Moreover, with the end of the war, many of the partners in the Agency Houses and servants of the Company in India were withdrawing their money and returning to England, thus reducing the amount of capital held by the Houses. The failure of one or two of the smaller Houses to meet their commitments in 1827 caused anxiety in the money market. With loss of confidence in the Houses, less money was invested and therefore less capital was available to meet demands. Panic withdrawals caused Palmer & Co. to collapse on 4th January, 1830. This was the largest and most important of the Agency Houses. John Palmer was known as 'the indigo king of Bengal' yet his company failed for over £2 million sterling. The Calcutta Bank, which had been formed by Palmer & Co. had failed a short time before. The crash brought poverty to many. A majority of parents whose children were in the Marshmans' boarding schools could no longer pay the fees and relied on the missionaries' charity not to turn their pupils away.

This in itself was a big enough strain on the finances of the Mission but there was further anxiety to come. When Lord William Bentinck had assessed the financial chaos he had inherited from his predecessor, he began a programme of retrenchment. Fort William College was the first to feel the axe. It was reduced from a teaching academy to a purely examining body. The teaching staff, including Carey, were made redundant. Although he was, very creditably, given a pension equivalent to half his salary, Carey's income was nonetheless reduced by Rs. 500 (£62.50) per month.

The plight of the Serampore missionaries was now acute. They did not worry for their personal needs; they had done without before and could do so again. But how to support their nineteen mission stations? How to find the money to send for the maintenance of William's sisters in England, one of whom was paralysed? How to support the beloved Charlotte's sister in France, or the orphan whom Carey had sent home to England to be educated? As always in times of stress, the missionaries accepted their plight humbly as a sign of God's chastening. William Robinson who had come out to India in 1806, had served for a time in Java and was now back at Serampore, described their reaction:

> The two old men were dissolved in tears while they were engaged in prayer, and Dr. Marshman in particular could not give expressions to his feelings. It was indeed affecting to see these good old men, the fathers of the mission, entreating with tears that God would not forsake them now grey hairs were come upon them, but that He would silence the tongue of calumny, and furnish them with the means of carrying on His own cause.[6]

Carey sent home an appeal to England. It concluded:

> But a few years have passed away since the Protestant world was awakened to missionary efforts. Since that time the annual revenues collected for this object have grown to the then unthought-of sum of £400,000. And is it unreasonable to expect that some unnoticeable portion of this should be intrusted to him who was amongst the first to move in this enterprise and to his colleagues?[7]

He added: 'Our present incomes even are uncertain.'

Almost immediately, need for further economy caused the Governor-General to withdraw even the Government translation work, bringing Carey a loss of income of a further Rs. 300 (£37.50) per month.

It may be that these anxieties helped Carey and Marshman to agree at last to fall in with the wishes of the Society at home and surrender their independence. They made their peace with the home Committee after sixteen years of bitter misunderstanding. All the Serampore properties were transferred to the care of eleven trustees in England. The only stipulation that Carey and Marshman made was to be allowed to live at Serampore rent-free for the remainder of their lives. In the context of the much greater battles they had had to fight, that for Serampore at last seemed unimportant.

'Blessed be God!' they are said to have cried, 'that we have lived to see this day! Now shall our grey heads go down to the grave in peace!'[8]

This submission and Carey's plea for aid did not go

unheeded. After all the bitterness that had rankled for so many years, the Society reached out in Christian love to rescue the work in India, bringing cheer to Carey and Marshman, bringing strength and encouragement to the younger men, like John Mack, who had joined them after the schism. £1,000 reached Carey in May, 1831 from the new Secretary, Christopher Anderson. The money arrived at a time when Carey's and Marshman's own means were exhausted; when allowances to the mission stations were two months in arrear. Carey had been ill with fever for the past month and the generous gift from England was as healing as any medicine. Even more healing were the letters which, for the first time in years, were gracious and kindly in tone.

Yet even during the crushing anxiety of these months, Carey's application to his work did not falter. In his reply to Anderson he said 'I have still two or three years' work to do, particularly in putting my last corrections to my Bengali and Sanskrit versions of the Bible.' The Bengali Bible (his fifth edition of the Old Testament, the eighth of the New Testament) was completed within the year. 'I have done all in my power to make it correct,' he wrote in June, 1832.[9]

He was nearly seventy-one and the years in India were taking their toll. Hannah Marshman, writing to her daughter in March 1832, says 'Dr. Carey is very poorly, very weak & sinking, particularly in the evenings but is generally up and out in the mornings.' Carey himself wrote to Jabez: 'I am exceedingly emaciated. This does not appear particularly in my face, but is so great in all other parts that my clothes hang about me like bags.'[10]

He took even greater pleasure in his garden where, even at the beginning of the century, he could claim to have 427 different species growing. He worked on the Linnaean system and every plant in his garden carried a metal label with the plant's Latin name. As a tribute to his great friend, the late botanist, Dr. Roxburgh (whose *Flora Indica* he had published) Carey took over the editing of his *Hortus Bengalensis*.

There was to be no peace. Carey's entire life was a struggle and even at this late hour the pattern did not change. The relief gained by the generosity of the Society was soon swallowed up in further financial turmoil.

When Palmer & Co. failed, the other Agency Houses appealed to the Government for help. Business, trade and shipping – all depended on their stability. Realising that there would be a further run on the banks unless confidence was restored, Bentinck agreed to Government loans to the Agency Houses. Even these were not sufficient to stop the slide. One after another, the Banks and Agency Houses collapsed – Scott & Co., then the Bank of Hindostan and the Commercial Bank. The Government refused further aid and the British in India, officials and merchants alike, were reduced to universal poverty.

Towards the end of 1832 a further drop in the price of indigo brought about the collapse of Alexander & Co. for £3½ millions. Carey lost every last penny in the crash. Three weeks later, Macintosh & Co. failed for £2½ millions. The £3,000 Grace Carey had inherited from her first husband was lost. So were all Joshua Marshman's savings; the £1,600 legacy Mr. Fernandez had left for Dinadjpur; £720 of the Jessore School Fund; £800 put aside for a school in Delhi.

'How we are to carry on the stations, I know not,' wrote Marshman in near-despair. 'As a Missionary Committee we have nothing; as individuals, nothing. Yet we dare not faint . . . (great areas of India) . . . have not a soul from whose lips they can hear the Word of Life, save our own workers. We dare not recall them.'[11]

The situation was indeed desperate. Expenditure was cut to the bone and Serampore managed to exist on a small loan. The out-stations were asked to forego their allowances for the time being and to support themselves with 'lay' work, just as Carey had done during his first seven years in India.

God did provide. Three separate sums of £500 reached Serampore from England – fortunately too late to be lost in what proved to be almost the last of the Agency House collapses, that in April, 1833 of Colvin & Co. They were unable to meet demands of over £1 million.

The fatalism of the Indian must be in part due to his country's constantly-recurring disasters. In May 1833 a typhoon hit South Bengal leaving a trail of misery – drowned men and beasts, wrecked vessels, polluted drinking water, devastated crops. Once again Carey's beloved garden suffered. Great mahogany trees that had survived the ruinous floods of 1823 crashed onto his glasshouses and once again destroyed the patient work of the past ten years.

Two months later there was yet another disappointment when the Bible Society withdrew its support from the Mission. Non-Baptist subscribers in Calcutta objected to the use of the word 'baptise' in the sense of 'immerse' in the translations, rather than some less specific word! It is scarcely credible that the life of the Mission could be jeopardised by such minutiae yet such was the case. As early as 1812, Andrew Fuller was writing to Christopher Anderson describing in detail a long argument he had had with another minister on precisely this point.[12] Truly a case of 'straining at a gnat'.[13] This withdrawal by the Bible Society, quite apart from undermining the morale at Serampore, threatened further the Mission's precarious financial balance. However, as so often happens, a setback in one direction brought progress in another. What Baptists in England considered the wrong-headedness of the Bible Society stimulated them to provide further financial support for their maligned colleagues in Serampore! The response was instant and generous, and by 18th September, 1833, John Mack was able to write to one of the out-stations: 'We are now able to restore all your former salaries. God has supplied all our wants. . .'[14]

One thing needed to be done during 1833 – the drawing up with Dr. Marshman and his son of 'the unalterable Statutes of the College' as required by its Charter. It was, as with so many other of Serampore's ideas, forward-thinking. It decided that, 'as learning and piety are the monopoly of no single denomination' that only four of its five Council members need be Baptist. This early step in the direction of ecumenism could not but help the Christian church to give a united witness. Moreover, appreciating the depths of poverty suffered by the majority of Indian people, the Statutes laid down that all degrees conferred by the College should be free of charge. Marriage should not be a bar either to student or teacher; nor should caste, colour or creed disqualify any student. It was, however, laid down that the staff of the College should be professing Christians.

What changes Carey had seen in India! Where at first he had worked illicitly under the cover of being a 'manufacturer', now he and his colleagues were respected allies and co-workers in the social improvement programme of the Government. Where once all Indians had been forbidden any share in the administration of their own country, now the colour-bar had been removed in the Indian Civil Service. *Sati* had been made illegal, and child murder, and in September 1833 news came from England of free trade with India and of the abolition of slavery in the West Indies. This last Carey had prayed for most earnestly ever since his early years in Paulerspury. Could he dare to hope now that slavery could also be abolished in India? Also in 1833, the first mails from home to be brought by steamboat arrived after only sixty-four days' journey. It was another age from the five to six months' hazardous voyage of 1793. Carey had completed all the translations he had planned. He could well say he had 'scarcely a wish ungratified'.[15]

From July 1833 onwards, he suffered a series of strokes which left him progressively more frail, though still clear in mind and, though paralysed for a short period in October, still able to speak. His wife, Grace, cared for him devotedly. When he was too weak to walk, he had wheels fitted to a chair so that he could be pushed around his garden. When he became too frail even to go outside, he sent for the gardeners to talk with him about the plants, and had a painting of a beautiful shrub propped up near his couch so that he could look at it constantly. His last months were passed quietly, reading, writing, sleeping; occasionally, even, protesting humorously: 'After I am gone, Brother Marshman will turn the cows into my garden!'[16] He was very weak, but free from pain.

Always, after Christ, his thoughts were with his garden . . .

with the English daisies that surprisingly appeared in his Bengal garden after shaking out the last fragments of soil and seeds sent by Lord Milton's gardener . . .

with the 'tulips, daffodils, snowdrops, lilies' that he had asked John Sutcliff to send him . . .

with the 'blubils, kings fingers, jonkils, tilips, and snapdragons' sent by a gardener in Pury End . . .

with the foaming hawthorn and green hazel thickets of the Whittlebury Forest of his childhood. . .

His three surviving sons came to be with him: William from Cutwa; Jabez from Rajputana; Jonathan, now an attorney of the Calcutta Supreme Court and treasurer of the Serampore Mission. Lady Bentinck, the Governor-General's wife, was a frequent visitor.

On 8th June, Dr. Marshman – Carey's companion and fellow-worker for thirty-four years – knelt beside the bed of the dying missionary.

'Do you know, dear, who is praying with you?' asked Grace Carey of her husband.

'Yes, I do,' Carey whispered and responded to the gentle touch of Marshman's hand.

A few hours later, at sunrise on 9th June, William Carey slipped peacefully away to join the Lord he had served so faithfully.

He was buried at Serampore alongside the tomb of his beloved Charlotte. At his own request, only a simple tablet marked his grave, bearing the words:

WILLIAM CAREY
Born August 17th, 1761
Died June 9th, 1834
A wretched, poor, and helpless worm,
On Thy kind arms I fall.

Later, contrary to the instruction left in his will, a monument was erected next to his grave and the inscriptions commemorating his death and those of his three wives were fixed to it. This is one of the few tangible memorials to this great and modest man. He had nothing material to leave behind him except his books (which were sold for the benefit of Grace and Jabez Carey) and his collection of shells, insects and other natural objects which were left to the College. His wife received what little money survived the Agency House crashes. The couch on which he died is in the library of Regent's Park College, Oxford.

What else remains?

Two portraits, also at Oxford; an empty cottage and a church minute-book at Moulton; an interleaved copy of *Hortus Bengalensis* (with his notes and additions in small, neat handwriting) in the headquarters of the Baptist Missionary Society in London; his *Journal*; and hundreds of letters.

There is little left, either, of the Serampore and Calcutta where he spent so many dedicated years. Decay soon touches every building in Bengal, and what rain and sun and nature do not destroy falls before the onward march of industry. The College still stands. That was built to last and to this day its classical portico welcomes students from all over India – about two thousand in 1977 although, alas, only seventy of those were studying theology. And in Calcutta, the chapel in Lall Bazaar is still used and has been re-named Carey Baptist Church in the missionary's honour.

But of the Trio's extensive Mission at Serampore, nothing remains but the original tiny church (now part of the Church of North India) where services are held in Bengali in the morning and in English in the evening every Sunday. The large house in which Carey died, which stands next to the College, has been converted into four flats for members of the teaching staff. All else has disappeared, the land having been sold many years ago. In its place are the mills of the India Jute Company whose smoking chimneys dominate the Serampore skyline and whose dust settled in a grey film on the trees in the College gardens. Where once the warehouses stood on the river bank that were used to house the printing-presses after the fire, there are now wharves and cranes to accommodate the busy traffic of barges that breast the muddy river. The schools the Marshmans created have long since disappeared, save for the relic of the main entrance to Hannah Marshman's school for girls. The house where William and Charlotte spent so many happy years was lost in the floods of 1823 and what of Carey's beloved garden survived that and subsequent inundations now lies beneath the foundations of the jute mills.

Far from being 'one of the most beautiful places . . . in India . . . pleasant and healthy'[17] described by Carey's contemporaries, Serampore today is dirty and over-crowded, its population swollen by refugees after Partition in 1947 and now taking the overspill from Calcutta's millions. Where Carey crossed the river by paunceway, today workers pack the train to Howra and cross the river into Calcutta by bridge.

Opposite Serampore, where the Governor-General had his country residence amid 'a park of uncommon beauty'[18] at Barrackpore, there are still gracious gardens for the Governor's residence is today a Police Training College. And the obelisk of the Gandhi Memorial is there, a place of pilgrimage for today's Indians.

The Hooghli still runs grey-green between its low mud-banks, bearing its flotsam of torn foliage and swollen carcases after the monsoon rains. Still also, as in Carey's day, the swift current whirls away the brightly coloured images of Hindu gods consigned to the waters of the sacred river after, so the worshippers believe, the spirit of the god has gone out of them.

For the Indian sub-continent is still largely non-Christian. Indeed, the two faiths Carey fought so strenuously have riven the continent into Hindu India and Moslem Pakistan and Bangladesh. Yet surely Carey's great vision was more than a 'pleasing dream'?

No-one can measure his achievement. But his mark is surely left on India – on its Christian church, still a minority religion but even so upwards of fifteen millions strong. The Baptist Missionary Society which his persistence brought into creation still works in cooperation with the native church in thirty-three stations in the Indian sub-continent, demonstrating through its churches, its schools, its hospitals, its clinics, its agricultural projects that the God of the Christian church is a caring God who knows each sparrow's fall. Carey's Bible translations may have been superseded by more accurate versions but they were the tools he provided for later scholars to reap a harvest for God. Other missionaries from other denominations worked in India both before and after Carey and his colleagues and sought to fulfil Christ's missionary charge in similar ways. Among these, however, the Serampore team were unique as to the form in which they built up their Mission and in the wide-ranging scope of its activities. Theirs was the pattern that others have followed; and though Marshman, Ward and the rest of the Serampore team worked on the building up of the Mission, the plan, the vision was Carey's alone – the plan clearly conceived, the details already worked out as early as his *Enquiry* of 1792.

Out of his abounding faith, Carey always expected 'great things from God' and that faith was not disappointed. All that he received, he spent for his Lord: the money he earned was ploughed back into the Missions; the talents with which he was endowed were used unstintingly in the labour of translation. His family, his possessions, his own life were offered freely. If he did indeed achieve great things *for* God, it was no surprise to him – only the natural consequence of his great expectations.

Carey had a remarkable intelligence which he used with remarkable application. He was patient, persistent, stubborn and humble and faithful. The unsuccessful schoolteacher of Moulton developed into the translator, orientalist and college professor of Serampore. The shoemaker of Northamptonshire took the gospel to India even as the tent-maker of Tarsus did to Europe. It is at once a glory and a wonder that faith in God can so transform a man.

'*Can* any good thing come out of Nazareth?'[19] – or out of Paulerspury?

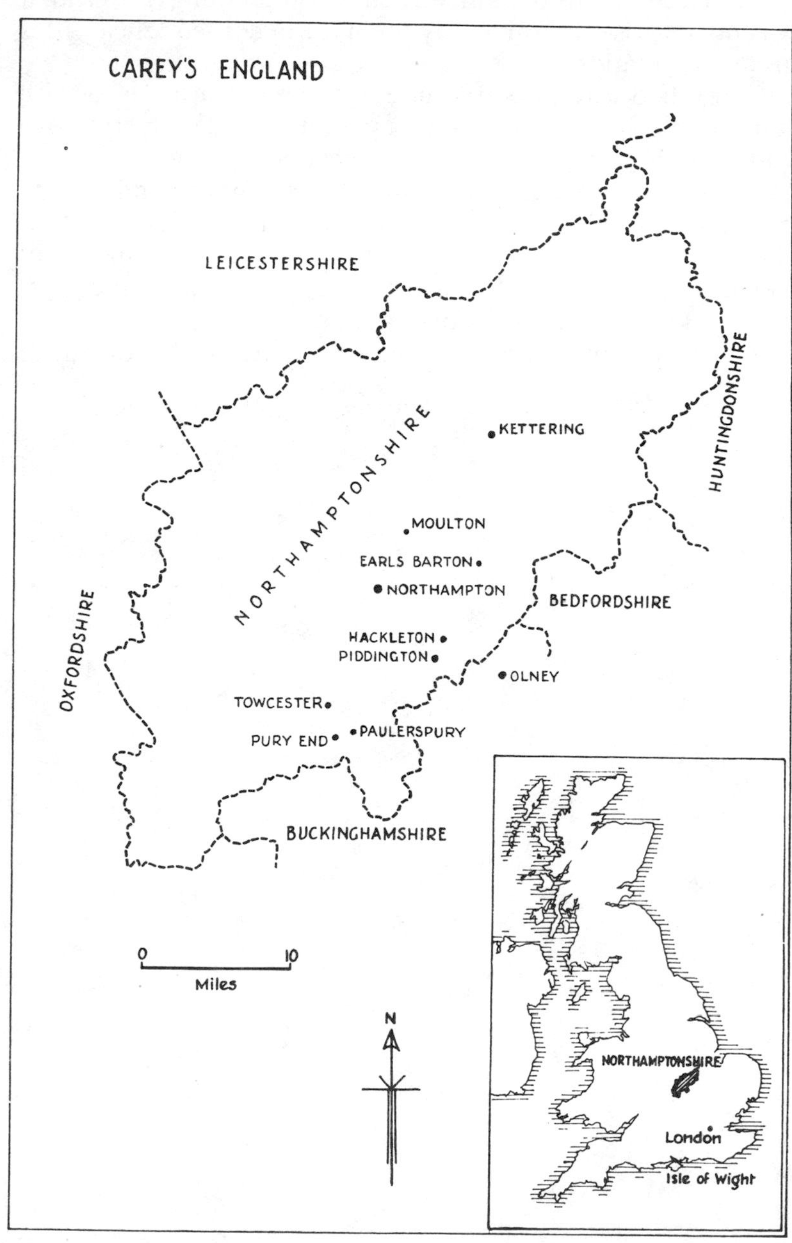
CAREY'S ENGLAND
LEICESTERSHIRE
HUNTINGDONSHIRE
NORTHAMPTONSHIRE
KETTERING
MOULTON
EARLS BARTON
NORTHAMPTON
BEDFORDSHIRE
OXFORDSHIRE
HACKLETON
PIDDINGTON
OLNEY
TOWCESTER
PURY END
PAULERSPURY
BUCKINGHAMSHIRE
0
10
Miles
N
NORTHAMPTONSHIRE
London
Isle of Wight

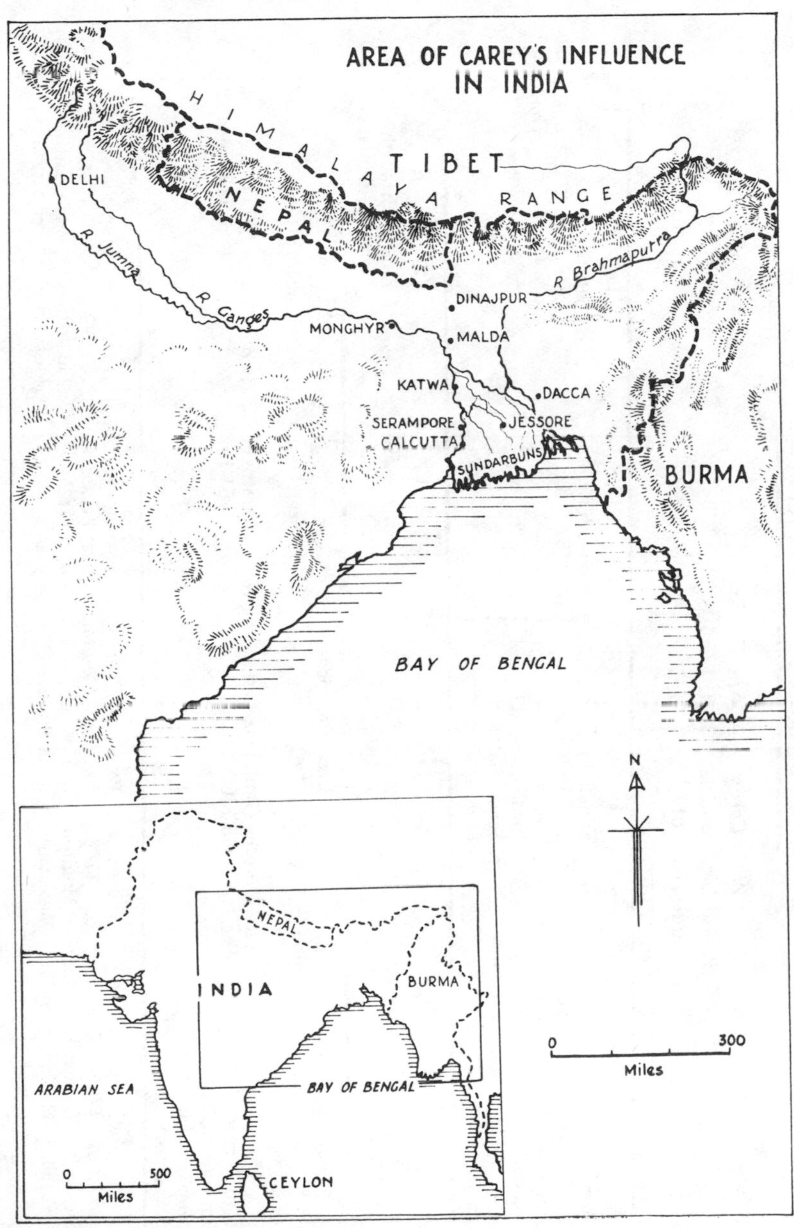
AREA OF CAREY'S INFLUENCE IN INDIA
HIMALAYA RANGE
TIBET
NEPAL
DELHI
R Jumna
R Ganges
R Brahmaputra
DINAJPUR
MONGHYR
MALDA
KATWA
DACCA
SERAMPORE
JESSORE
CALCUTTA
SUNDARBUNS
BURMA
BAY OF BENGAL
N
0
300
Miles
NEPAL
INDIA
BURMA
ARABIAN SEA
BAY OF BENGAL
CEYLON
0
500
Miles

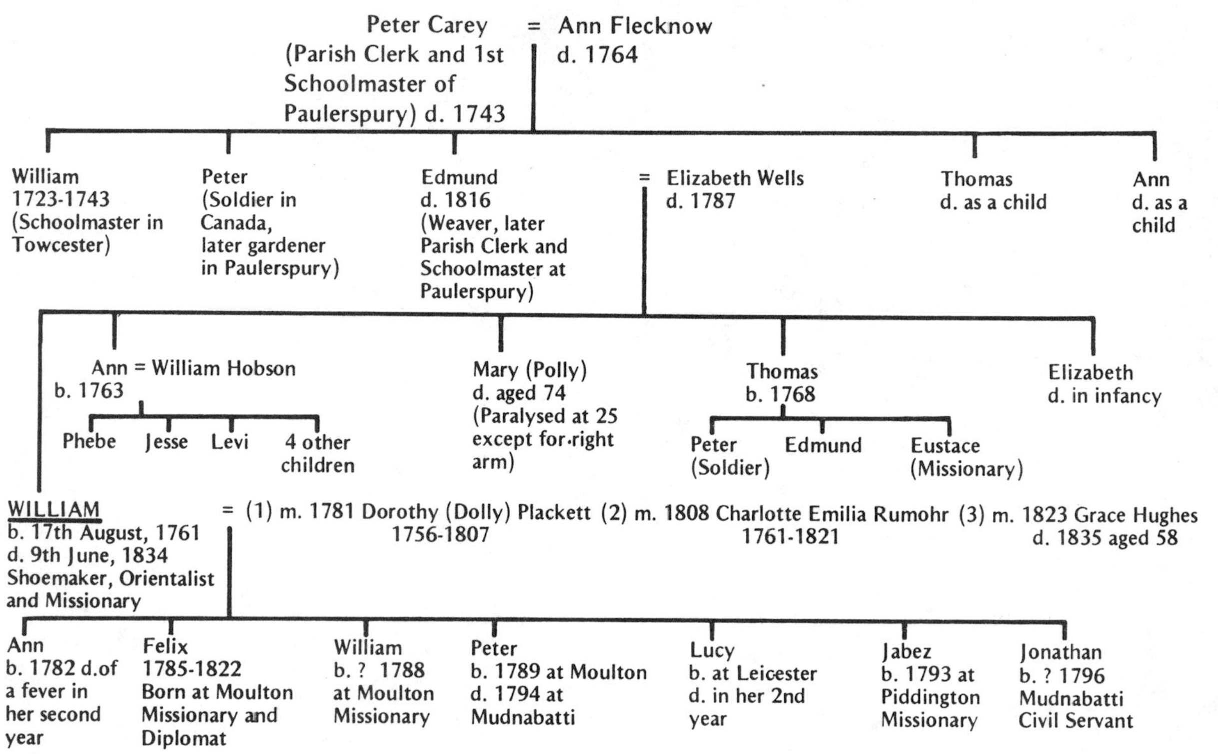
WILLIAM CAREY AND HIS FAMILY
Peter Carey (Parish Clerk and 1st Schoolmaster of Paulerspury) d. 1743
= Ann Flecknow d. 1764
William 1723-1743 (Schoolmaster in Towcester)
Peter (Soldier in Canada, later gardener in Paulerspury)
Edmund d. 1816 (Weaver, later Parish Clerk and Schoolmaster at Paulerspury)
= Elizabeth Wells d. 1787
Thomas d. as a child
Ann d. as a child
Ann b. 1763 = William Hobson
Phebe
Jesse
Levi
4 other children
Mary (Polly) d. aged 74 (Paralysed at 25 except for right arm)
Thomas b. 1768
Peter (Soldier)
Edmund
Eustace (Missionary)
Elizabeth d. in infancy
WILLIAM b. 17th August, 1761 d. 9th June, 1834 Shoemaker, Orientalist and Missionary
= (1) m. 1781 Dorothy (Dolly) Plackett 1756-1807 (2) m. 1808 Charlotte Emilia Rumohr 1761-1821 (3) m. 1823 Grace Hughes d. 1835 aged 58
Ann b. 1782 d. of a fever in her second year
Felix 1785-1822 Born at Moulton Missionary and Diplomat
William b. ? 1788 at Moulton Missionary
Peter b. 1789 at Moulton d. 1794 at Mudnabatti
Lucy b. at Leicester d. in her 2nd year
Jabez b. 1793 at Piddington Missionary
Jonathan b. ? 1796 Mudnabatti Civil Servant

Notes

1 – Schoolboy and Shoemaker, 1761–1784

1. *The Life of William Carey: Shoemaker & Missionary* by George Smith, C.I.E., LL.D. first pub. 1885 (1913 Edition pub. J. M. Dent & Sons Ltd.) p. 6.
2. Letter from Mary Carey to Rev. John Dyer quoted in *Memoir of William Carey, D.D.* by Eustace Carey (pub. Jackson & Walford, 1836).
3. Ibid.
4. Ibid.
5. Letter from Wm. Carey to Andrew Fuller – 14th August, 1804.
6. See 2, op. cit.
7. Ibid.
8. *Daily Life in England in the Reign of George III* by André Parreaux (pub. Geo. Allen & Unwin Ltd., 1969).
9. See 5, op. cit.
10. See 2, op. cit.
11. See 5, op. cit.
12. Ibid.
13. Ibid.
14. See 2, op. cit.
15. See 5, op. cit.
16. Ibid.
17. Ibid.
18. Ibid.
19. Letter from Wm. Carey to Dr. Ryland quoted in Eustace Carey, op. cit.
20. Quoted in *The Nabobs: A Study of the Social Life of the English in 18th Century India* by Percival Spear. O.U.P. 1963 (1st Ed. 1932).
21. See 2, op. cit.
22. See 5, op. cit.
23. See 2, op. cit.
24. See 5, op. cit.
25. Newspaper cutting of 1806 in Beaumaris Gaol, Anglesey.
26. See Hawkin's *Pleas of the Crown*, Vol. i and Holdsworth's *History of English Law*, Vol. xi, 533–4.
27. See 5, op. cit.
28. Ibid.
29. See Smith, op. cit., p. 12.

30. Letter from Rev. Thomas Scott to Mr. Ivimey – 31st January, 1815.
31. See 2, op. cit.
32. See Smith, op. cit., p. 16.
33. *William Carey* by John Brown Myers (pub. S. W. Partridge & Co. Ltd., 1887), p. 19.
34. Quoted in *William Carey, D.D., Fellow of Linnaean Society* by S. Pearce Carey (pub. Hodder & Stoughton, 1923) 5th Ed. 1924, p. 37.
35. See 2, op. cit.
36. Ibid.
37. Ibid.
38. Ibid.
39. See 5, op. cit.
40. Ibid.
41. Published 1781.
42. See 5, op. cit.
43. Ibid.
44. Acts ix, vv. 36–37.
45. See 5, op. cit.

2 – Young Radical, 1785–1792

1. Letter from Mary Carey to Rev. John Dyer quoted in Eustace Carey, op. cit.
2. Quoted in Eustace Carey, op. cit.
3. Eustace Carey, op. cit., p. 623.
4. See 1, op. cit.
5. Smith, op. cit., p. 22.
6. S. Pearce Carey, op. cit., p. 51.
7. Smith, op. cit., p. 22.
8. Eustace Carey, op. cit., p. 626.
9. Per Mr. Thomas of Clipstone, quoted in S. Pearce Carey, op. cit., p. 49.
10. S. Pearce Carey, op. cit., p. 57.
11. *England in the Eighteenth Century (1714—1815)* by J. H. Plumb (pub. Penguin Books Ltd., 1950).
12. *Letters of Anna Seward*, pub. 1811.
13. S. Pearce Carey, op. cit., p. 7.
14. Luke ix, v. 51.
15. Smith. op. cit., p. 22.
16. John vi, v. 9.

3 – '*No power on earth can hinder you . . .*', January–May, 1793

1. Letter from Wm. Carey to Edmund Carey – 17th January, 1793.
2. *William Wilberforce* by Robin Furneux (pub. Hamish Hamilton, 1974), p. 120.
3. Eustace Carey, op. cit., p. 85.
4. Letter from John Thomas to Andrew Fuller – Buddaul, 10th March, 1794.
5. Letter from Andrew Fuller to John Thomas, William Carey, &c. – Kettering, 25th March–25th May, 1794.
6. Letter from Wm. Carey to Andrew Fuller – Ryde, 21st May, 1793.

7. Letter from Wm. Carey to Dorothy Carey – Ryde, Isle of Wight, 6th May, 1793.
8. See 5, op. cit.
9. Matthew vi, v. 8.
10. Letter from John Thomas to Friends in London, 13th June, 1793, quoted in S. Pearce Carey, op. cit., p. 130.
11. Letter from Wm. Carey to the Society – Bay of Bengal, 17th October, 1793.

4 – Passage to India, June–November, 1793

1. Letter from Wm. Carey to the Society – Bay of Bengal, 17th October, 1793.
2. Letter from Wm. Carey to his Sisters – Bandell, 4th December, 1793.
3. The storm is described in detail in Carey's letter, see 1, op. cit.
4. 'Journal' of Wm. Carey – 9th November, 1793.
5. *Memoirs*, Vol. IV (1790–1809) by William Hickey (pub. Hurst & Blackett, 1925).

5 – In the Wilderness, November 1793–May 1794

1. *The Embassy of Sir Thomas Roe*, ed. by W. Foster (Hakluyt Society), vol. ii, p. 344.
2. *History of British India*, by P. E. Roberts (3rd Ed. completed by T. G. P. Spear) (O.U.P., 1952).
3. *History of the Freedom Movement in India*, by R. C. Majumdar (pub. Calcutta, 1962).
4. *The Indian Awakening and Bengal*, by Nemai Sadhan Bose (pub. Calcutta, 1960).
5. Ibid.
6. 'The Christian Missions & Their Impact on Modern India in the Pre-Mutiny Period', by H. L. Gupta (paper delivered at Delhi University, November, 1964).
7. 'Journal' of Wm. Carey – 9th November, 1793.
8. Letter from Wm. Carey to the Baptist Missionary Society – Calcutta, 25th November, 1793.
9. 'Journal' of Wm. Carey – 13th January, 1794.
10. Letter from Wm. Carey to Rev. John Sutcliff – Manicktullo, 3rd January, 1794.
11. 'Journal' of Wm. Carey – 13th January, 1794.
12. See 10, op. cit.
13. 'Journal' of Wm. Carey – 15th, 16th January, 1794.
14. Ibid.
15. Ibid., 22nd January, 1794.
16. Ibid., 23rd January, 1794.
17. Ibid., 19th January, 1794.
18. Ibid., 21st January, 1794.
19. Ibid., 22nd January, 1794.
20. Ibid., 28th January, 1794.
21. Ibid., 5th February, 1794.
22. Ibid., 5th March, 1794.

23. Ibid., 19th April, 1794.
24. Ibid., 18th April, 1794.
25. Ibid., 25th–28th March, 1794.
26. Ibid., 22nd April, 1794.
27. Ibid., 19th April, 1794.

6 – Manufacturer and Missionary, May 1794–April 1795

1. For a detailed account of this incident, see Hickey, op. cit., Vol. iv (1790–1809).
2. 'Journal' of Wm. Carey – 1st March, 1794.
3. Ibid., 25th May, 1794.
4. Ibid., 29th, 30th, 31st May, 1794.
5. Ibid., 7th June, 1794.
6. Ibid., 12th, 13th, 14th June, 1794.
7. Ibid.
8. Ibid., 17th, 18th June, 1794.
9. Letter from Wm. Carey to Rev. John Sutcliff – Mudnabatty, 9th August, 1794.
10. 'Journal' of Wm. Carey – 28th June, 1794.
11. Ibid., 12th, 13th July, 1794.
12. Ibid., 5th July, 1794.
13. Ibid., 5th, 6th, 7th August, 1794.
14. Ibid., 4th July, 1794.
15. Ibid., 5th July, 1794.
16. Ibid., 1st September–1st October, 1794.
17. Smith, op. cit., p. 70.
18. Letter from Wm. Carey to B.M.S. – Mudnabatty, 5th August, 1794.
19. 'Journal' of Wm. Carey – 28th January, 1795.
20. Hickey, op. cit. (Vol. iv).
21. Letter from Wm. Carey to his Sisters – Mudnabatty, 11th March, 1795.
22. Letter from Wm. Carey to B.M.S. – Mudnabatty, 5th August, 1794.
23. Letter from Wm. Carey to the Society – Mudnabatty, 27th January, 1795.
24. Jesuits' Bark (also called Peruvian Bark or Quinquina) – the bark of species of *Cinchona*, introduced into Europe from the Jesuit Missions in South America; used as a tonic and febrifuge.
25. 'Journal' of Wm. Carey – 22nd October, 1794.
26. Ibid., 7th December, 1794.
27. Ibid., 19th, 20th December, 1794.
28. Ibid., 22nd–31st December, 1794.
29. Ibid., 7th February, 1795.
30. Ibid., 23rd February, 1795.
31. Letter from Wm. Carey to Rev. John Sutcliff – Mudnabatty, 16th January, 1798.
32. 'Journal' of Wm. Carey – 9th May, 1795.
33. Letter from Wm. Carey to John Williams – Calcutta, 2nd March, 1803.
34. 'Journal' of Wm. Carey – 3rd February, 1795.

7 – '*Attempt great things . . .*', May 1795–January 1798

1. Letter from Wm. Carey to the Society – Malda, 11th January, 1796.
2. Letter from Wm. Carey to Samuel Pearce – 2nd October, 1795.
3. Ibid.
4. Ibid.
5. Ibid.
6. Letter from Wm. Carey to the Society – Malda, 11th January, 1796.
7. Letter from Andrew Fuller to Wm. Carey – Kettering, 9th August, 1796.
8. Letter from John Thomas to the Society – 13th January, 1796.
9. Ibid.
10. Letter from Wm. Carey to Andrew Fuller – Mudnabatty, 17th June, 1796.
11. Ibid.
12. Letter from Wm. Carey to Samuel Pearce quoted in S. Pearce Carey, op. cit., p. 170.
13. Letter from Wm. Carey to Andrew Fuller – Mudnabatty, 16th November, 1796.
14. Ibid.
15. H. Spencer: *First Princ*. II, ii para. 43, pub. 1862.
16. Letter from Wm. Carey to John Sutcliff – Mudnabatty, 22nd November, 1796.
17. Letter from Wm. Carey to Andrew Fuller – Mudnabatty, 25th March, 1797.
18. Letter from Andrew Fuller to Wm. Carey – 6th September, 1797.
19. Letter from Andrew Fuller to Wm. Carey – 18th January, 1797.
20. Ibid.
21. Letter from Wm. Carey to Andrew Fuller – Mudnabatty, 22nd June, 1797.
22. Ibid.
23. Letter from Andrew Fuller to Wm. Carey – Kettering, 18th April, 1799.
24. Letter from Andrew Fuller to J. Thomas & Wm. Carey – Kettering, 25th March–25th May, 1794.
25. Letter from Andrew Fuller to Wm. Carey – Kettering, 12th April, 1800.

8 – Growing Confidence, 1798–1799

1. Letter from Wm. Carey to John Sutcliff – Mudnabatty, 16th January, 1798.
2. Letter from Andrew Fuller to Wm. Carey – 6th September, 1797.
3. Letter from Wm. Carey to Andrew Fuller – Mudnabatty, 17th July, 1799.
4. Hickey, op. cit., Vol. iv.
5. Letter from Wm. Carey to Andrew Fuller – 1st April, 1799.
6. Letter from Andrew Fuller to Joshua Marshman – 26th November, 1802.
7. Letter from Wm. Carey to Andrew Fuller – Mudnabatty, 17th July, 1799.

8. Letter from John Fountain to Andrew Fuller – Moheepal, 5th September, 1799.

9 – Serampore, October 1799–October 1800

1. Letter from Andrew Fuller to Wm. Ward – London, 13th June, 1800.
2. Diary of Wm. Ward – Lord's Day, 1st December, 1799.
3. Letter from Wm. Carey to Dr. Ryland – Serampore, 17th January, 1800.
4. *Sketches in India by an Officer to Fireside Travellers at Home*, 4th Ed., 1826.
5. Letters from the Missionaries to the Society – Serampore, 25th January, 1800.
6. Ibid.
7. Letter from Wm. Carey to Andrew Fuller – Serampore, 5th February, 1800.
8. Diary of Wm. Ward – 18th January, 1800.
9. Letter from the Missionaries to the Society – Serampore, 10th October, 1800.
10. Letter from Andrew Fuller to Wm. Ward – London, 13th June, 1800.
11. Reported by Andrew Fuller on 29th November, 1802.
12. Letter from Andrew Fuller to John Sutcliff – Olney, 10th May, 1804.
13. Diary of Wm. Ward – 8th October, 1800.
14. Memoir by Mrs. Rachel Voigt in Library of B.M.S., London.
15. Letter from Wm. Carey to Andrew Fuller – Serampore, 23rd November, 1800.
16. Letter from Hannah Marshman to A Friend in Bristol – Serampore, 13th October, 1804.
17. Letter from Hannah Marshman to Dr. Ryland – Serampore, 5th June, 1802.
18. Letter from Hannah Marshman to A Friend in Bristol – Serampore, 13th October, 1804.
19. John Clark Marshman: *The Life & Times of Carey, Marshman and Ward. Embracing the History of the Serampore Mission*, 2 Vols., 1859.
20. Luke X, vv. 8, 9.

10 – A Wonderful Year, 1800–1801

1. Luke V, vv. 4–6.
2. *A History of England*, by Keith Feiling (Pub. Macmillan & Co. Ltd., 1959), p. 934.
3. Letter from Wm. Carey to John Sutcliff – Serampore, 27th November–29th December, 1800.
4. Letter from Wm. Carey to his Sisters – Serampore, November, 1801.
5. Letter from Wm. Carey to his Sisters – 23rd August, 1804.
6. Smith, op. cit., p. 136.
7. Letter from Wm. Carey to John Sutcliff – Serampore, 27th November–29th December, 1800.
8. Ibid.
9. *History of Bengali Literature in the Nineteenth Century, 1800–1825*, by Dr. Sushil Kumar De (pub. Calcutta University, 1919).

10. Letter from Lord Wellesley to Lord Dartmouth – 5th August, 1802.
11. Letter from Wm. Carey to Dr. Ryland – Serampore, 15th June, 1801.
12. Ibid.
13. Ibid.
14. Hickey, op. cit., Vol. iv.
15. Ibid.
16. Spear: 'The Nabobs', op. cit., p. 23.
17. Letter from Wm. Carey to his Sisters – Calcutta, 2nd December, 1802.
18. Letter from Wm. Carey to Andrew Fuller – 7th September, 1803.
19. Letter from Wm. Carey to John Sutcliff – Calcutta, 21st September, 1803.
20. Letter from Wm. Carey to John Sutcliff – Serampore, 8th April, 1801.
21. Letter from Wm. Carey to his Sisters – Serampore, November, 1801.
22. John XV, vv. 1, 2.

11 – Conflict with Government, 1802–1807

1. Hickey, op. cit., Vol. iv.
2. 'Journal' of John Thomas – 2nd January, 1796.
3. S. Pearce Carey, op. cit., p. 238.
4. *British Baptist Missionaries in India, 1793–1837*, by E. Daniel Potts (pub. Cambridge U.P., 1967), p. 22.
5. J. Brown Myers, op. cit., pp. 82–84.
6. Letter from Wm. Carey to John Sutcliff – Calcutta, 22nd August, 1805.
7. Letter from Wm. Carey to Andrew Fuller, 1803, quoted in S. Pearce Carey, op. cit., p. 244.
8. Smith, op. cit.
9. MSS Journal II of Wm. Ward – 10th February, 1805.
10. Letter from Wm. Carey to John Sutcliff – 8th February, 1805.
11. Letter from Wm. Carey to Andrew Fuller – Calcutta, 27th February, 1804.
12. *History of British India*, by P. E. Roberts, 3rd Ed. completed by T. G. P. Spear (pub. O.U.P., 1952).
13. Letter from Wm. Carey to John Sutcliff – Calcutta, 22nd August, 1805.
14. Hickey, op. cit., Vol. iv.
15. Ibid.
16. Letter from Wm. Carey to Andrew Fuller – Calcutta, 15th May, 1806.
17. Letter from Wm. Carey to Andrew Fuller – Calcutta, 17th July, 1806.
18. Letter from Wm. Carey to Andrew Fuller – 10th December, 1805.
19. Letter from Wm. Carey to Andrew Fuller – Calcutta, 15th May, 1806.
20. Letter from Wm. Carey to Dr. Ryland – Calcutta, 12th June, 1806.
21. J. H. Reilly, retired Chief of Detective Dept. speaking with S. Pearce Carey's brother, 17th May, 1892, quoted in S. Pearce Carey, op. cit.
22. Letter from the Missionaries to the Society, written by Mr. Carey – Serampore, 2nd September, 1806.
23. Letter from David Brown to Charles Grant – Calcutta, 2nd September, 1806.
24. See 22, op. cit.

25. Ibid.
26. Letter from Wm. Carey to Andrew Fuller – Calcutta, 18th November, 1806.
27. Commonwealth Relations Office (India Office Library) MSS Eur. F.89, Box 2c, Pt.5, Minute 'On Missionaries'.
28. Letter from Wm. Wilberforce, M.P. to Dr. Ryland – Brighton, 28th August, 1807.
29. Commonwealth Relations Office (India Office Library) MSS Gov.Gen. Minto in Council to J. Krefting – Fort William, 15th September, 1807.
30. CRO, etc., MSS J. Krefting to Lord Minto – Fredericksnagore, 20th September, 1807.
31. The Treaty (of 22nd February, 1845) is transcribed in *Treaties, Engagements and Sanads*, by C. U. Aitchison (pub. 1930), vol. 2, pp. 276–281.
32. Letter from Wm. Carey to Andrew Fuller – Calcutta, 14th October, 1807.
33. Letter from Wm. Carey to his Sisters – Jan. 1808.
34. Ibid.
35. Ibid.

12 – Indian Idyll, 1808–1811

1. John Clark Marshman, op. cit.
2. Clara Rebecca Southwell: Diary of a Tour in India October 1907–March 1908.
3. Wm. Ward's MSS Journal – 18th January, 1800.
4. National Library of Scotland MSS – Letter from Lord Minto to Lady Minto – Barrackpore, 24th May, 1808.
5. Extracts from Letters written by Charlotte Carey to Wm. Carey from Monghyr where she had gone for her health.
6. Letter from Wm. Carey to Andrew Fuller – Mudnabatti, 16th November, 1796.
7. Letter from Wm. Carey to Wm. Carey, Jnr. – 3rd August, 1811.
8. S. Pearce Carey, op. cit., p. 280.
9. Ibid., p. 280.
10. Ibid., p. 204.
11. J. H. Reilly, retired Chief of the Detective Dept. speaking to S. Pearce Carey's brother, 17th May, 1892.
12. Letter from Andrew Fuller to Wm. Carey – Kettering, 8th February, 1804.

13 – Phoenix Rising, 1812–1813

1. Letter from Joshua Marshman to Mr. Harrington – 14th March, 1812.
2. Reported in a letter of Rev. Thomas Thomason.
3. Letter from Wm. Carey to Dr. Ryland – 25th March, 1812.
4. J. C. Ghose: *Bengali Literature* (pub. London, 1948), p. 103.
5. Claudius Buchanan: *Christian Researches in Asia* (11th Ed., London, 1819), p. 87.
6. Matthew XXVIII, v. 19.

7. Judges VI, v. 15.
8. Judges VI, v. 16.
9. Wm. Ward's MSS Journal II – 5th August, 1805.
10. Letter from Andrew Fuller to Wm. Ward – 17th August, 1809.
11. Joshua Marshman's MSS Journal (fragment) – 26th June, 1805.
12. Sushil Kumar De: *History of Bengali Literature*, op. cit.
13. Letter from Wm. Carey to Andrew Fuller – Calcutta, begun 30th July, 1812.
14. Eustace Carey, op. cit., p. 623.
15. Letter from Andrew Fuller to Joshua Marshman – 26th November, 1802.
16. Hickey, op. cit., Vol. iv.
17. Letter from Andrew Fuller to Serampore Missionaries – January, 1813.
18. Letter from Wm. Carey to Andrew Fuller – Calcutta, 5th May, 1813.
19. Letter from Andrew Fuller to the Brethren Carey, Marshman & Ward – 56 Lothbury, 4th August, 1814.
20. Letter from Andrew Fuller to Wm. Ward – Kettering, 6th February, 1809.
21. Furneaux *William Wilberforce*, op. cit., p. 322.
22. Letter from Andrew Fuller to the Brethren Carey, Marshman & Ward – Kettering, 4th February, 1814.
23. Smith, op. cit., p. 252.
24. *The Life of William Wilberforce*, Vol. iv, p. 124, by Robert Isaac Wilberforce and Samuel Wilberforce, 5 Vols. (pub. John Murray, 1838).

14 – Backbiting and Building, 1814–1820

1. Letter from Andrew Fuller to Wm. Ward – Kettering, 15th July, 1812.
2. Letter from Andrew Fuller to Wm. Ward – London, 5th March, 1813.
3. C.R.O. MSS Bengal Despatches Vol. 74, pp. 361–3.
4. Smith, op. cit., p. 126.
5. Letter from Andrew Fuller to Wm. Ward – Kettering, 15th July, 1812.
6. Mark XVI, v. 15.
7. Letter from Wm. Carey to Dr. Ryland – 14th October, 1815.
8. Quoted in S. Pearce Carey, op. cit.
9. Letter from Carey and Others to the B.M.S. – Serampore, 2nd April, 1816.
10. Letter from Wm. Carey to Andrew Fuller – Calcutta, 4th October, 1809.
11. Letter from Wm. Carey to Andrew Fuller – Calcutta, 4th August, 1814.
12. Letter from Wm. Carey – 22nd April, 1817.
13. Letter from Wm. Carey to Dr. Ryland – September, 1817.
14. Ibid.
15. Letter from Wm. Carey to Dr. Ryland – 30th March, 1819.
16. Ibid.

17. C.R.O. MSS 'Bengal Public Consultations', vol. 636, 16 February, 1826. J. C. Marshman to Lord Amherst – Serampore, 9 February, 1826.
18. Quoted in *Twelve Indian Statesmen*, by Dr. George Smith, 1897.
19. Quoted in S. Pearce Carey, op. cit.
20. Letter from Wm. Carey to Jabez Carey – 15th August, 1820.
21. Letter from Wm. Carey to the Society – Bay of Bengal, 17th October, 1793.
22. John VI, v. 9.
23. Letter from Wm. Carey to Jabez Carey – Serampore, 26th January, 1824.
24. S. Pearce Carey, op. cit., p. 329.
25. Ibid.
26. Letter from Wm. Carey to John Sutcliff – Mudnabatti, 16th January, 1798.
27. Letter from Wm. Carey to John Chater, 1807.
28. Letter from Rev. John Dyer to Wm. Ward – Reading, 6th July, 1819.
29. Letter from Wm. Carey to Dr. Ryland – Serampore, 23rd October, 1820.
30. Letter from Wm. Carey to Rev. J. Dyer – Serampore, 9th December, 1825.
31. Letter from Wm. Carey to Andrew Fuller – Calcutta, 25th March, 1812.

15 – Bitter Disputes, 1821–1827

1. Letter from Wm. Carey to Dr. Ryland, 1821.
2. Letter from Wm. Carey to Jabez Carey, June, 1821.
3. Letter from Andrew Fuller to Wm. Ward – 31st December, 1803.
4. Letter from Wm. Carey to Rev. J. Dyer – Serampore, 9th December, 1825.
5. Letter from Wm. Carey to Dr. Ryland – Serampore, 22nd December, 1823.
6. Letter from Wm. Carey to Jabez Carey, quoted in S. Pearce Carey, op. cit.
7. Galatians VI, v. 9.
8. Letter from Wm. Carey to Rev. J. Dyer – Serampore, 15th July, 1819.
9. S. Pearce Carey, op. cit., p. 349.
10. Ibid.
11. Letter from Andrew Leslie to R. R. Sherring – 7th June, 1824.
12. G. E. Pearce: 'Reminiscences'.
13. John XVII, v. 21.
14. Letter from Wm. Carey to Christopher Anderson – Quoted in S. Pearce Carey, op. cit., p. 350.
15. Letter from Wm. Carey to Andrew Fuller – Mudnabatty, 20th December, 1796.
16. Letter from Wm. Carey to – Steadman, 1830.
17. Letter from Wm. Carey to the Society – 11th January, 1796.
18. Sydney Smith: *Edinburgh Review*.

16 – Undefeated, 1828–1834

1. 'Oriental Translations of the Scriptures', Asiatic Journal, xxviii (September, 1829), pp. 297–8.
2. Wm. Greenfield: *A Defence of the Serampore Mahratta Version of the New Testament* (London, 1830).
3. Smith, op. cit., p. 298.
4. Information regarding the collapse of the Agency Houses taken from S. B. Singh: *European Agency Houses in Bengal, 1783–1833* (pub. Calcutta, 1966).
5. Letter from Wm. Carey to Andrew Fuller – Moypal, 21st December, 1799.
6. Smith, op. cit., p. 297.
7. Ibid., p. 298.
8. S. Pearce Carey, op. cit., p. 351.
9. Ibid., p. 378.
10. Ibid., p. 377.
11. Ibid., p. 369.
12. Letter from Andrew Fuller to Christopher Anderson – 27th January, 1812.
13. Matthew XXIII, v. 24.
14. Letter from Robert Mack to L. Mackintosh – 18th September, 1833.
15. S. Pearce Carey, op. cit., p. 377.
16. Smith, op. cit., p. 308.
17. Letter from Andrew Leslie to R. R. Sherring – 7th June, 1824.
18. *Sketches in India by an Officer to Fireside Travellers at Home*, 4th Ed. 1826.
19. John I, v. 46.

Index

Note: As the whole of this book is about William Carey, only the main points in connection with him have been indexed under 'Carey, William'. Other references are under the appropriate subject headings. For example, although there is a mention of '*sati*' under Carey, the full details of the campaign against this practice are indexed under '*sati*'.